ONTARIO

Lake
Nipigon

ke of
he Woods

Prince Arthur's Landing

Lake Superior

Sault Ste. Marie

OTA

MICHIGAN

DULUTH

w Wing   • Brainerd

warab

• Sauk Rapids

• St. Anthony

LIS   • Stillwater

ST. PAUL

WISCONSIN

Lake Michigan

Milwaukee

Mississippi River

Dubuque

CHICAGO

WA

ILLINOIS   INDIANA

Awakening Continent

THE LIFE OF LORD MOUNT STEPHEN

'Tis always morning somewhere, and above
The awakening continents, from shore to shore,
Somewhere the birds are singing evermore.

Lord Mount Stephen's mother wrote her name
and date of birth opposite these lines in a
Longfellow Birthday Book belonging to Eliza Cantlie,
Keithmore, Dufftown, who was visiting Montreal.

SIR GEORGE STEPHEN
by Frank Holl, 1887
(In the possession of Mrs. Robert W. Reford)

Heather Gilbert

Awakening Continent

THE LIFE OF LORD MOUNT STEPHEN

Volume 1 : 1829-91

Aberdeen University Press

Printed in
Great Britain at the
Aberdeen University Press

For my family
and for my teachers at
Lumphanan School

Preface

THE fact that no full-length biography of Lord Mount Stephen has been written appears to call for some comment. It is said that he did not wish to be immortalized in this manner, and one can readily believe that the custom, current in his day, of dictating reminiscences to a biographer did not appeal to him, reluctant as he was to speak of his achievements, believing that his work would be his memorial. After his death, however, there were discovered in his desk at Brocket Hall some brief notes in his own handwriting descriptive of his boyhood days, and a list of dates of the important events in his life. This would seem to betray a hope that some day someone would complete the tale. Yet practically all his private papers were destroyed by his own instructions. His nephew, General Frank S. Meighen, compiled a short biographical sketch, but this has remained in manuscript. The only published account, *The Story of Lord Mount Stephen*, by Keith Morris, devotes some forty pages to the subject and the remainder of a slim paperback to his notable contemporaries.

Awakening Continent is based on my Ph.D. thesis *The Life of Lord Mount Stephen, 1829-1921* (University of London, 1952), written under the supervision of Professor Gerald S. Graham, Rhodes Professor of Imperial History, and recorded under my maiden name, Heather Donald. To Professor Graham I owe my best thanks not only for technical advice (on both original and revised versions) but for his continuing interest and help. It is planned to complete a second volume when the private papers of J. J. Hill, with whom Mount Stephen corresponded over many years, are made available in 1981.

The publication of the present volume has been made possible by the generosity of the Louis W. and Maud Hill Family Foundation of St. Paul, Minnesota, and I should like to record my thanks to them, and to Dr. Grace Lee Nute who first drew my work to their attention. The original research was made possible by grants from The Mary Davidson Smith Clerical and Educational Fund for Aberdeenshire and The Carnegie Trust for the Universities of

Scotland, and by the award of the Ida Smedley Maclean Junior British Scholarship of the Federation of University Women.

For the provision of, and for permission to include, photographs of portraits in their possession I am indebted to Mrs. Robert W. Reford, Mrs. Aubrey Geddes and Mrs. H. G. Lafleur. For the photograph on which the drawing of Lord Mount Stephen's Drummond Street house was based I have to thank Mr. Eric Reford.

The originator of the whole project was my father, the Reverend Francis Cantlie Donald, a native of Auchindoun, Banffshire, who first told me of George Stephen's part in the building of the Canadian Pacific. Later he helped me to collect oral evidence in Mortlach and Glenrinnes. The witness with the longest memory was Miss Margaret Thompson, daughter of Provost Symon's sister Jane, who died on 16 December 1964, in her 102nd year.

I am indebted to Mrs. Aubrey Geddes also for allowing me to see the few remaining Stephen papers, largely of a personal nature, and her father, General Meighen's manuscript.

The most productive of manuscript sources was without doubt the Macdonald collection in the Public Archives of Canada, which includes five volumes containing some eight hundred letters from Stephen to Sir John Macdonald. I was directed to these by Professor Donald G. Creighton, whose two-volume biography of Macdonald was then in preparation (*John A. Macdonald, The Young Politician*, Toronto, 1952; *John A. Macdonald, The Old Chieftain*, Toronto, 1955). I am the more grateful to Professor Creighton because our work on the later period was obviously destined to overlap, while our viewpoints were inevitably different.

I should like to acknowledge the assistance given me by Dr. W. Kaye Lamb and his staff of the Public Archives of Canada, and by Mr. J. L. Johnston of the Provincial Archives of Manitoba and Miss Lucile Kane of the Minnesota Historical Society, also by Miss D. E. Eldred, representative of the Public Archives of Canada at the Public Record Office, and the late Mrs. Joan Reynolds. I am indebted to the *Montreal Gazette* and *The Star*, and to the *Banffshire Journal* for making their files available to me, and to the Bank of Montreal for permitting me to see early Reports.

For help at various points I am grateful to Mr. F. D. Blackley, of the University of Alberta, Mrs. M. E. M. Beattie, Aberdeen, Mrs. Helen Brown, Portgordon, Mr. James E. Cumming, Dufftown, Mrs. Robert Hampson, Montreal, Miss Rosemary McNutt, Cults, the late Dr. Charles S. McPherson, Banff, Mr. and Mrs. Elgin Melvin, Mather, Manitoba, Mrs. John Melvin, Aberdeen, the late Mrs. J. E. Scott Riddell, Aberdeen, the late Mrs. Margaret Stephen, Doonies Farm, Nigg, and Mrs. Charlotte Walker, Aberdeen.

The final tasks of preparation for publication were willingly shared by my husband, Ian Grant Gilbert.

Forest Hill   HEATHER GILBERT
London, 1965

Contents

Illustrations

I

George Stephen : The Formative Years

THE year 1829 stands out in the history of the North East of Scotland as something of an *annus mirabilis*. It was the year of the 'muckle spate'. For twenty-four hours in the month of August such ordeal by water was experienced that, in the words of a contemporary poet,

> We thocht the warl', owerga'en wi' age,
> Drew near the crack o' doom.

Contrary to expectation, the world rolled on, destined to see even greater wonders than in the past. And in the flood-soaked howes of upper Banffshire farmers and crofters, millers and householders salvaged their property as best they could and went about their daily work unaware that there was growing up in their midst a boy who was to play a leading part in bringing one of these wonders to pass.

George Stephen was born on 5 June 1829, at Stephen's Croft, near Croftglass in Inveraven, the first child of William Stephen, a carpenter, and his wife Elspet Smith. Croftglass was the family home; one of a group of holdings round the burn of the Coulalt, it looked across the valley to the site of the battle of Glenlivet. There, in October 1594, Patrick Gordon of Auchindoun and Gordon of Gight, fighting under the Earls of Huntly and Errol, had lost their lives upholding the old religion in face of the Protestant army of the Earl of Argyll.

The Stephens themselves traced their ancestry to the Danish invaders whom Malcolm II had finally defeated in battle in the neighbouring parish of Mortlach in 1010.

Traditionally, the eldest son of the family farmed Croftglass, but the younger Stephens sometimes settled nearby. George's grandfather, William Stephen, was born near the Coulalt in 1769. On his marriage to Elspet Cameron of Coull, Morinsh, he became the tenant of Lint Pots, now known as Bedaugh, a holding across the burn from Croftglass, named after the pot-shaped holes by the waterside in which lint was soaked before being stripped for use in the weaving of linen. But being a builder or mason to trade William Stephen moved in 1817 to Dufftown, the village founded by James Duff, 4th Earl of Fife, in the parish of Mortlach and the year of Waterloo. Only a pardonable family egotism, wrote John Symon, a famous Provost of Dufftown, saved it the cheap dignity of an afflicting commemorative title. 'Waterloo!' scoffed the Earl,'that will be the name of every cadger's cart and every fishwife's creel in the country. I'll call it after myself.'

William Stephen set up in business in Church Street. His grandson George once recalled that he had heard him say that his was the third 'reek' in Dufftown—that is, the third chimney to smoke there.

Meanwhile, a son who had been born in 1801 at Lint Pots—also William—had married in 1828 Elspet, daughter of John Smith of Knockando, Morayshire. This young couple set up house at Stephen's Croft until William the elder had built for them a cottage in Dufftown where the son could continue to ply his trade of carpenter. The house to which they came with their infant son George was a small stone dwelling of which the first floor faced Church Street slightly above ground-level—there were two or three steps up to the front door—while a lower floor, with its carpenter's shop, opened into a close at the back. Water had to be carried from the public well in the village square, and after dark the kitchen would be lit by a 'cruisie' lamp.

Across Church Street lived John Symon, saddler. His son John, who later took over the business and became Provost, was a contemporary of George Stephen, while little Jane Symon was the latter's childhood sweetheart. On new year's day, 1835, the saddler took Jane, then aged four and a half, and George Stephen, her senior by a year, to the first Dufftown Boys' Ball, now an institution, and George was enrolled as a member of the Juvenile Society,[1] entry fee one penny. From then on, Jane and George went together to each successive new year ball, until presently the years brought to both a self-consciousness that forbade the continuance of this routine.

THE SCHOOL AT THE KIRKTON

At the age of five George Stephen went to the parish school at the Kirkton of Mortlach. His first schoolmaster was the Rev. James A.

[1] See *People's Journal*, Dundee, 31 January, 1953.

Cruickshank, M.A., who in 1837 became minister at Mortlach. Then came John Macpherson, M.A., who had taken the first prize in mathematics at the University of Aberdeen,[1] '. . . a splendidly built, athletic, fine-looking man, about six feet high . . . an excellent sportsman, being a fine shot and an extra good fisher'.

Macpherson, who was to become known to generations of pupils as 'Mac', conducted the school at the Kirkton unaided, so that much of the more advanced work of the senior classes was done out of school hours. And when a boy had produced a Latin version that pleased even this stern critic, or had tackled a 'problem' with conspicuous success, his reward was an invitation from the master to go on a salmon-fishing expedition. As Macpherson numbered George Stephen among the three best mathematicians he encountered in his thirty-odd years at Mortlach, it seems likely that this was how the latter came to love the sport that was his only recreation in later days.

But schooldays at the Kirkton were not entirely idyllic. 'Mac's' mathematicians were brought up the hard way, as John Symon (the Provost) was to testify in an article in the *Banffshire Journal* in 1901, which conjured up the scene in the Mortlach schoolroom:

'Please, sir!' . . . quaver . . . 'My question winna come oot! Fat dae I dae wi' the fraction?' 'Find . . . you . . . that . . . out!'

This 'staccato roar' of Macpherson's became famous in the district, and one particular incident established it in the unofficial annals of the parish and, incidentally, showed that even this Olympian figure had his weaknesses. The occasion (described by Symon) was one of those dramatic performances by local school children which were, in their day and in their own way, equally as entertaining as many a professional presentation.

Old Mac, sitting in scholarly seclusion in one of the wings as prompter, was suddenly called upon by a perspiring performer wearing a long cock's tail in his hat (he was Haystone of Bucklaw, I think, but the legitimate drama of those days demanded a cock's tail of nearly everybody) for his cue.

'Fat comes next?' he asked in a frenzied sough, getting as near Mac's hidden post as the stage trauchle of swords and corpses would let him. 'Quick, fat is't?' There was a rather terrible silence. A bottle clinked emptily, and then 'Find . . . you . . . that . . . out!' floated out to stage and audience alike, chill, dignified, reproachful, . . . old Mac at his best.

[1] William Barclay, *Schools and Schoolmasters of Banffshire*, Banff, 1925.

It was Macpherson who protested when, at the age of ten, George Stephen was 'fee'd' to a local farmer and taken away from school. By this time there were six Stephen children: three girls, Elizabeth, Eleonora and Elsie, and two other boys, James and William. (Later there were two more boys, John and Francis.) In 1839 this meant a severe strain on the purse of a village carpenter; at that time even elementary education had to be paid for, although it was not compulsory. It was therefore not unusual for a boy to leave school at an early age to earn his own living.

The story goes that 'Mac' took his protest in person to George's father. William Stephen listened sympathetically to the schoolmaster's point of view, for he had the traditional Scottish respect for 'learning', but he explained that he had five other children to keep in clothes and winter boots, not to mention school fees, and George must now be self-supporting. When Macpherson pressed his case, however, it was finally agreed that if the Stephens but gave George his bowl of brose at home, his further schooling would cost them nothing.

So George Stephen went back to school, at least for six months in the year. It was common practice then for a number of pupils to absent themselves from school as soon as the annual inspection was over—in April or May—and to stay away until after harvest. George Stephen once told a friend that in these months he would earn ten shillings, sufficient to pay for his winter boots. During the months he attended school he was given a small wage by the minister, Mr. Cruickshank, for helping with his cattle out of school hours.

In the churchyard of Mortlach there is a stone with these words:

In memory of John Macpherson, M.A., for thirty years parochial schoolmaster of Mortlach. . . . Erected by a few of his earlier pupils in affectionate and grateful remembrance. . . .

This is said to have been chiefly the work of George Stephen. Although in the days of his munificence he did much for the parish where he got his first chance, all he could then do for the schoolmaster was to write his name in stone.

ABERDEEN – GLASGOW – LONDON – MONTREAL

At the age of fourteen George Stephen finally left school, and worked for a time as ostler at the Fife Arms Hotel in Dufftown, then in the hands of the Collie family. In 1844, along with young Patrick

Collie, he set out for Aberdeen, where both youths apprenticed themselves to one Alexander Sinclair, draper and silk mercer.

At Mr. Sinclair's house of business in Union Street, known as the Bonnet Emporium, he stocked 'everything replete, new, fashionable, chaste, elegant, useful, economical'; so ran his advertisement in the local Press. Apprentices began by dusting, sweeping, window-cleaning and delivering parcels, often by handcart, and gradually were entrusted with more responsible tasks such as carrying the day's drawings to the bank.[1]

They were seldom idle. In 1901 when, as Lord Mount Stephen, George Stephen returned to Union Street, but this time to the Town House to receive the freedom of the City, he spoke thus of his years of apprenticeship:

I had but few wants and no distractions to draw me away from the work I had in hand. It was impressed upon me from my earliest youth by one of the best mothers who ever lived that I must aim at being a thorough master of the work by which I had to get my living, and to be that I must concentrate, I was told, my whole energies on my work, whatever it might be, to the exclusion of every other thing. . . .

Even an interval of enforced idleness in 1846, when he was admitted to hospital with a broken arm, was hardly welcome. He said of the Aberdeen Royal Infirmary of that time: 'It was by no means a cheering place, and I was mighty glad to get out of it.' When in later days this institution became one of his favourite charities it was not because he cherished happy memories of his sojourn there, but because he wanted it to have better facilities than it could afford when he was a patient.

In 1848, having finished his apprenticeship, Stephen set out for Glasgow in search of employment. The outlook was not promising; trade was depressed and the Chartist agitation was at its height. Before very long he had moved on to London, where he found work, first with a firm of drapers in Fore Street, then at the wholesale dry goods house of F. Pawson and Company in St. Paul's Churchyard.

A story is told of Stephen's arrival at one of these establishments, probably the former, in search of work. It was stocktaking day, the store was in chaos and no one had time to talk to the youth who eventually turned away disappointed. On his way to the door he stooped to pick up a pin, which he stuck carefully behind the lapel of

---

[1] A. S. Cook, *Old Time Traders and their Ways*, Aberdeen, 1902.

his coat. The foreman, who had been watching him, called him back and gave him employment.

One day in 1848, that year of revolution when more than one royal head in Europe lost its crown, George Stephen was on his way to work at Pawson's when he noticed an unusually large crowd outside the Mansion House. He stopped to investigate. Someone was obviously being accorded a civic welcome, and the nineteen-year-old boy, in a mischievous impulse, mingled with the reception committee and in his turn solemnly shook hands with the unknown guest. He learned afterwards that this was none other than Louis Philippe, being congratulated on his escape from France.

Changes had come, meanwhile, to the Stephen family in Dufftown. William I's elder brother George had a son William who had emigrated to Canada and established a wholesale dry goods business in St. Paul Street, Montreal. It was probably at his suggestion that William II, the carpenter, set out for Canada in 1847 with his eldest daughter Elizabeth. They sailed from Aberdeen on the barque *St. Lawrence*, a vessel of 352 tons owned by Rose and Company. The following year they were joined in Montreal by Mrs. Stephen and the other children, except George, who was still in London.

This was a great adventure for the very young Stephens. Eleonora spent her last night in Dufftown at the Symons' house and wept with terror at the thought of the impending voyage. She declared that she 'wid raither traivel ten miles roon than pit ae fit in the sea'. Elsie, on the other hand, was more sanguine, remarking of the Atlantic Ocean 'It canna be bigger than Crachie Pot'. This well-known salmon-pool on the Dullan, near Dufftown, was the largest area of water she had so far come across, or could imagine. Eleonora was the truer prophet. They had an unpleasant voyage of two months, with smallpox aboard.

The family was soon to be completely reunited. George had been at Pawson's for over two years, had become a departmental senior and seemed in a fair way to becoming Lord Mayor of London, when one day his father's cousin from Montreal came into the store to place an order. It was George who served him, and, seeing his young kinsman's name on the receipt and being struck with his efficiency, William Stephen made himself known and offered to take George back with him to Montreal.

So on 16 March 1850, George Stephen sailed from London in the *John Bull*, a regular Montreal liner of 436 tons. He arrived at Quebec on 20 April, but stayed there for a week as there was still ice on Lake St. Peter. He reached Montreal on May Day.[1]

DRY-GOODS MERCHANT

George Stephen joined the firm of 'William Stephen, importer of British and foreign dry goods, 226 St. Paul Street'. Before long he became junior partner, and travelled regularly to England in the capacity of buyer. On one of these trips he made the acquaintance of James Morrison, M.P., of 'Morrison's Millions' fame, who had made a fortune by working on the principle of small profits, quick returns. His firm, Morrison and Dillon, dry goods merchants in Fore Street, dealt extensively with the produce of the East, and at Basildon Park in Berkshire where Stephen was an occasional guest the millionaire had an interesting collection of Oriental works of art.[2] It may have been these glimpses of the Far Eastern trade that, many years later, led Stephen to see the possibilities of trans-Pacific communications.

When the Crimean War loomed up Morrison advised Stephen, who was then in England, to buy up all the cotton and woollen goods he could lay hands on and ship them to Canada in anticipation of scarcity and high prices. Stephen took the advice, of necessity without consulting his senior partner, for this was five years before the laying of the first Atlantic cable. Several times previously he had alarmed his cousin by his willingness to take such risks. Beckles Willson wrote in 1915:

There are some still living in Montreal who remember Mr. William Stephen and his uneasiness over some of his young relative's financial excursions. Not infrequently his consent to some arrangement or other would be prefaced by the half-serious comment, 'Well, it is clear George is going to ruin the firm, so it might as well come now as at a later time.'[3]

This time William Stephen no doubt prepared for the worst, but George's wisdom in improving this opportunity was soon apparent. *The Times* of 5 January 1855, commented thus on the situation:

A crisis of war and one of trade have come at the same time. The same month that brings Western Europe to the very walls, and, we trust, into the city of Sebastopol, exhibits also the greatest check that our commerce has received for an unusually long period. . . .

. . . half the transports now on the surface of the Black Sea, or hastening to and fro on the long track from England to the Crimea, carrying

---

[1] Mount Stephen to Frank S. Meighen, 7 August 1908.
[2] John Murray Gibbon, *Steel of Empire*, London, 1935, pp. 118-19.
[3] Beckles Willson, *Life of Lord Strathcona*, Toronto, 1915, p. 141.

soldiers, stores, cannon, shot and all the apparatus of war, would have been freighted with calicoes, linens, silks, haberdashery, hardware, crockery and such-like vulgar stuff of peace. . . .

Montreal had particular reason to regret this state of affairs, for the newly-established Montreal Ocean Steamship Company—later to be known as the Allan Line—had had to suspend operations on the Atlantic while its liners steamed on the Black Sea.[1] This check to the commercial life of Montreal, coming just as that port was getting a chance to compete with Boston and New York, that is, with the fast Cunarders, was happily of short duration, and when the Grand Trunk Railroad was opened in 1856, connecting the seaboard with Sarnia on Lake Huron in the 'West' (Ontario), the Canadians began in earnest to fight for their share of the Atlantic trade.

THE GIANTS OF MONTREAL

In March 1853, during his visit to England, George Stephen was married at Woolwich to Annie Charlotte, daughter of Benjamin Kane, Controller of the Naval Arsenal at Portsmouth. As William Stephen, head of the firm which was now known as William Stephen and Company, had taken up residence on Drummond Street, the young couple moved into the dwelling above the St. Paul Street warehouse. 1860 saw them established at 4 Beaverhall Square, and later they moved to Mountain Street.

On 8 July 1862, the senior partner died and was succeeded by his young cousin, who then took Francis, his youngest brother, into the business. Their parents were then living in Montreal, in Clontarf Place. By this time George Stephen was recognized as one of the leading young merchants of the city. Practically all his attention was still devoted to his business. His name seldom appears in the Press of those days as taking part in social activities or recreations, although in August 1860, he had attended a levee held at the Advocates' Library for the Prince of Wales who was then touring Canada. In any mercantile or charitable project, however, the name of George Stephen was added to those of his contemporaries.

And his contemporaries were a remarkable group. There were indeed giants in those days, and the city's 'commercial and social four hundred'[2] balanced Montreal, and to some extent the whole of

---

[1] Gibbon, op. cit. p. 115.
[2] John Irwin Cooper, *Montreal, The Story of Three Hundred Years*, Montreal, 1942.

WILLIAM STEPHEN

Father of Lord Mount Stephen, artist unknown
(In the possession of Mrs. H. G. Lafleur)

'old' Canada, on the palms of their Olympian hands. In what Professor Cooper terms the 'mid-century madness' of 1849, quite a number of them had signed the Annexation Manifesto; the important thing, in whatever they did, was to do it in good company.

The 'mid-century madness' gave place to a solid conservatism which was, in its way, unique. After the great fire of 1852, the Corporation of Montreal had brought out a by-law requiring all new houses to be built of stone or brick instead of the customary timber, and then it was that the prominent citizens began to 'build for eternity'. With the growing reputation of the city as the emporium of the Province, there was found in embryo that circumscribed society which garrisoned itself in massive limestone piles on the slopes of the mountain.

In the *Montreal Gazette* of 13 January 1863, the following notice appears:

We, the undersigned, respectfully invite those favourable to the establishment of a Protestant House of Industry, to attend a public meeting, to be held in the Mechanics' Hall, on Tuesday, 13th inst., at 2 o'clock p.m.

The first signature is that of John Bethune, Dean of Montreal, and the last that of George Stephen.[1] The meeting duly took place, being 'a large and influential one, comprising many of the leading merchants and business men of the city, clergymen of different Protestant denominations and members of Parliament, all taking, apparently, a deep interest in the proceedings'.[2] The objects of the House of Industry were outlined by the Dean, and included 'providing facilities and encouragement for the cultivation of industrious habits', which doubtless had the wholehearted support of George Stephen. It was pointed out that the sick of the city were provided for, but not the 'healthy but unemployed'. The House was to be residential, and work would be found, either there or elsewhere, for those who had a trade, while training might be arranged for those who had none. A provisional committee was appointed to canvass for contributions. It included Peter Redpath, Junior (son of Peter Redpath, importer and general merchant of St. Paul Street), John Torrance (of the firm of John Torrance and Company who ran steamboats between Montreal and Quebec in competition with the

[1] Sometimes mis-spelt 'Stephens' or 'Steven' but a study of others of that name in Montreal and their mode of signature enables one to distinguish the subject.
[2] *Montreal Gazette*, 14 January 1863.

Molson Line), the Hon. John Rose (M.P.P. for Montreal City, and seldom absent from any committee, social, recreational or otherwise), and George Stephen. The last-named, having contributed $500, was automatically elected a Life Governor at a meeting on 12 September, the minimum donation to qualify for this honour being $400.[1]

So successful were the canvassers that by the following year a temporary organization was functioning, and a site purchased on Dorchester Street for the permanent building. This was completed in due course and the Protestant House of Industry and Refuge figures in later guides to Montreal as one of the points of interest in the city. Thus was achieved an object which had recurred on the agenda of the City Council at intervals since 1808, when John Conrad Marsteller had bequeathed all his real estate towards erecting a House of Industry in Montreal. It was found then that the amount of the bequest was not sufficient, and although attempts had been made in 1818, 1827 and again in 1860, it was left to George Stephen and his contemporaries to carry out the scheme.[2]

Having thus provided for their more unfortunate fellow-citizens, the merchants turned their energies to a project for the benefit of such as themselves. In December 1863, the Mercantile Library Association of Montreal launched a scheme to secure a new building which would contain, in addition to a good library, lecture and study rooms where the young merchants and clerks could, after business hours, further their education and fit themselves for the higher positions into which some of them would haply rise and others inevitably fall. Again George Stephen figures on the executive committee, along with the redoubtable John Rose and Peter Redpath and John and David Torrance. At a meeting of the Association, presided over by the Hon. John Young, M.P.P., they were charged with the duty of 'ascertaining how far, and to what extent, the merchants of the city approve of the plan'.[3]

The Mercantile Library Association had had a somewhat peripatetic existence since its inauguration in 1840.[4] From a room in a Methodist Chapel in St. Sulpice Street it had removed in 1843 to rooms above the St. Ann's Market. These premises had to be abandoned some months later when the upper flat of the market became the Parliament House. From St. Joseph Street they moved in 1851 to what had formerly been Tetu's Hotel in Great St. James

[1] *Montreal Gazette,* 15 September 1863.
[2] Ibid. 21 April 1864.   [3] Ibid. 8 December 1863.
[4] Alfred Sandham, *Sketches of Montreal Past and Present,* Montreal, 1870.

Street,[1] but five years later the quantities of books which the Association had been amassing, by gift or purchase, had to be given refuge in a room belonging to the Merchants' Exchange.

Once more Stephen and his colleagues were able to display their financial wizardry. As a result of an appeal by circular letter, most diplomatically worded and calculated to touch the hearts and open the purses of all who approved of the hard-won leisure of their juniors being devoted to their moral and intellectual development, a sum of over \$20,000 was subscribed.[2] A site was procured for the new Library between Bonaventure and St. Joseph Street, and the three-storey building of Ohio sandstone was completed in 1866.[3] Succeeding generations of young merchants hardly emulated the industry of their elders, judging by a column on the subject of the Association in the *Gazette* of 11 April 1872, headed 'Billiards versus Books'.

The subjects of the lectures delivered before the Association were various, but one paper, to which George Stephen listened on 18 March 1858, is worthy of mention. It was given by Alexander Morris, later Lieutenant-Governor of Manitoba, and was entitled *Nova Britannia, or The Consolidation of the British North American Provinces into the Dominion of Canada*. The paper concluded with these prophetic words, spoken nine years before Confederation:

And now, my hearers, we have travelled in company from the Atlantic to the Pacific. What think you of our journey, and of these Britannic possessions in which your lot is cast? Is there not here the germ of a mighty people? I . . . believe that a line of railway will yet pass up the Ottawa valley, and present, through British territory, a highway to the Pacific.

Twenty-six years later the lecture was published, along with others,[4] and the author sent a copy of the book to George Stephen, who wrote in acknowledgment:

. . . Time and events have shown that the forecast of your younger manhood of Canada's future was wonderfully accurate even to detail. Little did I think when listening to your lecture in the early spring of '58 that fate had in store for me the instrumentality for the building of what you called the Atlantic and Pacific Railway. . . .[5]

[1] *Montreal Gazette*, 21 April 1864.
[2] Ibid. 2 January and 10 May 1864.   [3] Sandham, op. cit.
[4] A. Morris, *Nova Britannia; or Our New Dominion Foreshadowed*, Toronto, 1884.
[5] Morris Papers, Q. I. Stephen to Morris, 14 December 1884.

AN EARLY STEAMSHIP LINE

In December 1863, George Stephen made his first but fleeting entrance into the shipping world. For some time the import merchants of Canada had been dissatisfied with the shipping facilities available to them on the Atlantic. Ocean freight rates from Liverpool to New York were much lower than to Quebec, although the latter was 300 miles nearer. This was hardly surprising considering that the Cunard Line was subsidized by the Governments of both Great Britain and the United States, whereas the Allan Line, which carried most of the Canadian trade, received only a mail subsidy from the Provincial Parliament. Moreover, public confidence in the Allan Line had been considerably shaken by the fact that since 1856 no fewer than seven of its vessels had been lost, an average of one a year.

In a lecture to the Mechanics' Institute of St. Catharine's, Ontario, in 1857, the Hon. William Hamilton Merritt, M.P.P., had suggested that the merchants of Quebec, Montreal, and Toronto should forget their rivalry and join together, along with such English capitalists as they could interest, to establish a line of screw steamers to ply between ports in Great Britain and Quebec or Portland, Maine. The last-named was the terminus of the Grand Trunk Railroad.

It looked, in December 1863, as though this would actually come to pass. The *Montreal Gazette* published the prospectus of a new venture, the North American Steamship Company, and George Stephen figured on the provisional board. The *Gazette* of 15 January 1864, reported that the organization of the Company had been completed, and a week later notice was officially published of its proposed application to Parliament for an Act of Incorporation. By the end of the month, however, rumours were getting about of dissension in the provisional board, several members having resigned. One of these was George Stephen.

It is not clear why these men withdrew from a project which appeared so promising. No one suggested that a new steamship line was unnecessary; on the contrary, shipping companies seemed suddenly to spring up overnight, all agog to remedy the shocking position of the unfortunate Canadian ports. For some time rival prospectuses jostled one another in the press, while neighbouring eyes watched developments in Montreal with more than casual interest. The *Boston Post* concluded that the business men of Montreal were determined to have a steamship line of their own and at whatever cost. This phrase suggests a recklessness that would hardly have commended itself to George Stephen.

By July, the project from which Stephen had considered it advisable to withdraw had been abandoned. A second company shortly afterwards died a natural death and the field was left clear for the British Colonial Line, which had a London directorate and the backing of Glyn, Mills and Company. By the end of the year this line had three fine iron screw steamers, the *Thames*, *Hector*, and *St. Lawrence*, on an Atlantic upon which the shipping storm, had, at least for a time, subsided. And there grew up a tradition in Montreal that, while it was not positively unwise to attach oneself to a project with which George Stephen had not a connection, it was sure wisdom to embrace a scheme with which he had one.

At its quarterly meeting in July 1864, Stephen was elected a member of the Montreal Board of Trade. Two years later a new dry goods firm, George Stephen and Company, came into being, and in 1867 the old business was sold to Robertson, Stephen and Company. The partners in the latter concern were Andrew and John A. Robertson, Robert Linton and Francis Stephen.

INCENTIVES TO INDUSTRIAL DEVELOPMENT

October 1864 saw the Province acutely embarrassed by the incident of the St. Albans Raid. A number of Confederate soldiers who had been given asylum in Canada recrossed the boundary into the United States, robbed three banks in St. Albans, Vermont, murdered a cashier and returned to their northern refuge. Their subsequent arrest was followed by a farcical trial at which the Canadian judge discharged them, despite an indignant protest in Court from the Hon. John Rose, Q.C.

The business men of Montreal, aghast at the thought of possible American reactions, and fearing for the Reciprocity Treaty which then existed between the two countries, prepared a Memorial praying the Governor-General for a speedy inquiry. The document, which was signed by many prominent men including Peter Redpath, then President of the Board of Trade, David Torrance, George Stephen, Hugh and Andrew Allan of the shipping line, and Robert Esdaile, President of the Corn Exchange, called for increased vigilance on the part of the Government and all subordinate authorities, so that Canada's neutrality might be effectively and honestly maintained. The signatories felt that the result of the recent proceedings had been such as to cast doubts upon the good faith of the Province in carrying out her treaty obligations.[1]

It was several years before the matter was finally settled, but in the short term the premonitions of the Montrealers proved only too correct. It seems certain that along with the 'Trent Affair' and the Underground Railway activity of Canadians during the Civil War, the St. Albans Raid was the cause of the anti-British sentiment which resulted in 1866 in the refusal of the United States to renew the Reciprocity Treaty.

The erection of a tariff barrier along the 49th Parallel was not without beneficial consequences to Canada. It was a challenge to such men as George Stephen. In a report to the United States Senate in 1850 the American Consul in Canada had compared, with some complacence, the progress of the two countries in manufacturing with particular reference to the textile industry. While in Canada there was a scarcity of investment capital and of labour, the United States lacked neither, and had several factories in production.

There had, at one time, been woollen manufacturing establishments in both Quebec and Ontario, but these had closed down and Canadian wool, which was of excellent quality and fine texture, generally found its way to American factories whence the finished products returned to Canadian warehouses.

There were other reasons besides shortage of capital and labour for the tardy development of Canadian manufactures. One was the problem of poor communications; another was what one writer describes as 'a dogged indifference, if not direct obstruction on the part of the whole population of the country to anything bearing the stamp of home production'.[2]

The impetus provided first by the dislocation of trade during the Civil War, then by the cancellation of the Reciprocity Treaty, produced the opposite reaction. The 'idea of national exclusiveness'[3] permeated the Canadian mind already charged with thoughts of political development. Nor can one discount the effect of a change in British policy which no longer sought to discourage local manufacturing in the Colonies; nor the growing realization that one of

---

[1] *Montreal Gazette*, 15 November, 14 and 23 December 1864.
[2] A. Walshe, Lecture at Montreal printed in *Canadian Merchants' Magazine*, May 1857.
[3] D. G. Creighton, *Economic Nationalism and Confederation*, in Transactions of the Canadian Historical Association, 1942.

Canada's most valuable assets—unlimited waterpower—awaited exploitation.

By 1866, capital and labour were becoming more plentiful, and rail communication existed between the main centres of the Province. It only remained for men of enterprise to grasp the opportunity so patently within reach. As George Stephen's firm had begun to specialize in the sale of Canadian tweeds, which he saw were advancing in popularity, he decided to have an interest in their manufacture.

In Lanark county, Ontario, where suitable waterpower abounded, and where it so happened that the first settlers were weavers, displaced in the old country by power looms,[1] Bennett Rosamond and his brother William had in 1862 leased the wool mills built by their father at Almonte. Four years later, having achieved a measure of success and doubled the capacity of their mills, they admitted George Stephen as a partner.

In 1868 Stephen became associated also with the Paton Company of Sherbrooke, Quebec. Andrew Paton, a mill owner from Galt, Ontario, had set up a plant at Sherbrooke in 1866. Seeking to expand the business, he invited the co-operation of a group including George Stephen, Donald A. Smith (a cousin of Stephen), and Richard B. Angus who shortly afterwards became general manager of the Bank of Montreal. Together they formed a joint-stock company, and at the first board meeting on 18 July 1868, Stephen was elected Vice-President. Expansion first took the form of incorporating the neighbouring Lomas Woollen Mill; later the Quebec Worsted Company was purchased.

From woollens George Stephen turned next to cotton manfacturing. On 30 January 1872, the *Montreal Gazette* hailed the Canada Cotton Manufacturing Company as another step in the industrial progress of the Dominion. The promoters included Sir Hugh Allan, Edward Mackay (of a wholesale dry goods firm; like Stephen he had in 1865 withdrawn from the North American Steamship Company; he later became President of Canada Cotton); Bennett Rosamond, George Stephen and Donald A. Smith. Their prospectus stated that they aimed to achieve for the manufacture of cotton goods the same success that had attended the production of Canadian woollens. The town of Cornwall, Ontario, was chosen as a suitable locality for the

[1] Innis and Lower, *Select Documents in Canadian Economic History 1783-1885*, Toronto, 1933, pp. 290 and 608.

company's operations, partly because its population was sufficiently large to supply the necessary operatives.

Although chronologically other events in Stephen's career intervene here, it may be well, before leaving the subject, to complete the recital of his manufacturing ventures, which did not stop short at textiles. Along with Sir Hugh Allan, Edward M. Hopkins (Chief Officer of the Hudson's Bay Company in Montreal) and Charles John Brydges (Manager of the Grand Trunk Railway), Stephen took over the Montreal Rolling Mills Company. Among the directors subsequently elected were Peter Redpath and E. H. King, then President of the Bank of Montreal.[1] In 1870 the Canada Rolling Stock Company was formed, in which Stephen's co-directors included Donald Smith, E. H. King and Robert Reekie. The last-named had also been involved in the North American Steamship Company and had retired with Stephen; he was well-known as a railroader in Quebec and Ontario. Both Sir Hugh and Andrew Allan were also associated with the rolling stock enterprise. Stephen had an interest, too, in the Canadian Locomotive and Engine Company of Kingston, of which Reekie was managing director.

THE FREE TRADE CONTROVERSY

It was in 1866 that Stephen first became acquainted with his cousin, Donald Alexander Smith, son of Elspet Stephen's brother Alexander. Smith was then with the Hudson's Bay Company in a Labrador outpost. Their first meeting, as described by a Chief Factor of the Company, was decidedly inauspicious.[2]

I first saw Donald Smith on his visit to Montreal in 1866. He had been spending some days at Lachine with his wife and two children, where his mother-in-law, Mrs. Richard Hardisty, then resided.

One morning he said, 'I have a cousin in Montreal, Mr. George Stephen, whom I have never seen. Do you know anything about him? He's a prominent man in the woollen trade, I believe.'

I said I had heard of Mr. Stephen, who had been a junior partner with his cousin William Stephen, in a firm of wholesale drapers, and was now established for himself.

As Mrs. Smith had some shopping to do, we all went into the city together. I gave him Mr. Stephen's address, and we parted company. A couple of hours later I met all the Smiths in St. James's Street loaded

---

[1] *Montreal Gazette*, 7 May 1869.　　　　[2] Willson, op. cit. pp. 140-1.

down with parcels and Mr. Smith carrying a rather gaudy carpet bag. He stopped to show me the bag, and asked my opinion of it.

'It's just the thing for the Labrador,' he said, 'It'll make a great hit with the Indians there.'

I enquired if he had met his cousin, Mr. Stephen. 'Oh, yes,' he said, 'I went in and had a few moments conversation with him.'

'I suppose he was glad to see you, eh?'

Mr. Smith seemed a little embarrassed at the question, but his wife burst forth, 'He wasn't glad at all. Why should Mr. Stephen be glad to see country cousins like us—all the way from Labrador? I wish,' she added shyly, 'I wish he had waited until he had met Mr. Stephen before buying that red carpet bag. But he wouldn't let me carry it, and the rest of us waited outside.'

If the sudden blast of Labrador air that blew both Donald Smith and a red carpet bag into his line of vision at one and the same time had been too much for George Stephen, his cousin was soon to forget his coolness, for before he left Montreal Smith was to see Stephen in a new light. The occasion was a public meeting called to protest against A. T. Galt's Budget of June 1866, the main feature of which was a proposed reduction in the tariff on imported goods and the complete removal of the duty on certain industrial raw materials. The duty on manufactured goods had originally been imposed not in pursuit of a policy of protection, but solely for revenue purposes. Many manufacturers had counted on its continuance, however, as a form of protection for the growing native industries.

Donald Smith was present at the meeting where, after several people had spoken against Galt's proposals, George Stephen (who, in after years at least, never cared for Galt himself) rose and defended the Budget in 'a strong Free Trade speech which was received with a storm of hisses and other signs of disapproval'.[1] He was told afterwards it was a wonder he wasn't lynched.[2] Smith was 'profoundly impressed, as much by his cousin's bearing and courage as by his arguments'. The result was that Smith became interested both in the government's fiscal policy and in industrial enterprise, and through Stephen had made several business contacts in Montreal before coming to that city in 1868 to take charge of the Montreal Department of the Hudson's Bay Company.

George Stephen continued, at every opportunity, to defend the Government's policy of bringing down the cost of living. He maintained that any branch of industry that could not exist under the

[1] Willson, op. cit. p. 142. [2] Ibid. p. 143.

2

reduced protection ought to be given up; certainly manufacturers who could not compete with the United States in their then over-burdened condition ought, he said, to abandon the attempt. The new proposals offered the great advantage of duty-free machinery and raw materials and promised larger markets, 'the best, safest and only enduring kind of protection'.[1]

The controversy raged for some time, the division of opinion in Montreal bearing no relation to political affinities. It was finally stilled when, on Galt's resignation over the question of the Lower Canada School Bill in August, John Rose became Finance Minister. In a previous term in that office Rose had shown a tendency to favour protective measures, so that the protectionists welcomed his appointment.

Stephen's views on Free Trade as an academic question, leaving aside any particular application of the principle, were stated in a letter to Sir John Macdonald in 1872:

I am by conviction in favour of what is called Free Trade, that is a tarriff based on our fiscal necessities and imposed for the purposes of revenue alone.[2]

If he appeared in later years to depart from this stand it was because of his keen appreciation of changing circumstances. What was appropriate when the tide of commercial prosperity was flowing high could not be blindly adhered to when the waters ebbed, leaving more than one mercantile mariner high and dry.

CONFEDERATION: A DISCONNECTED DOMINION

A somewhat disunited and disconnected Canada achieved Dominion status on 1 July 1867. In the autumn of 1869 John Rose (a native of Turriff, Aberdeenshire) left Canada to join the firm of Morton, Rose and Company, financiers, of London, England. But he by no means lost interest in the new Dominion. In London, acting as a 'missionary of Empire in an England in which there was still a *laissez-faire* indifference to the colonies and often a positive hostility to them as an unprofitable burden on the mother land',[3] he served Canada even more effectively than before. He was, in effect,

[1] *Montreal Gazette*, 2 and 3 July 1866. See also 6, 11 and 13 July.
[2] Macdonald Papers (hereafter 'Macd.P.') 'Stephen' 267, Stephen to Macdonald, 22 February 1872.
[3] Morden H. Long, 'Sir John Rose and the informal beginnings of the Canadian High Commissionership', *Canadian Historical Review*, 1931. (Rose was knighted in 1870.)

Canada's first High Commissioner in all but name, and the fact that he had not been officially appointed did not prevent the Colonial and Foreign Offices from taking advantage of his special knowledge of Canadian affairs.

It seems likely that it was Rose who first brought together Sir John Macdonald,[1] Canada's first Prime Minister, and George Stephen, and by the time of Rose's departure they were on intimate terms. Macdonald wrote to Stephen on 8 November 1869:

. . . I have several letters from our friend Rose since he left us. He seems to have gone to work with his usual energy. I am glad to believe that he has left behind him a friend in yourself who will act with me as cordially as he did.[2]

Stephen at no time took an active part in politics (except for some electioneering at Huntingdon on Rose's behalf, which taught him that it was no use to try to interest a farming community in Free Trade). He adhered to the Conservative Party, but had good friends on either side of the House and was extremely averse to political considerations intervening in any commercial transaction. As a pillar of the Conservative Party, therefore, he was unsatisfactory; the mere survival of one particular group in power meant very little to him, although he had an almost unbounded admiration for Macdonald and an equal contempt for certain members of the Liberal Party. It was not as a politician that Macdonald valued him, but as a far-sighted man of business. With Rose in London and Stephen in Montreal with his finger on the commercial pulse of the Dominion, the Prime Minister had two useful allies.

At the farewell banquet given in his honour at Montreal, Rose had referred to the appointment of William McDougall, Member for North Lanark and late Minister of Public Works, as the first Lieutenant-Governor of the North-West, the region lately handed over to the Government of Canada by arrangement with the Hudson's Bay Company and in accordance with the British North America Act of 1867. Said Rose:

I confess I am a little inclined to envy my friend and former colleague, Mr. McDougall, in *his* new pursuit, for I know no more interesting occupation than that of laying the foundation of a new nationality. I can only content myself with the reflection that as it is said no one who has lived in

[1] See Donald Creighton, *John A. Macdonald : The Young Politician*, Toronto, 1952; *The Old Chieftain*, Toronto, 1955.
[2] Macdonald Letter Book (hereafter 'Macd.L.B.') 13.396, Macdonald to Stephen, 8 November 1869.

America will be happy in Heaven unless there be some new place west of it to go to, there will be an unexplored west in store for me when I reach the land of spirits, while he will have had it in his life. . . .[1]

Whether John Rose ever found his El Dorado can never be known; it was very soon to be clear that McDougall was to be denied his. Within a few weeks his position was anything but enviable, for his entry into the North West was the signal for a rising of half-breeds under Louis Riel, who claimed that the new arrangement had been made without consulting them, and was an infringement of their rights. It is not proposed to deal at length with this question here; it is mentioned because the 1869 Riel Rebellion was the first recorded crisis on which George Stephen made a recommendation to Sir John Macdonald.

Donald Smith was at this time chief officer of the Hudson's Bay Company in Montreal, and Stephen suggested to Macdonald that as Smith was in almost daily communication with Governor McTavish at Fort Garry, the chief Hudson's Bay post and the focal point of the Rebellion, he might be able to give some useful information on the situation.[2] Macdonald accordingly invited Smith, whom he had never met, to see him at Ottawa. During the interview Macdonald mentioned that it was the Government's intention to send up some influential French Canadians to the North West to try to smooth over the difficulties. Smith suggested that George Stephen might be sent along with them; as a Protestant unconnected with office, and known to be an independent man of business, he might be 'exceedingly useful'.[3]

As Macdonald had expected, Stephen declined the mission, but wrote that if Smith was to go, Colonel Wolseley was anxious to accompany him, having followed the situation with much interest.[4] Garnet Wolseley was then Deputy Quartermaster-General on H.Q. Staff, Canada. On 13 December Macdonald wrote to Stephen that Smith had left that day for Fort Garry, but that it would not have done to send Wolseley:

Smith goes to carry the olive-branch, and were it known at Red River that he was accompanied by an officer high in rank in military service, he

---

[1] *Montreal Evening Star*, 29 September 1869.
[2] Macd.P. 'Stephen' 267, Stephen to Macdonald, 27 November 1869. Also Macd. L.B. 13.621, Macdonald to Stephen, 29 November 1869.
[3] Macd.L.B. 13.630, Macdonald to Stephen, 1 December 1869.
[4] Macd.P. 'Stephen' 267, Stephen to Macdonald, 10 December 1869.

would be looked upon as having the olive-branch in one hand and a revolver in the other. [1]

This decision Stephen admitted to be a wise one.[2]

Macdonald fully expected that the whole affair would be speedily and peacefully settled, but the situation at Fort Garry became so threatening that the following spring Colonel Wolseley was indeed despatched, and with an armed force, to Red River. Such a force could not have been sent earlier even if required, as winter communication on Canadian soil did not exist. Smith and his party had gone by rail south of the Lakes via Chicago to St. Paul, Minnesota, thence northward by trail, but troops could not pass over American territory. Wolseley arrived at Fort Garry in August, after a journey of which he afterwards said, 'I have campaigned in many parts of the world, but I never before saw men go through such incessant labour'.[3] Much of the three months was spent in roadmaking. and in carrying their provisions and equipment and dragging their boats over numerous portages. Forty-six of these were negotiated in one stretch of seven miles. Fortunately it was not necessary for them, on arrival, to go into battle, for by then Smith's mission had succeeded and a peaceful settlement been reached.

RED RIVER: A NORTH-SOUTH TRADE ROUTE

It was not every day that an armed force had to find its way from Eastern Canada to Red River. It was obvious, however, that some satisfactory line of communication should be established to link this newly-acquired territory with the seat of Government, and to transport thither the 'vulgar stuff of peace'. Long before Confederation a transcontinental railroad had been visualized; the 'journey from Halifax to the Pacific'[4] had set many minds thinking in an east and westerly direction, But in 1869 the settlers of Red River lived in a world that ran from north to south; Canada was a foreign country, Minnesota their near neighbour.

The mace of the Provincial Parliament of Manitoba was fashioned out of the hub of a Red River cart wheel, and appropriately so, for

---

[1] Quoted in Pope, *Correspondence of Sir John Macdonald*, Toronto, 1921, p. 112.
[2] Macd.P. 'Stephen' 267, Stephen to Macdonald, 15 December 1869.
[3] Speech by Wolseley, *Montreal Gazette*, 30 September 1870.
[4] A phrase often quoted from a speech by Joseph Howe at Halifax in 1851: 'I am neither a prophet nor the son of a prophet, but I believe that many in this room will live to hear the whistle of the steam engine in the passes of the Rocky Mountains and to make the journey from Halifax to the Pacific in five or six days.'

the 'prairie schooners' were the heart, soul and lifeline of the old order. Drawn by oxen, they formed sociable caravans on the trail between St. Paul and Fort Garry, the leisurely journey punctuated by regular halts to rest the animals and prepare the 'pemmican'—the staple and easily carried food of the travellers. Often the day ended with violin music round an evening campfire.

Steamboats on the Red River supplemented this romantic form of transport. The Hudson's Bay Company operated a line which was later transferred to the St. Paul agent, Norman W. Kittson, a patriarchal personage known as the Commodore. *The Nor' Wester*, published at Fort Garry, printed, somewhat uncertainly, the advertisement:

> General Red River Agency.
> N.W. Kittson will at
> tend to
> The Purchase of Goods etc. of Freight to
> and from New York, Canada and Liverpool etc.
> St. Paul, Minnesota

With the coming of Confederation, merchants both east and west of Lake Superior were beginning to see how fantastic was the circuitous trade route by which the products of the west—buffalo robes, beaver and mink marten—reached Montreal by way of St. Paul and New York, while the hunters, trappers and voyageurs imported their heavy clothing from England. In course of transit either way, American customs duties added anything up to 16 per cent to the original price of the commodity. The incongruity of the position was pointed out in a *Nor' Wester* article reprinted in the *Montreal Gazette* of 20 December 1867, with the comment:

We commend the following article to the earnest consideration of the merchants and manufacturers of the Dominion. They will only have themselves to blame if they do not soon entirely engross the large and growing trade of the North West, and with this object in view, they should insist on the immediate completion of the Canadian route to Red River.

The isolated position of the Red River settlement in relation to the rest of the Dominion had not escaped the notice of George Stephen, for especially after Donald Smith in 1871 became Member of Parliament for Selkirk, Manitoba, and a member of the Legislative Assembly of that Province, his cousin was to hear a great deal of talk on the subject. Knowing little of the area, however, Stephen let Smith take the initiative. The *Canada* (Official) *Gazette* of 16 December 1871, published the formal notice of an application to be made to Parliament at its next session by Donald A. Smith, A. T. Galt, George Stephen, George Laidlaw and others, for a Charter to build a railway from the United States boundary, at or near St. Vincent or Pembina, to Fort Garry. The same group, with the exception of Laidlaw, also gave notice in the *Gazette* of 24 February 1872, of their intention to apply for an Act to incorporate a company for the construction of a railway from a point on Lake Superior at or near Prince Arthur's Landing to Fort Garry, 'with power to construct the same either continuously or by railways connecting the navigable waters along the said route, and to build, own and operate steam and other vessels upon the same . . .'.

The railway to the American boundary was no doubt planned to connect up with the railroad then building from St. Paul northward, subsidized by a land grant from the Minnesota Legislature. The line to Lake Superior promised to provide an outlet on Canadian soil and then by Canadian waters for the produce of the West, and at the same time would admit the manufactures of Quebec and Ontario to that area. Rail connection would also encourage an influx of settlers into the North West and thus ensure the expansion of this two-way traffic. Already development on these lines was taking place in the American Middle West; the 49th Parallel was but an arbitrary barrier mirroring a similar picture on either face. There were even signs that for some the barrier scarcely existed.

The Canadian Prime Minister was not unaware of the fact that American railway builders were casting covetous, if not possessive eyes northwards. On 28 January 1870, Macdonald wrote to C. J. Brydges, manager of the Grand Trunk Railroad:

It is quite evident to me from advices from Washington, that the United States Government are resolved to do all they can, short of war, to get possession of the western territory, and we must take immediate and vigorous steps to counteract them. One of the first things to be done is to show unmistakably our resolve to build the Pacific Railway.[1]

Although the Grand Trunk Company declined to undertake the task of building the transcontinental road, surveys were begun by the Government, and Stephen and his associates were not permitted to proceed with their projects on the grounds that the lines they

[1] John Macnaughton, *Life of Lord Strathcona*, Makers of Canada Series, London and Toronto, 1926, vol. X, p. 209.

planned would compete with the Canadian Pacific Railway.[1] For the
moment, therefore, these men of enterprise left the western arena, to
return when others had failed, on either side of the boundary, to
give Manitoba rail communication with the outside world.

One of the group which had planned the Pembina—Fort Garry
line, George Laidlaw, had already been making a name for himself
as a pioneer of narrow-gauge railway building in Ontario. An honest
man with a good deal of vision, his efforts to develop communications in that Province did not always meet with the success they
deserved, partly because of Laidlaw's tendency to get involved in
financial difficulties, partly because of the opposition of the Grand
Trunk Railroad Company. The latter was out to stop anything that
might conceivably be regarded as poaching on what it considered to
be its preserves, as Laidlaw found when, in 1870, he tried to find
purchasers in London for the bonds of the Toronto, Grey and Bruce
Railway. Such was the influence of the Grand Trunk that it proved
impossible to place the bonds until by chance George Stephen arrived
in England and succeeded in arranging for their disposal.[2]

OPENING UP THE LAURENTIANS

From the shores of Georgian Bay Stephen's interest was next
diverted to the small Laurentian village of St. Jérôme, thirty-three
miles north of Montreal, a French-Canadian community presided
over by the Mayor, M. Laviolette, and a most enlightened curé,
Antoine Labelle. Labelle, who came to be known as the Apostle of
Colonization,[3] devoted much of his life to the development of the
'back-country', the Laurentian hinterland, a task which he began in
practical fashion by leading an expedition to explore the area (which
he found to be rich in timber and minerals) and which was finished
by the construction, after many days, of the St. Jérôme Colonization
Railway. But before the first locomotive, named *Rev. A. Labelle*,
steamed out of Montreal not only the curé but men such as George
Stephen had become involved in one of the problem railroads of the
time.

In 1869 the Northern Colonization Railway Company had been
formed with the avowed intention of building a wooden line from

[1] Macd.P. 'Stephen' 271, Stephen to Tupper, 12 May 1888.
[2] *Montreal Gazette*, 15 September 1870.
[3] *Cyclopaedia of Canadian Biography*, ed. Rose, Labelle, Francois Xavier Antoine.
See also *Dictionary of Canadian Biography*, ed. Wallace, Toronto, 1926, quoting E-J.
Auclair, *Le curé Labelle*, Montreal, 1930.

Montreal to St. Jérôme—it became known as the 'chemin à lisses de bois'—its chief object being the transport of firewood into the city, where large quantities of that commodity were required during the severe winters. Three years later, when nothing further had been done to promote this enterprise (nothing, that is, by the Company; the curé had not been idle. 'I wish you would send your curé to his parishioners', a Cabinet Minister is reported to have said to the Member for Terrebonne. 'You can do that yourself', was the reply; 'if he annoys you, give him what he asks, otherwise you will never get rid of him') the *Montreal Gazette* published the prospectus of a new company who intended to apply for a Charter (unless arrangements could be made to transfer the existing one) to construct the Montreal and St. Jérôme Colonization Railway.[1] George Stephen's name was included in the published list of provisional directors, and the first report of the Company bears the stamp of his authorship.[2] The *Gazette* adopted at first a very pessimistic attitude towards the project, influenced, no doubt, by the original Company's failure to give practical effect to their proposals. Adverse rumours, too, suspected of emanating from Grand Trunk sources, propagated the information that what the Company really intended to do was to obtain money under false pretences of interest in St. Jérome, and spend it in the construction of a line along the north shore of the Ottawa River.

What the Company had in mind, as a deputation of directors explained to the inhabitants of the Laurentian village, was that one day the road would connect, via the Canada Central Railway, with the transcontinental line which at that moment Sir Hugh Allan was planning to build, under charter from the Dominion Goverment, from Lake Nipissing (the terminus of the Canada Central) to the Pacific. Sir Hugh had gone up to St. Jérôme, in fact, to impress upon the inhabitants that this was the precise reason for his lately having joined the Board of the new Company. Had it been merely a local road for carrying firewood he would not have been interested. The people of the village were highly delighted. The 'steam whistle in the Rockies', so often heard in those days as people listened to after-dinner speeches, blew full blast through Grignon's Hotel as the Municipal Council entertained the deputation. The menu cards were embellished with the mottoes: 'C'est le Grand Tronc du Nord que nous voulons depuis l'Atlantique jusqu'au Pacifique et non seulement l'embranchement de St. Jérôme.' 'Vaincre ou perir avec

[1] *Montreal Gazette*, 14 February 1872.   [2] *Montreal Gazette*, 16 February 1872.

elle.' 'L'energie, la perseverance et la patriotisme de nos amis ompteront l'injustice et le fanatisme de nos adversaires.' Father Labelle rounded off the evening with a speech which one would scarcely have expected to fall from the parochial Quebec curé of tradition. He looked forward to the day, seemingly not so far distant, when by the construction of a railway across the continent Lachine was proved indeed to be, as the early explorers thought it, the road to China.[1]

Just when the enterprise appeared to be succeeding beyond doubt, two events intervened. On 2 April 1873, in the Canadian House of Commons, Lucius Seth Huntington moved for an inquiry into the matter of the charter granted to Sir Hugh Allan and others for the building of the Canadian Pacific Railway. The ensuing 'Pacific Scandal' which led to the cancellation of the charter and the downfall of the Macdonald Government was probably partly responsible for the cessation of railway activity in the Laurentians. It coincided with an international financial crisis which discouraged, if it did not completely stop, investment in long-term projects such as railways. It was not until July 1883, that Sir Hugh Allan was able to inform Father Labelle that the contract for the colonization railroad had at last been signed. Meanwhile the Provincial Government of Quebec had undertaken the construction of the north shore line to Montreal, —the Grand Trunk Railroad followed the south shore—of which more will be heard in later chapters.

'THE BAD TIMES' AND THE BANK OF MONTREAL

The period of financial crisis ushered in by the 'Vienna Crash' of May 1873, and assured of a prolonged stay by Wall Street's 'Black Friday' in September, did not at once bring disaster to the flourishing commerce and industry of Eastern Canada, but there was evidence among business men of a marked disinclination to take any form of risk. Investors on either side of the Atlantic tended, on the contrary, to realize their capital. Private finance not being forthcoming for the construction of the Pacific Railway, the Liberal Government, under Alexander Mackenzie, undertook the task as a Government work, but was determined to build no faster than extreme caution dictated.

It was in 1874 that Terrill, the Pepys of Montreal, recorded: 'What will long be known as the "bad times" begin this year.' Even

[1] *Montreal Gazette*, 17 February 1872.

then there prevailed in the city an atmosphere not so much of apprehension as of unwonted calm; 'a drowsiness which had in it more or less of dejection; of mourning for the moneymaking activity which was gone . . .'.[1] Firms failed and went quietly out of business; no sensation shattered the gloom of St. James's Street; commerce was in the doldrums.

And in St. James's Street was an establishment which registered every rise and fall of the commercial mercury. In the transactions of the Bank of Montreal, Canada's 'Old Lady' of the Place d'Armes, was reflected the history of the times. Directors' reports and presidential speeches at the annual general meetings form a commentary on the period, and it so happened that during the critical years the President of the Bank of Montreal was none other than George Stephen.

A substantial shareholder, Stephen had been elected a director in 1871. Edwin H. King was President then, and R. B. Angus, general manager; all was well with the business world and the Bank was paying a dividend of 16 per cent. Two years later, King was succeeded by David Torrance, who had just established the Dominion Line on the Atlantic and was also doing an extensive trade with the West Indies, and George Stephen became Vice-President.

On 7 June 1875, in the absence through illness of the President, Stephen for the first time took the Chair at the Annual General Meeting. A decrease in net profits was reported, attributed to the impossibility of profitably employing money in the United States, and to the extremely low rates of interest prevailing in Canada. The dividend was reduced to 14 per cent, so that a balance might be held in reserve against the possibility of bad debts. In his speech, however, Stephen struck an optimistic note; in his opinion the state of stagnation could not long continue, but until it did pass away he considered that the business of the Bank ought to be confined within the narrowest possible limits.

David Torrance died in January 1876, and it was as President that Stephen faced the shareholders on 5 June. There was no improvement to report in the commercial situation. The general depression had continued to deepen, and the Bank was finding its activities severely restricted by the lack of desirable investments. The Report congratulated traders and manufacturers on the stability they had displayed in adverse circumstances, cutting down imports and

[1] James Hedley, 'The Financial Situation in Canada', in Rose-Belford's *Canadian Monthly*, Toronto, July 1880.

curtailing production. The President, still optimistic, referred to this as 'a painful but health-restoring process', which, 'if vigorously persisted in, until the volume of imports is brought down to the limits prescribed by the diminished buying capacity of the country, must soon make its influence felt in every department of our trade and commerce. It is only by such a reduction that business can again be made profitable.'

Again the Bank declared a dividend of 14 per cent, and a substantial sum was reserved for emergencies. The situation was under control. But it was the security of stalemate; nothing was ventured, nothing lost, but neither was there anything to be gained by an indefinite vigil on the fence.

The following year brought no confirmation of Stephen's prophecy. In February 1877, he wrote to Sir John Macdonald, who was still in Opposition, regarding some project which a friend of the latter was planning:

At present there is d . . . . d little encouragement to risk anything in Canadian enterprises, which are nearly all equally bad. I do not suppose the Government will deal with the depression which daily becomes deeper and darker. . . .[1]

When the crisis had come in 1874, bringing financial problems for the Government, Sir Richard Cartwright, Finance Minister in Mackenzie's administration, had raised the tariff on manufactured goods, reduced in 1867 from 20 to 15 per cent, to $17\frac{1}{2}$ per cent. Both Britain and the United States were unloading their surplus stocks on the Canadian market at very much reduced prices, so that revenue from *ad valorem* duties dwindled, while the Canadian product was at an immense disadvantage. Cartwright's proposal in 1875 to halt this trend by restoring the 20 per cent tariff was frustrated by Alexander Mackenzie's honourable decision to abide by the Party's declared policy, a decision which ultimately led to the eclipse of his Government by the Conservative phenomenon, the National Policy. On the point of resigning office, for he contended that it was a question not of Protection or Free Trade but of 'providing revenue for the public needs',[2] Cartwright was persuaded by Mackenzie to remain and find revenue from other sources to tide them over. The Finance Minister agreed that the depression could not last—that it was but a 'passing cloud'.

---

[1] Macd.P. 'Stephen' 267, Stephen to Macdonald, 2 February 1877.
[2] Sir Richard Cartwright, *Reminiscences*, Toronto, 1912, pp. 153-8.

But the cloud only grew blacker. The 1877 Budget, while it did not raise the tariff on manufactured goods, laid heavy duties on malt, ale, and tea. This was the point at which Stephen emerged as a Protectionist, in the sense in which that term was incorporated in the National Policy. Having read in the *Montreal Herald* that the Member for Montreal West, Thomas Workman, had told Parliament that as a manufacturer he considered it judicious to vote against a duty on coal (it was later found, on reference to *Hansard*, that this had been incorrectly reported), Stephen took up an indignant pen and wrote to that paper that as a manufacturer himself he was perfectly willing that a duty of 75 cents a ton should be imposed on bituminous coal, although his own concerns consumed a considerable quantity of this commodity. He pointed out that Nova Scotia had all the natural facilities for the production of coal and iron as cheaply as any country in the world; what she required was equally favourable conditions of market. Similarly, each of the other Provinces had its own special advantages for the production of certain commodities, either natural or manufactured. He concluded:

Hence it seems to me that what the country needs most today . . . is a Government who will try to estimate aright the capacities of the country, and decide what Canada can do successfully for herself, and what she cannot do, and ought not to attempt, and who would then so frame the Customs Tariff, that those industries for which we have a natural and special aptitude might have the advantage of an assured market within the Dominion.

I do not ask that the volume of taxation should be increased one single cent beyond the sum absolutely required to carry on the Government of the country.

The lighter the burden of taxation the better for all, but I do ask that the burden should be so adjusted to the back of the bearer, that the interference with his onward progress shall be reduced to the minimum. . . .[1]

In April Stephen wrote to Macdonald that the situation had not improved. After commenting on the success which George Laidlaw was, unaccountably, having with a new short line, the Credit Valley, from Toronto to St. Thomas[2] Stephen concluded:

Nothing new here—dull times and unprofitable trade on all hands. Cartwright's 'passing cloud' doesn't pass.[3]

[1] See Debates of the Canadian House of Commons (hereafter 'D. of C.H.C.') 6 March and 15 March 1877.
[2] See *Toronto Mail*, 16 February 1884, also quoted on page 154.
[3] Macd.P. 'Stephen' 267, Stephen to Macdonald, 23 April 1877.

FINANCIAL STAGNATION AND A RISK THAT PAID

4 June 1877, brought another Annual General Meeting of the Bank of Montreal. The tone of the Report was, the President said, 'somewhat more apologetic than usual'. (The Canadian *Monetary Times* of 8 June observed: 'It shows . . . what a handsome return had grown to be expected from the institution when 13 per cent dividend was regarded as a result requiring to be excused. . . .') The 'bad times' remained and their effects had been intensified by the previous year's poor harvest and by the tendency of importers to depart from the 'health-restoring process of contraction'. The depressed state of affairs had meant still less business for the Bank, rates of interest at home and abroad were low and, in addition, unusually large losses through bad debts had had to be met from the reserve laid aside for the purpose.

Stephen warned businessmen against incurring new liabilities. The markets were overstocked as a result of increased importations, and were still subject to 'spasmodic raids from the other side of the line whenever any accumulation of stocks takes place over there'. He feared, moreover, that owing to the continued expenditure of large sums of money on railways and other public works, the full measure of the reaction from the period of inflation from which the country had been suffering had not yet been reached. The state of the Bank itself was, under the circumstances, not unsatisfactory; indeed, the President remarked, the Bank was never in a better position to undertake any sound and legitimate business that might offer, in Canada or elsewhere, than it was at that time.

But where was that business to be found? The need to channel this dammed-up river of wealth in some useful direction was strongly urged in the Montreal *Journal of Commerce* of 19 October:

Money, floating capital, unused funds, are more abundant than ever; the cash-boxes overflow; the large banks literally sweat with gold; and this excess, this plethora of unemployed capital, causes the public funds to advance and the price of money to decrease. It is business that is wanting; it is the employment of capital that is in default. . . .

In his speech to the Annual General Meeting of the Bank on 3 June 1878, Stephen gave a faint indication of a solution that was in his mind. Although, he said, the period of abnormally heavy losses from bad debts had passed, it was likely to be followed by one of diminished earnings, and he prophesied that the difficulty of finding safe and profitable employment *in Canada* for all the means at the disposal of the Bank was more likely to increase than to diminish. Printed records do not show the words 'in Canada' in italics, but it seems certain that the President gave them mental, if not vocal emphasis. The Report pursued the theme even further. The previous year's abundant harvest had, it said, stimulated a 'healthful movement of unemployed labour from the cities and older settlements to the new lands of the Western Provinces', a tendency that had been even more marked in the neighbouring country than in Canada. The opening up of the Middle West had in America been accompanied by a decided improvement in mercantile affairs south of the boundary which the directors hoped would not be without a favourable influence in Canada. As token of their faith, that year saw the founding of a branch of the Bank in Winnipeg, the new prairie city growing up around the old Hudson's Bay post at Fort Garry. It was the more advanced development south of the line, however, of which immediate advantage was to be taken.

The Report under discussion at the Bank's General Meeting on 2 June 1879, showed that Canada's economic recovery still lagged behind that of the United States, although the position of the Bank itself remained satisfactory. The President, in his speech, held out the hope of diminished losses if not of increased earnings. He went on

I am happy to believe that the position and credit of the Bank, both at home and abroad, never stood higher than it does today. The past two years, and more particularly the one just ended, have, as you all know, been exceedingly disastrous to the commercial and financial interests of the country, and it is not to be wondered at that we, with our widely extended business, and large aggregate of loans, should have shared in the misfortune and losses which have been all but universal. . . .

The President's speech was followed, as always, by 'question time', and the first shareholder to raise his voice took his cue from Stephen himself, but put up a plea for positive, rather than comparative achievement. The speech of John Crawford, President of the Montreal City Passenger Railway, was a regular feature of these meetings; his was the voice of the shareholder who, in reality pretty well satisfied with the conduct of affairs, likes to remind the directors that they are under observation. At the 1876 meeting George Stephen had cast an eye round the gathering and remarked, 'I am sorry to see that Mr. Crawford is not here, but I hope his mantle has fallen upon someone who will ask some questions'. In 1879, however, questions were not lacking. When, having taxed the Board with accommodating insolvent rather than solvent customers, rated his fellow-shareholders for contributing to the downward progress of the institution by their ill-advised business methods and declared the Banking Act to be a fraud, Mr. Crawford returned satisfied to his seat, another shareholder rose, with sterner gleam of battle in his eye.

Mr. John McDonald hoped he would get a straightforward answer to the question he was about to ask, with regard to granting so much accommodation in certain quarters. Was it true, what he had heard on the street, that some of the directors held a railway in the West and required large accommodation for it? Here Mr. Crawford intervened again, with a mild observation that he would have the names of parties by whom it had sustained loss placarded on the walls of the Bank.

Unperturbed, George Stephen rose and quietly expressed the pleasure he felt that the remarks of his friend Mr. McDonald had given him an opportunity to reply to the statement that 'someone ran a railway', bowing, in his choice of phrase, with mock gravity to the current conception of a railway as being a form of lottery. No railway, he declared, had ever owed the Bank one dollar that could not be collected whenever the Bank declined to lend.

One may judge the effect of this terse rejoinder from the fact that although it could hardly be judged a straightforward answer, Mr. McDonald resumed his seat murmuring defensively that he had heard the rumour outside from time to time, and had thought it was well to look after the directors.

The general manager, however, was prepared to supplement the President's understatement, made in the spirit of perverse taciturnity which was destined frequently to animate Stephen when called upon to justify a course of action which he himself knew to be only for the benefit of his critics. With regard to the directors' loans, R. B. Angus said that it would, in his opinion, be a misfortune to the Bank if the shareholders were to get impatient, and it would not be judicious at any time to give a detailed statement of that account. The Bank had no right to give figures of other peoples' business, but if the shareholders got unreasonable and did not trust their directors in that respect, and wished these loans to disappear from the books it could be done. They had just to say so, and in a very few days the loans represented by the directors would be withdrawn; but he could only say that the Bank would then lose some of the most desirable business in Canada, and simply transfer to rivals the opportunity of making money of which the Bank then had the monopoly. He concluded:

The Bank has not a railway account that is not amply covered, and it holds securities of an unquestionable character for anything connected with railways.

The railway in question was the St. Paul, Minneapolis and Manitoba, which was destined to turn its proprietors into millionaires, and which undoubtedly provided the Bank of Montreal with one of the most profitable transactions of its history.

II
Railroading in the Middle West

NEW SETTLERS AND A BANKRUPT RAILROAD

To provide the background for the entrance of George Stephen and his associates into the railway theatre of the West, it is necessary at this point briefly to bring the history of transport in the Red River Valley up to date. Railway-building, like a slow-moving tide, had since the sixties been edging up towards the Red River, at every advance shortening by a few more miles the trail of the ox-train. In 1867 the St. Paul and Pacific, heading northwest from Minnesota's capital, reached St. Cloud, and the Red River cart was known no longer south of that point. In 1871 the Northern Pacific, building westward from Duluth, tapped the traffic stream at Moorhead, across the river from Fargo, the normal head of navigation, and in less than two years the 'prairie schooner' had disappeared completely from the Minnesotan scene.

Nor was it only the inanimate 'vulgar stuff of peace' that was finding its way from the east into Minnesota and Manitoba by the ever-accelerating route of rail and river steamer. Immigrants, no longer deterred by the discomfort of travelling long distances through unknown territory with all their worldly possessions stacked on the tedious carts, began to pour into the promised land, settling on the rich acres both north and south of the 49th Parallel.

Not unnaturally, most of the immigrants coming in via Duluth halted south of the boundary; with an abundance of good farming land there it seemed superfluous to undertake the second stage of the journey up the Red. Owing to financial difficulties, the Northern Pacific Railroad had stopped short at Moorhead; writing to Sir John Rose in March 1872, Sir John Macdonald expressed the fear that the Northern Pacific would crash before completing a connection to Pembina, on the Canadian border.[1] At that time this American company also had on its hands the St. Paul and Pacific (later to become

---

[1] Macd.L.B. 17.370, Macdonald to Rose, 5 March 1872.

the St. Paul, Minneapolis and Manitoba) which like the wounded snake was dragging its slow length along the northern valley of the Mississippi. In order to clarify later events, and to indicate clearly the nature of the enterprise with which in 1877 George Stephen became connected, the history of the St. Paul and Pacific must be traced through twenty years of misfortune.

In 1857, when the connection between agriculture, immigration, producers' and consumers' markets and communications had become apparent, the Congress of the United States passed an Act making a grant of land to the Territory of Minnesota to aid in the construction of railroads there. Four railroad companies then received land grants from the Territorial Legislature, one of which, then called the Minnesota and Pacific Railroad Company, undertook to build 'from Stillwater by way of St. Paul and St. Anthony, to a point between the foot of Big Ston [*sic*] Lake and the mouth of the Sioux Wood River, with a branch via St. Cloud and Crow Wing, to the navigable waters of the Red River of the North, at such point as the Legislature of said Territory may determine'.[1] The lands were granted solely on condition that they should be applied exclusively in the construction of the road specified, and that they should be handed over only as the work progressed.

The fact that the work did not progress, on any of the four lines, would inevitably have meant the forfeiture of the land grants when, in 1860, all four companies became insolvent, had not the Territorial Government been extremely anxious to have railways built. The companies themselves were not entirely to blame; the times were not propitious for railway investment, badly as the lines were needed, and the Government decided to give them another chance.[2] Then came the Civil War. Money for railway-building became scarcer than ever, and by the end of 1861 the Minnesota and Pacific Railroad Company had ceased to exist.

Such were the potentialities, however, of railroading in this new field of settlement that in 1862 another company, calling itself the St. Paul and Pacific, accepted from the Legislature the rights and properties of the defunct corporation. Two years later, when construction was still lagging, the company was by special Act of the Legislature resolved into two parts; a separate interest was given

[1] Statutes at Large and Treaties of the U.S.A., vol. XI, 34th Congress, Session III, chapter 99, 3 March 1857 (Boston, 1867).
[2] William Watts Folwell, *A History of Minnesota*, St. Paul, 1926, vol. III, pp. 184, 420–2 and 441; vol. II, p. 330.

power to issue special and preferred stock with the object of hastening the construction of those sections of the line which traversed populated areas and thereby earning their land grant, while the primary company retained its franchises and was to build through unoccupied country, earning its land grant at greater leisure. Variants of this 'construction company' device were to become not uncommon in railroading.

In 1866 one Edwin B. Litchfield of Brooklyn, who had bought most of the special and preferred stock of the St. Paul and Pacific, acquired from the Company the surveyed lines from St. Paul to Watab and from St. Anthony to Breckenridge, including the land grant and other rights, and undertook to complete these lines and to organize a board of directors to administer the property under the name of the First Division of the St. Paul and Pacific Railroad Company. Soon afterwards Litchfield disposed of his interest to E. Darwin Litchfield of London, who in 1870 sold out completely to the Northern Pacific Railroad Company for $500,000 cash and $1,500,000 in second mortgage bonds of the St. Paul and Pacific primary company whose stock and franchises the Northern Pacific had meantime acquired. By 1871, therefore, when its own line reached Moorhead, the Northern Pacific controlled practically the entire St. Paul and Pacific system, a property of potential rather than present value.

The next chapter in the history of the enterprise was to introduce a group of investors destined to play a prominent part at the time when George Stephen and his friends became interested in it. An Act of Congress approved a change of location for the northbound line; instead of following the Mississippi to Crow Wing and the navigable waters of the Red River, it was to run via Alexandria, Fergus Falls and Crookston to St. Vincent, while an extension was to be completed from St. Cloud to Brainerd.[1] 'Extension' bonds were disposed of to a firm of bankers in Amsterdam, Lippman, Rosenthal and Company, probably with little difficulty as at that time the Northern Pacific's credit still stood high. The purchasers were further encouraged for a time by the regular payment of interest.

But the money realized from the sale of the bonds was spent extravagantly, and in October 1872 the contractors stopped work, with over half a million dollars owing them. About a hundred miles of the main line had been completed and were in operation, but the

[1] Statutes at Large, vol. XVI, p. 588.

Brainerd extension had not been touched. In May and June of the following year no interest was paid to the bondholders. To obtain the land grant, the roads had to be finished by December 1873, but when that time came the prospect of seeing a group of foreigners laying claim to Minnesota land prevented the Courts from ordering foreclosure proceedings.[1]

That was the year that saw the beginnings of the world depression. The Northern Pacific itself fell into the hands of a receiver and was powerless to help its subsidiary. To make matters worse, another type of cloud appeared on the horizon and the Rocky Mountain locust descended upon the Middle West. The 'hoppers', as they were termed by those not troubled by the pedantries of entomology, made farming literally impossible, even on land where 'weeds ten feet high spring when the soil is stirred'.[2] They consumed every variety of grain and vegetable except beets; even rhubarb was not spared their ravages. To drive a team through them was like cleaving the waters in a boat. As one writer put it, they left the country looking like the top of an old rusty stove.[3] This was Minnesota as George Stephen first saw it, and nothing can have looked more desolate than the miles upon miles of prairie in monotone, robbed of all evidence of the promise that was to be so richly fulfilled.

Yet once again the St. Paul and Pacific found a backer. In 1874 the stock was once more in the hands of E. B. Litchfield, with the Dutch group and various other individuals holding the majority of the bonds. Now events began to move more swiftly. Although the Minnesota Legislature was for the moment and under the circumstances inclined to turn a blind eye to the lack of building activity, the patience of the Dutch bondholders was exhausted. They decided to go to law.

They appointed as their agents John S. Kennedy and Company of New York, who duly filed a Bill in equity in the United States Circuit Court in Minnesota against the two St. Paul and Pacific Companies, and demanded the appointment of a receiver. The man chosen for this office was Jesse P. Farley of Dubuque, Iowa, formerly connected with the Dubuque and Sioux City Railroad. Farley was authorized to borrow $5,000,000 with which to complete the extensions, but was able to raise only $100,000, to which the Dutch

[1] Folwell, op. cit. vol. III, pp. 444, 446.
[2] Finlay Dun in Bertha L. Heilbron, 'A British Agricultural Expert in the Red River Valley, 1879', in *North Dakota Historical Quarterly*, January 1933, p. 108.
[3] John Moody, *The Railroad Builders*, New Haven, 1919, p. 169.

contributed not a cent. In February 1876 the directorate of the First Division Company was reorganized, and Farley was appointed general manager and superintendent. But although the balance sheets began to show a surplus of receipts over operating expenses, there was a yearly interest charge of nearly $2 million on a bonded debt of over $28 million. The Dutch bondholders decided to send a personal representative, Johan Carp, to investigate the situation on the spot.[1]

SMITH AND HILL SEE THE POSSIBILITIES

The slow progress of railway construction south of the boundary had given food for thought to Donald A. Smith, now representing Selkirk, Manitoba, in the Dominion Parliament. There was still no immediate hope of rail communication between Manitoba and the Eastern Provinces on Canadian territory, but Mackenzie's Government had in 1874 introduced legislation to provide for the construction of a branch of the Pacific Railway from St. Boniface south to Pembina: the route of the line planned by Smith and his colleagues in 1871. But unless this branch could connect, on completion, with an American road, it would be something of a blind alley.

As early as 1870 Smith had discussed this particular problem with James Jerome Hill of St. Paul, whom he had encountered by chance on the trail between St. Paul and Fort Garry while on his way to Red River.[2] Hill, a Canadian by birth, was to become one of the giants of American railroading. He was then associated with Norman W. Kittson in the Red River Transportation Company, which had its own short line from Glyndon to Fisher's Landing via Crookston, but as the days of the steamers' monopoly were numbered, these men of enterprise were anxious to have a stake in the new order.

Stephen's attention was first directed to the St. Paul and Pacific in 1873 or 1874, when Smith, who had occasion to make frequent journeys through Minnesota to Winnipeg and the North West, used to return to Montreal and bore his cousin exceedingly with his pipe-dreams of rail connections between the older Provinces of the East and the new territories of the West. He talked at length of the part the Minnesota lines must play, and plagued Stephen to join with

[1] Folwell, op. cit. vol. III, pp. 446-7, 450.
[2] Joseph G. Pyle, 'J. J. Hill' in *Minnesota History Bulletin*, vol. II, no. 5, February 1918.

him in some plan for acquiring the properties of the St. Paul and Pacific. He was already in touch with J. J. Hill on the subject, but prior to 1876 no particular scheme was discussed. Stephen was not enthusiastic; he had never seen either Minnesota or the Canadian West, had heard unfavourable reports of the latter and thought, in short, that Smith was being a little less than realistic.

By the spring of 1877, however, even Stephen was beginning to be convinced by the persistent reiterations of his cousin regarding the possibilities of the territories in question, and when J. J. Hill came to Montreal to meet them with a definite proposal they all three came to the conclusion that if the St. Paul and Pacific properties could be acquired on something like the terms proposed it would be a very good stroke of business. Already Hill had some idea of the terms on which the Dutch group would part with their bonds, for in January of that year he and Kittson had made a tentative offer to Johan Carp, in terms which virtually precluded acceptance, with the object of obtaining this information.[1]

At the Montreal meeting a provisional price was set against each class of bonds and it was decided that in the event of the bond-holders accepting the total figure—they were to be free to alter the details—Stephen would endeavour to obtain a loan in London with which to finance the purchase. Having once got control of the bonds, the plan was to gain possession of the property by means of fore-closure proceedings. It would also involve the acquisition of the stock held by Litchfield, if complete autonomy were to be achieved.

On 26 May 1877, a letter was addressed by Hill and Kittson to Johan Carp at Utrecht, cancelling their previous offer and stating the terms under which they and their Montreal associates would consider purchasing the bonds. This was not intended to be a definite offer; they could not finally commit themselves until Stephen should have negotiated the necessary loan. But owing to the admittedly ambiguous wording of the proposition the Dutch group construed it as such, and their hopes rose.

Stephen, meanwhile, had resolved to make a personal inspection of the properties in Minnesota. Late in August 1877 he and R. B. Angus had occasion to visit Chicago on Bank business, and took the opportunity of proceeding to St. Paul. The story is commonly told that this was not pre-arranged, but that having a day to spare after completing their business they spun a coin in order to determine

[1] J. G. Pyle, *Life of James J. Hill*, New York, 1917, vol. I, p. 212.

whether they should visit St. Paul or St. Louis. It is even alleged
that Stephen favoured the latter, but that the coin decreed St. Paul.
Documentary evidence refutes this; before leaving Montreal
Stephen had received a letter from Hill saying how much he looked
forward to Stephen's visit, as he felt sure that only then would he
fully appreciate the extent and value of the property. The die was by
then virtually cast that was to mould George Stephen's future; often
as the hand of fate showed itself throughout his career it was not, at
this point, the spinning of a coin that set his feet towards his third
St. Paul.

It is to Donald Smith that we owe an account of the visit, for both
he and J. J. Hill accompanied Stephen on his journey over the completed portion of the St. Paul and Pacific on 1 September. The tale
was told many years later by the then Lord Strathcona to Archbishop Ireland, the pioneer of Catholic colonization in Minnesota:

All went well at first. Between St. Paul and Litchfield there were settlers
and villages. But beyond Litchfield it was almost nothing but wild, un-
tenanted prairie. Mr. Stephen shook his head ominously. Whence was
business to come to the railroad? When would there be settlers in this
barren waste? At last the station of De Graff was reached. It was Sunday
morning. Around a rude but good-sized structure there were crowds of
people; the trails leading toward it were covered with conveyances, most
of them drawn by oxen. 'What is all this?' inquired Mr. Stephen. 'Why,'
answered quickly his friends, 'this is but an instance of what is soon to
occur along the whole line of the railroad. This is a colony opened by
Bishop Ireland one single year ago. Already the settlers brought in by the
Bishop are counted by hundreds, and hundreds of others are coming to
join them from different parts of America and Europe. This is Sunday
morning, and the settlers are going to Mass.' The certain rush of immigrants to the West was pictured to Mr. Stephen in glowing terms. He
already saw enough to make the prophecy credible. From that moment
he was won over to the new enterprise.[1]

In mid-September, before Stephen left for England, John S.
Barnes, representing the Dutch group's agents in New York, came
to Montreal to confer with the associates. The bondholders had
suggested some minor modifications of Hill's and Kittson's proposal
of 26 May, to which Stephen and his friends were ready to agree.
Nothing definite could be concluded, however, until the purchase-
money was in sight.

[1] Pyle, op. cit. vol. I, p. 205.

STEPHEN CONVINCED BUT FINANCIAL MISSION FAILS

Evidence regarding the first interest in, and subsequent acquisition of the St. Paul and Pacific properties is, fortunately for the historian, available in great detail as a result of the unfortunate attempt of Jesse P. Farley, the Company's receiver, to make something for himself out of the unexpectedly successful coup.[1] In spite of the nature of his office, Farley claimed that by a private arrangement he had been promised a fifth share in the profits, and when this was not forthcoming he took his case to law. There is always a section of public opinion ready to impute unworthy motives and methods to anyone who has achieved outstanding success in a business transaction, and it seems clear that Farley's object in bringing the suit was not unconnected with blackmail. The defendants, having nothing to hide, let the law take its course, which it did through twelve long years, during which both Kittson and Farley died. In Stephen's testimony, given in 1888, the whole tale is unfolded, incident by incident.

No very definite agreement was at first made as to the associates' financial shares in the project; there was a sort of tacit understanding that if the scheme were carried through all four—Hill, Kittson, Smith, and Stephen—should have an equal interest. Asked by the judge what understanding, if any, there was between them as to Stephen's authority to dispose of any interest in the enterprise to the persons to whom he applied in England for financial support, Stephen replied:

It was generally understood that it might take a share in the profits that it was supposed might be realized of one fifth to secure the financial aid necessary to carry the thing through. That is to say, Sir Donald Smith, myself, Mr. Kittson and Mr. Hill would each have one fifth, leaving one fifth to be disposed of to secure the money necessary to buy the Company's bonds. . . . It was understood in a general way that I was in a position to concede any reasonable terms that might be exacted in order to attain our object.[2]

Stephen sailed for England at the end of September. Before making any attempt to negotiate a loan in London he crossed to Amsterdam and made himself personally acquainted with most of

---

[1] Case of Jesse P. Farley, *v* N.W. Kittson *et. al.*, U.S. Circuit Court, District of Minnesota, in Equity, Ent. 131. C. Ch. Unless otherwise attributed, all the evidence in the preceding pages comes from Stephen's Testimony, hereafter Step. Test.

[2] Step. Test. p. 169.

the Dutch group, explaining to them in general terms what he planned to do.[1] This personal meeting only served to increase the confidence of the bondholders that they were to be able to make a reasonably profitable withdrawal from Minnesota railroading.

In London, however, Stephen experienced a setback. In spite of his offers of all the security they could muster, and a fifth share in the profits, the response he met with was not enthusiastic. In his own words:

After considerable negotiation I utterly failed. Nobody believed—or at least I failed to induce anybody to believe—that the property was good for anything.[2]

At the Canadian end, meantime, affairs were moving rapidly. In October Farley warned the New York agents, John S. Kennedy and Company, that the Northern Pacific, once more in control of its resources, was negotiating with the Canadian Government for exclusive rights over the branch line from Fort Garry to the boundary. The Pacific was planning to build an extension from its terminus at Moorhead to St. Vincent, and to have a forfeiture declared on the St. Paul and Pacific line from Crookston to the boundary. It was even taking steps to 'pack' the Minnesota Legislature to ensure the success of the scheme. Seeing that the Dutchmen were in danger of losing everything, their agents advised them to accept Hill's and Kittson's proposition as it stood.[3]

The Dutch were only too anxious to take advantage of the only chance they had of avoiding total loss on their property; to those who knew the circumstances, the very fact that someone had offered to relieve them of it on any terms seemed incredible: they 'thought they were seeing the ghost walk' is Pyle's way of expressing it. Now they were suddenly faced with the intelligence that owing to Stephen's failure to find the wherewithal, that opportunity was completely withdrawn.

CONTROL OF ST. PAUL AND PACIFIC

It was characteristic of Stephen that once he had made up his mind to a thing he did not easily renounce it. A short time before he

---

[1] Step. Test. A 74, p. 169. Stephen added, 'I dare not venture to name them'. They were: Chemet & Weetjen, Kerkhoven & Co., Lippman, Rosenthal & Co., Wurfbain & Son, Tutein Nolthenius & De Haan (all of Amsterdam), H. C. Voorhoeve & Co. of Rotterdam and Johan Carp of Utrecht.

[2] Ibid. p. 170.   [3] Pyle, op. cit. vol. I, pp. 210 and 222.

had refused to take any interest in the potentialities of the West; now that he was convinced he threw himself into the task of realizing them. Shortly after his return from England early in January 1878, he went to New York where he met John S. Kennedy for the first time, and submitted a new proposal on an entirely different basis.[1] The new plan, which was his own idea,[2] was to buy the bonds on credit, depositing only such a sum as the associates could themselves supply, and paying up the balance after the foreclosure proceedings had been completed. The new proposal was subsequently put to the Dutch group and duly accepted.[3] On 13 March by a formal agreement, the associates assumed control of the St. Paul and Pacific.[4]

The initial sum required, although much smaller than that which would have been necessary to buy the bonds outright, was still considerable; the actual payment to Amsterdam was in fact the smallest item, amounting to $100,000. In addition, $280,000 was spent in clearing the standing debts of the Company, and $140,000 was required to pay the first half-yearly dividend; $1 million besides had to be raised for the completion of extension lines, to fulfil an agreement with the Courts.[5] Moreover, it was estimated that it would take $500,000 to get possession of the stock still held by Litchfield. After all this, there remained the main line to St. Vincent to be built.

It was a tall order. As a last resort, Stephen consented to use his credit with the Bank of Montreal. When asked by the judge whether at any time prior to 13 March 1878, it was expected that any part of the money required should be obtained from or through the Bank of Montreal, Stephen's answer was: 'No, never thought of such a thing.'[6] Only the fact that the reduced sum could be covered by the securities of the associates, possibly supported by the knowledge that if the scheme succeeded it would provide just that fillip to its business for which the Bank had been waiting, could have persuaded the President to agree to this course of action. The only risk involved was to the personal fortunes of the associates, and to their reputations as astute men of business. At this stage they were ready to take that risk.

Inevitably, rumours got about regarding the Bank's part in the transaction; more will be said of this presently. Certainly one great

[1] Step. Test. A 84, p. 171.   [2] Step. Test. A 98, p. 174.
[3] Pyle, op. cit. vol. I, pp. 258-9 and Appendix 5.   [4] Defendant's Exhibit 122.
[5] Pyle, op. cit. p. 249.   [6] Step. Test. A 115, p. 181.

advantage of obtaining money from this source was that strict secrecy was guaranteed. At that point it was vitally important that the actual state of the Company's finances should not become known in two quarters: to Edwin B. Litchfield or to the Northern Pacific Railroad Company.

On 27 March 1878, a written agreement concerning their share in the enterprise was formally signed by the associates. The profits and losses accruing from the reorganized Company were thereby apportioned in the following manner:

George Stephen, two fifths, Donald A. Smith one fifth, Norman W. Kittson one fifth, and James J. Hill one fifth; it being, however, understood and agreed between us that one half of the said two fifths interest so set off to the said George Stephen as above, shall be held by him for the purpose of securing the necessary means to carry out and complete our said agreement.[1]

This document also provided for the redivision of the stock of the Red River Transportation Company, all the associates thereafter having an equal share. Although the Transportation Company and its associated railway interest, the Red River Valley Company, operating the short line from Glyndon to Fisher's Landing, maintained their separate identities they were thus henceforward under the same control as the St. Paul and Pacific; the rumour-mongers called this 'monopoly'.

According to an 1878 amendment to the Act of the Minnesota Legislature governing the Company's franchises, in order to qualify for the land grant the St. Paul and Pacific was required to complete by December 1878 the lines from Melrose to Alexandria. For the construction of the section from Crookston to St. Vincent more time was allowed, but the associates were anxious that this too should be finished that year so as to connect with the Canadian Government's Pembina Branch of the Pacific Railway. They proposed to finance this work by means of Receiver's Debentures, hoping to succeed where Farley had failed to raise the authorized loan. All the financial arrangements were entrusted to Stephen.

Farley was retained in his capacity as general manager, Stephen having told John S. Kennedy, who pending the foreclosure proceedings remained the Dutch group's representative, that he and his friends thought highly of the receiver's capabilities and would make

[1] Pyle, op. cit. vol. I, Appendix V. B.

it worth his while to stay until the lines were completed. Asked how it was intended to reward Farley for his services, Stephen replied:

What I proposed to do for him, when the foreclosures and everything were settled up, was to give him what the Dutchmen would call a 'bonification' and it was perfectly competent for me to do so, because I had the means of doing it at my own disposal.[1]

As time went on, however, it became evident that confidence in Farley had been misplaced. He himself doubted the wisdom of building to the boundary at that time; he told Stephen that it would be twenty years before such a line would pay, but added that if Stephen provided the money he had no choice but to spend it. This he did with little enthusiasm; it seemed, in fact, at one point, that the work would not be completed to schedule. He complained that the work was becoming too much for him, but grumbled more when Hill recommended a successor. Had the Company been in full possession of the property it would have been easy to dismiss the manager who was not only half-hearted about construction but careless regarding the operation of the completed sections. As it was, internal dissension had to be avoided, and Stephen wrote to Hill:

We . . . must all get along as best we can, tiding over things until we get into a shape to help ourselves. . . .[2]

MINORITY SHAREHOLDER BOUGHT OUT

The letter just quoted was written in reply to one from Hill in which he described the reckless operation of their railway. Hill concluded:

All this points to the advantage to us of an early settlement with Litchfield. . . . I do not see that we can prudently refuse paying him a liberal sum in order to get possession of the property, to enable us to run it as it should be run, and also to put us in possession of its revenues and in that way relieve us from the large personal liability for the sums necessary to carry out the undertaking.[3]

After the first Montreal meeting in 1877, Hill had gone to New York to try to come to some arrangement with Litchfield for the purchase of his First Division Company stock, but had been unsuccessful. This task had since been handed over with the other financial negotiations to Stephen.

[1] Step. Test. pp. 178-9.
[2] Defendants' Exhibit 34, Stephen to Hill, 3 January 1879.
[3] Defendants' Exhibit 131, Hill to Stephen, 26 December 1878.

In the summer of 1878 Stephen in turn set out for New York and introduced himself to Litchfield. To the Judge's somewhat superfluous question 'What was your object in going to see him and making his acquaintance?' Stephen replied with characteristic bluntness: 'My object in making his acquaintance was to endeavour to get possession of his stock.'[1] Litchfield received him kindly enough and they talked for some time together, but with no immediate result.

In November 1878, a meeting took place in St. Paul between Stephen, Hill, Kittson and three representatives of the Northern Pacific Railroad Company at which various differences were resolved, evidently to the great satisfaction of the President of the older road. He became confidential, telling Stephen that Litchfield had offered his St. Paul and Pacific stock to the Northern Pacific. He was confident that he could influence Litchfield to settle instead with Stephen, and even volunteered to act as intermediary. Billings and Litchfield quarrelled, however, before anything was achieved.[2]

Towards the end of the year Stephen saw Litchfield several times, and some correspondence passed between them. On 7 January 1879, Stephen wrote to Hill:

Nothing can be done with him by writing, so I go down with Mr. Smith on Thursday afternoon, to wait there until we either reach a settlement or give up the effort to effect one.[3]

They were successful. Stephen's letter to Hill of 17 January was referred to in Court. 'In this letter,' said the Judge, 'you state you "have settled with the old rat on the basis of $500,000." Who is meant in that letter by the term "old rat?"' Said Stephen: 'I am afraid it was Mr. Litchfield.'[4]

The transaction was not at once made public; Litchfield wished first to complete some business in St. Paul before the news were known there. There was, too, a further meeting in New York, attended by Hill, Stephen and Hill's attorney, R. B. Galusha, at which the final details were settled with Litchfield's representative, George L. Becker. On 3 March 1879, the *Montreal Gazette*, quoting the St. Paul *Pioneer Press*, announced that the new bond-holders of the St. Paul and Pacific had purchased Litchfield's common stock and bonds.

---

[1] Step. Test. p. 192.   [2] Step. Test. A 154, p. 191; A 157, p. 190.
[3] Defendants' Exhibit 36.   [4] Defendants' Exhibit 39 and Step. Test. p. 319.

For the first time in six years the railroad had no conflicting interests. Stephen became President of the First Division Company, and a new board of directors was chosen. The way was now clear for the foreclosure proceedings and the reorganization of the St. Paul and Pacific Company.

PLANS THREATENED BY RIVAL NORTHERN PACIFIC

The meeting referred to above between representatives of the St. Paul and Pacific and the Northern Pacific, at which so friendly an atmosphere prevailed, was in the nature of a peace conference, although its results were no more lasting than those of many another. It ended a war of bombast and bluff in which J. J. Hill only narrowly succeeded in out-bluffing and out-bombasting the leaders of the rival enterprise.

The *casus belli* cannot be better explained than by quoting the racy account in Frank P. Morse's *Cavalcade of the Rails*[1] of the position of the roads in March 1878, just after the Dutch bondholders had been bought out:

One last menace clouded the situation. The newly reorganised Northern Pacific turned a suspicious eye on its vigorous little rival. The interests back of the older road had expected to take over the St. Paul and Pacific at the psychological moment and dictate terms. They resented the evolution of the Manitoba[2] from the wreckage into which Hill and his friends had dived. They decided to put pressure on their small competitor; force a second bankruptcy and pick up the pieces they wanted. The Northern Pacific elected to build a competing line through this valuable territory and send trains to Winnipeg. . . .

The Northern Pacific did indeed make a survey for a branch line to run from a point across the Red from Moorhead northwards to the boundary, and twenty miles were actually built. In May 1878, Hill went to New York to see representatives of the pirate road who thought he had come to offer some concession if they would give up their plan to build the branch. On the contrary, Hill threatened to end the agreement whereby the Northern Pacific had been using the St. Paul company's line from Sauk Rapids to St. Paul at a *pro rata* charge; new terms would be made, imposing not only higher charges for the use of the line but also an additional charge for the use of the

---

[1] New York, 1940, p. 236.
[2] A slight anachronism, referring to the St. Paul, Minneapolis and Manitoba, as the road was later named.

St. Paul terminals. To this the Northern Pacific replied that, in that case, besides continuing their line to the boundary they would build their own road north from Minneapolis.[1]

To Stephen, who was somewhat alarmed at these extravagant statements, Hill wrote:

We do not think the Northern Pacific people intend to build any road in Minnesota, either in the Red River Valley or from Sauk Rapids to Minneapolis. If they had any money to spare they would be more apt to build west of Bismarck and save their land grant.[2]

Three months later the battle was still raging, Hill becoming more imperturbable as time went on. He reported to Stephen his latest thrust:

'I said to Mr. Wright' [general manager of the Northern Pacific] '. . . .if he persistently attacked us we would make a struggle for life and would not come off second best. We would at once survey a line from Grand Forks to Fort Buford at the mouth of the Yellowstone' [i.e. due west] 'which was on a good easy line all the way, through a country as good for agriculture as the very best portions of his road, and we would ask Congress for half his grant to the Rocky Mountains, and that he knew there were strong interests opposed to him who would be only too glad to help us; winding up by saying that our interests at present lay in developing Manitoba, but we would not sit quietly down and see him build lines that were unnecessary and only useful to injure us.'[3]

If the St. Paul and Pacific was at this time not over-affluent, the rival road was in no better condition. Mercifully ignorant of the true state of its enemy's affairs and fully aware of its own, the Northern Pacific bowed to the seemingly inevitable, accepted the St. Paul and Pacific as an established competitor and made overtures for peace.

The *Pioneer Press* of 20 November published a diplomatically-worded version of the terms of the agreement. The St. Paul and Pacific was to be left in undisputed possession of the Red River Valley—except for the belt adjacent to the Northern Pacific's westward line—and of the Manitoba trade. The Northern Pacific was to carry all freight coming to Duluth for either road, the revenues to be divided *pro rata* in the case of goods destined for Manitoba or points on the St. Paul road. By this compromise, the paper commented, the two roads recognized that there was ample room in the vast regions traversed by their lines for both their great enterprises; each had its

---

[1] Pyle, op. cit. vol. I, pp. 266-8.   [2] Ibid.   [3] Ibid.

distinct and independent mission, too grand in scope to be trammelled by any local disputes.

It may have been private relief at their release from the impossible commitments to which Hill and Wright had seemed to be driving their respective companies that led to the (albeit unproductive) coalition between Stephen and the President of the Northern Pacific, and to the latter's offer to mediate with Litchfield. At all events, the settlement precluded the possibility of hostile interference with the immediate plans of the St. Paul and Pacific for the purchase of Litchfield's stock and for the foreclosure on the property.

ST. PAUL, MINNEAPOLIS AND MANITOBA RAILROAD

The decrees of foreclosure were granted in March 1879, and by the middle of June the associates had acquired, by three separate sales under the decree, the main line of the St. Paul and Pacific from St. Paul to Morris, the branch from St. Paul to Watab and the extension lines from St. Cloud to St. Vincent. On 23 May, Stephen Smith, Hill, Kittson and John S. Barnes (representing John S. Kennedy and Company) met in a law office in St. Paul to reorganize the Company, which was to be known as the St. Paul, Minneapolis and Manitoba Railroad Company. Stephen was elected President, and Kittson Vice-President, the other directors being Smith, Hill, Barnes, R. B. Galusha and H. R. Bigelow (attorneys).

On becoming owners of the road, the associates made an issue of $8 million worth of bonds, secured by a first mortgage upon the entire property. Most of the former Dutch bondholders chose to take payment for the balance of what was due to them in these new bonds instead of in cash. Their satisfaction with the whole transaction was expressed in tangible form in the gift to Stephen of a valuable bowl. The fact that the said bowl had been fashioned in Holland to commemorate the Dutch victory over England in the Medway expedition in 1666 when the Dutch Admiral De Ruyter burned the best of the English Fleet, caused King George V, many years later, to say to Stephen: 'Why don't you destroy the damned thing?' Although opinion might be divided as to the suitability of the choice of gift, the gesture certainly appears to contradict the allegation which was to be made that the Dutch had been unfairly treated over their unfortunate American investment.

4

Of the remainder of the bond issue, $4 million worth were floated in New York and taken up by a syndicate of financial concerns of which one was the local branch of the Bank of Montreal. The disposal of its share of the bonds at a premium of about 5 per cent.—an operation undertaken in the ordinary course of business—constituted a profitable transaction for the Bank, but once again rumours got abroad. It was even alleged that the Bank had guaranteed the whole issue of $8 million.[1]

Matters were complicated at the crucial moment by the resignation of R. B. Angus from the position of general manager of the Bank of Montreal and his appointment as manager of the St. Paul, Minneapolis and Manitoba Railroad. It was said that the Bank's Board of Directors had been divided over the railway transaction. In vain did the Bank tell the *Montreal Gazette* (16 August) that Mr. Angus had resigned with a view to obtaining relaxation from work which had been very pressing of recent years, and that the most cordial relations existed between himself and the Board. The resultant fall in the Bank of Montreal stock was reported in *The Times* of 27 August 1879, with the comment:

Mr. Angus . . . is, it seems, going to assume the management of an obscure Canadian railway . . . which was formerly deeply in debt to the Bank of Montreal. It is, however, explained that this indebtedness has been extinguished by a successful issue of mortgage bonds of the line in New York. The only inference which can therefore be drawn from this step, as far as the reasons for it are known, is that it was very ill-timed, coming as it did on the back of a scare in banking credit that had very nearly involved the temporary suspension of half the banks in the Dominion.

More than once during his career Stephen was to experience a similar situation. Believing, even taking it for granted, that the private transactions of an individual or a company were his or its own affair and no one else's, Stephen rarely if ever made allowance for the reaction of public busybodies. Far from choosing a particular course because of its propaganda value, he preferred to go his own way, according as his not inconsiderable business instincts led him, prepared to let the results be his judge. Even knowing of the rumours that were going about concerning the financing of the railroad—and Stephen was ever regardless of such—he might still have seen nothing to prevent the St. Paul road from appointing the

[1] *Manitoba Weekly Free Press*, 4 October 1879, quoting *Chicago Tribune*.

manager of its choice. Those on the wrong side of the law are more inclined to be sensitive to public reaction than those who are not. If Stephen had decided obstinately to disregard public opinion —which would have been quite in character—it was more likely to have been because he had nothing to hide but considered the whole thing his own business and that of the Bank and Company.

The appointment of C. F. Smithers, formerly the Bank's New York agent, to the post of general manager stayed the panic and to some extent stilled the rumours, but the Annual General Meeting on 8 June 1880, brought inevitable criticism.

The Directors' Report, commenting on the continued depression of business, stated that but for the opportunity fortuitously offered the Bank of an outlet in the United States for some of its idle capital, the result of the year's operations would have been much less favourable than it was. Nevertheless, the moment 'question time' came, a shareholder rose to voice the opinion that the directors ought to be given an opportunity of explaining the relations of the Bank with the St. Paul, Minneapolis and Manitoba Company. It was understood, he said, that at one time the Bank had undertaken to run an unjustified risk in connection with that enterprise, and although the railway had turned out to be remarkably successful, it was suspected that had the President and other gentlemen connected with the Bank not been interested in the railway, the risk would not have been taken. Not content with Mr. Smithers's assurance that since he became manager the road had not owed the Bank a dollar, having on the contrary a large sum to its credit in New York, and that prior to that all reports concerning the advances made had been enormously exaggerated, the shareholders demanded a personal statement from Mr. Stephen, who accordingly rose to reply.

The President wasted no words. The previous year, by an admittedly evasive reply to a similar question, he had effectively silenced criticism of a transaction the wisdom of which was yet to be fully proved. On this occasion, secure in the knowledge that his action had been amply justified, and scorning to beg for the approval of those to whom a service had thereby been done, Stephen was equally terse:

It is not quite regular to bring up at any meeting of this kind private accounts, but, considering my own relations to the Bank, I have no objection to saying all that I think is fair and necessary on this question. The amount first loaned by the Bank of Montreal to myself and my associates, for which we had ample independent security, was $280,000. That loan was discussed at the Board. I was not present at the time it was made with the sanction of the Board of Directors. At no time did the Bank either here or in New York advance as much to myself and my associates as it had at times advanced to the late firm of George Stephen and Company. No advance was made in New York on which the Bank did not hold independent security. It never had a transaction in which it was safer or better secured, and the advance did not exceed something under $700,000.

RECEIVER ALLEGES BREACH OF UNDERSTANDING

On 13 June, the day before the last foreclosure sale took place, Jesse P. Farley brought suit in the District Court of Ramsey County against Kittson, Hill and the St. Paul, Minneapolis and Manitoba Railroad Company. He claimed that it was he who had conceived the original idea of purchasing the bonds of the road and of using them for the purpose of ultimately getting possession of the property, and alleged that there had been a mutual understanding between Hill, Kittson and himself that they should take an equal interest in the scheme. Hill, he said, was to persuade his friends from Montreal to furnish the major portion of the money, but in the final division of the concern all five were to have equal shares. It was on this understanding that the project had been launched, he averred, but shortly afterwards he had been 'dropped' from the consultations, and had never been asked to contribute his share of the purchase money, although he could have controlled just as much money as either Hill or Kittson.[1]

The judge of the District Court decided for Farley, holding that he was entitled to a hearing in Court. The defendants appealed to the Supreme Court of Minnesota. The case was heard during the summer of 1880, and when the decision was given on 24 August, that of the District judge was reversed.

In December 1881, Farley and his lawyers filed an amended Bill of Complaint in the United States Circuit Court for Minnesota, but on 15 July 1882, the Court dismissed the Bill, declaring that even if what Farley said was true, it was not the function of a court of equity to enforce the execution of a fraud, Farley's position as trustee for the Dutch bondholders precluding him from legitimate connection with such a transaction as he had described. Farley next appealed to the Supreme Court of the United States, the case not being brought

[1] Folwell, op. cit. vol. III, pp. 462-73.

forward until March 1886. On 2 February 1887, the Court refused to render a decision and referred the case back to the Circuit Court with directions to 'overrule the plea and to order the defendants to answer the Bill'.

The real trial opened at St. Paul on 17 October 1887. On 19 September 1889, the Circuit Court dismissed the Bill and on the same day Farley gave notice of appeal to the Supreme Court of the United States, where it came up on 30 October 1893. The Supreme Court endorsed the view of the Circuit Court regarding the inherent impossibility of the alleged understanding. Farley himself did not live to hear the judge's final summing-up:

A man of affairs would not be likely, in a matter of such magnitude, to rely upon a merely verbal agreement . . . the letters and conversations that we find in the record . . . do not point to or imply any subsisting agreement . . . It is not necessary to say, or to think that Farley . . . perpetrated intentional falsehood. It is altogether possible that, from desultory conversations with Kittson and Hill, and from an exaggerated sense of his own importance . . . Farley was led to believe that he was entitled to participate in the venture . . . But it is clear from his own evidence that he was not included in the actual transaction. . . .

Stephen had no idea of what was in Farley's mind in June 1879; the first he learned of the receiver's action was from the newspapers.[1] The only indication he had had that Farley was in the least dissatisfied was given in a conversation which took place in St. Paul about the time the Company was reorganized, between Farley, Kennedy and himself. Farley complained of not being appointed a director of the new Company, but Kennedy explained to him that as receiver he could not possibly hold that office. It was then, Stephen thought, that Farley had spoken of promises made to him by Hill and Kittson, but Stephen had the impression—and said so to Kennedy—that Farley was looking for nothing beyond such a 'bonification' of ten or twenty thousand dollars as Stephen already had in mind to give him before he retired to his native Dubuque.[2]

Earlier on, however, there had cropped up another source of friction between Farley and his employers. That the former had doubts about building the line to the boundary has already been mentioned. Probably resentful of the efforts of Stephen and Hill in late 1878 to hasten the work of construction in order to save the land grant, Farley had whenever possible asserted himself and acted

---

[1] Step. Test. p. 205.   [2] Step. Test. p. 204.

independently. One instance of this (and it is important historically as throwing light on contemporary Canadian railway progress) occurred over the fixing of rates. The Canadian Pacific branch to Pembina had been completed to the boundary in December 1878, but as the contractors were not obliged to hand it over to the Canadian Government for another year they were operating it themselves.[1] With them Farley's assistant Fisher, acting on Farley's behalf, had made arrangements which enabled him to quote through rates by rail from Eastern Canada to St. Boniface (across the Red from Winnipeg) the terminus of the Pembina Branch.[2] But Stephen was at this time trying to negotiate with the Government of Canada for a lease of the Pembina Branch, and Farley's plan put him at a great disadvantage. The contractors, making hay while the sun shone, were imposing excessive charges. As these must necessarily form part of a through rate, the total quoted by the St. Paul and Pacific was so high that the latter would inevitably share the blame for what was virtually putting an embargo on business.

The associates still had control of the Red River steamers, and when the navigation season reopened planned to use these to defeat the aims of the grasping contractors. Hill, writing to Stephen in January 1879 about the negotiations over the Branch, told him, as Pyle puts it, 'to put a flea in the Government's ear':

While we would very much prefer having the line to operate at once, I think we have command of the situation, and can charge the same rate to Pembina that we would charge to Boniface if we operated the road, until Red River opens; then we can make a rate of, say, $10 per car higher to Winnipeg than to Pembina, and all freight will go by boat, as it will be landed in Winnipeg.[3] The Winnipeg merchants will not stand the contractors' charge and will raise another Riel Rebellion![4]

This was the nicely-balanced plan across which Farley blundered with his through rates. Stephen immediately telegraphed the superintendent asking him to withdraw all rates north of the boundary, and as neither Farley nor Fisher appeared to grasp the importance of doing so he also wrote to Kennedy, who had more influence over Farley, asking for his support. In the end the through-rates were withdrawn, but Farley harboured a grudge against Hill, whom he regarded as responsible for over-ruling him.[5]

---

[1] Pyle, op. cit. vol. I, p. 281.   [2] Step. Test. p. 204.
[3] There was then no bridge across the Red River from St. Boniface.
[4] Pyle, op. cit. vol. I. p. 282.   [5] Step. Test. p. 202.

MANITOBA CONNECTED WITH EASTERN CANADA

The Speech from the Throne at the opening of the Dominion Parliament on 14 February 1879, contained the following item:

Communication by rail has been effected between Manitoba and the United States system of railways, by the junction, at St. Vincent, of the Pembina Branch of our railway with the St. Paul and Pacific Railroad.

If Lord Lorne's formal statement on behalf of Her Majesty barely did justice to an event which might have gone into history as the Relief of Manitoba, the exuberance of the contemporary press more than restored the balance. 'AT LAST!! RAIL COMMUNICATION ESTABLISHED': in triumphant headlines the *Manitoba Weekly Free Press* of 7 December 1878, had put on record the epoch-making achievement:

Manitoba, after many vexatious delays, which we can now afford to dismiss without a thought, is now connected by rail with the outer world. Manitoba takes another stride in the march of progress which will result in her assuming a higher and more influential position in the sisterhood of the Confederation.

Before going on to describe the ceremony with which the first train steamed out of St. Boniface on 3 December, the *Free Press* reviewed the cavalcade of transport that had served the western settlements:

From the York boat in summer, to and from Hudson's Bay, and the dogsled in winter; the primitive Red River cart freighting long and tedious journeys a thousand miles to the south-east, then as the railways were extended through the Gopher State, the trip reduced to five hundred miles; from the rudely constructed cart to the stage coach which yet faithfully performs its daily service, and the steamboat, at first running irregularly, but by rapidly increasing volume of trade expanding into a fleet of riverboats; from these to the happy culmination—the railway—the precursor of a great and glorious future for the Bull's eye of the Dominion! . . .

A week later, graced by the headline: 'First Epistle of St. Paul to the Winnipeggers', the *Free Press* published a letter from Henry H. Sibley, President of the St. Paul Chamber of Commerce, to the Mayor and City Council of Winnipeg, offering the Chamber's congratulations on the occasion of the union of the two cities 'by iron bands', and expressing the 'fervent desire that intimate social and business relations' would be the result, to which Thomas Scott, Mayor of Winnipeg, had made appropriate reply.

So much for Manitoba and her southern neighbours; the prospect opened by the new rail connection via St. Paul with the eastern province of Ontario was described in terms of extreme realism by the *Guelph Herald*:

Three days from Winnipeg! In mid-winter too! . . . The iron horse has opened up a new era for the Manitobans, and the blessings of civilisation will flow upon them in car loads, and at reasonable rates of freight. Oysters will tumble from $1 to $3 a can to a price at which as many as two may be used in an ordinary stew without bankrupting the restaurateur. Apples will cease to be objects of curiosity, and will be banished from private museums. The latest outrage in ladies' hats will appear on the Winnipeg tower of false hair but two days later than its appearance in Chicago. People with boots on their feet—absolutely wearing 'English shoes'—will debark at the railway station. Bachelors will be enabled to import and marry their 'Ontayreo' girls at all seasons of the year—or rather at any season of the year, without any regard whatever for the arrival of the 'first boat'. The last mentioned institution will be so utterly played out that dry goods clerks will be necessitated to unlearn the phrase 'We are just out, but will have a large lot in by first boat.' . . . And the great *Globe* will send in a special fast daily train to knock the *Free Press* into flinders or the valley of the Saskatchewan. . . .

Nor was one extremely important angle on the news neglected: the effect of this north-and-south connection on the future of the Canadian Pacific Railway. The same issue of the *Free Press* which quoted the above from the *Guelph Herald* added a parenthesis from the *Philadelphia Railway World*:

But it is manifestly not the desire of the British authorities that this sort of free trade should continue in any quarter, and they would greatly prefer to establish a system of communication through the new Dominion, which would eventually make the link just completed an avenue for the transfer of trade originating in the United States through British channels.

For the moment, however, it was to the north-and-south trade route that mercantile eyes were turned; the very fact that the United States–Canadian trade was subject to heavy tariffs would, it was thought, be proof against the monopoly of the American route once the Canadian Pacific was a *fait accompli*. Even in 1878 it was cheaper for Manitobans to buy many items in Montreal and have them shipped in bond across American territory than to order from St. Paul, although the promptitude of delivery from the latter market meant a quicker turnover for the Manitoba merchant.

THE PEMBINA BRANCH

Whichever route the freight might take—by the Northern Pacific and then the St. Paul and Pacific from Eastern Canada, or direct from St. Paul—the vital last link in the chain of communication with Winnipeg was the Pembina Branch, and it was the natural aim of the St. Paul and Pacific Company to acquire a lease of this important line. The scene therefore changes to the Canadian House of Commons, where, to go back a little in time, the Liberal Premier, Alexander Mackenzie, had on 18 March 1878, that is, before the St. Paul and Pacific had completed their line to the boundary, introduced a Bill empowering the House, without leave of the Senate, to lease the Pembina Branch to parties unspecified. The Bill itself was concerned chiefly with a point of principle; to effect such a lease some amendment was required to the Canadian Pacific Railway Act of 1874. No specific agreement could be entered into until the House approved the principle; Mackenzie stated, however, that the Government was in communication with Mr. Stephens [*sic*] of Montreal as the representative of the 'St. Paul and Northern Pacific Company'.

The members were not unaware of railway developments south of the boundary, although, as the speeches of even the best-informed indicated, they were not exactly clear as to which company was which. But they all knew that Donald A. Smith, the Member for Selkirk, Manitoba, was connected with one of them, and if the debate on the leasing of the Pembina Branch is to be followed with any degree of comprehension the fact cannot be disregarded that six years earlier Smith had made himself extremely unpopular with the leaders of the Conservative Party by turning against Sir John Macdonald in the affair of the 'Pacific Scandal'. The very name of Donald Smith was, to some members of the House, sheer anathema, nor was the Member for Selkirk disposed to make any conciliatory advances in order to regain the position in their esteem which he had been driven to forfeit by his utter disgust at their leader's excesses.

On 4 April Mackenzie moved the second reading of the Amendment Bill, whereupon Sir John Macdonald, Leader of the Opposition, raised an objection to the term of the lease being as long as ten years. Looking to the time when other American lines might possibly have built connections to the Canadian boundary, he asked to be assured that some precaution would be taken, when the contract was made, to prevent the St. Paul and Pacific having a monopoly of the Pembina Branch.[1] Mackenzie replied that the lease would contain simply a provision that there must be accommodation for the exchange of traffic, and that trains freighted at Winnipeg or Selkirk would have to go solely by the line with which traffic arrangements had been made.

There exists no correspondence between Stephen and Macdonald at this period, but ensuing events prove that they had remained on the most intimate and friendly terms. There seems to be nothing, apart from Macdonald's feeling towards Smith, which would account for his so bitterly opposing what was in the interests of the St. Paul company, even to the extent of advocating those of its present and potential rivals. There was to be later evidence in the debate that he was, in fact, pleading in favour of the Northern Pacific, and that others of his party were following his lead. Incredible though it may seem, it was to be left to Stephen, at a later date, to point out to Macdonald the full implications of allowing American lines to connect with the Canadian trunk road. The fact that the Canadian Pacific was at the time of the debate under Liberal management is neither here nor there; the transcontinental project was, and ever would be, until its completion, Macdonald's dream. At any moment the vicissitudes of political life might make it once more his responsibility. It seems unlikely therefore that Macdonald's attitude during the Pembina Branch debate was dictated by any desire to prejudice the future of the Canadian line, or by anything more than a passing desire to make things difficult for Donald Smith.

The debate continued. A Manitoba Member named Kirkpatrick hoped that the Government would guard the interests of the Province, reminding the House that the St. Paul and Pacific was virtually the same company that owned the Kittson line of boats which, he alleged, had 'ground down the people of Manitoba'. He was supported by Dr. Schultz, Member for Lisgar in the same Province, who proceeded to trace the connection of Stephen and his associates with the St. Paul and Pacific. No sooner, he said, had they purchased the bonds of the railway than it was announced at St. Paul that they had already obtained a lease of the Pembina Branch, the intention and effect of this false statement being to discourage the Northern Pacific Company, who were very anxious to connect with the Canadian line, and who could, by running a branch north-

[1] D. of C.H.C. 1878, p. 1675.

westward from their Duluth line, have given a more direct connection than the St. Paul company. Mr. Mackenzie Bowell thereupon observed that the 'St. Paul and Northern Pacific', having
bought the railroad for a song from Germany, was relying on the
Canadian Government to make it profitable.

It was Donald Smith himself who rose to reply to Dr. Schultz.
He dwelt at first upon the problem which had for so long exercised
his mind—that of providing rail communication between Manitoba
and Eastern Canada—referring to the difficulties experienced in the
past. Fortunately, he said, some gentlemen of enterprise were at
length induced to look into the matter. Those gentlemen went to the
Government and asked them that, in consideration of their building
an extension of their line from St. Paul upwards of seventy miles
through a district which was then without settlement, and from
which there could at first be no local traffic, they should obtain
running powers on certain conditions over the Pembina Branch. If
this offer were rejected, it might be many years more before railway
communication was provided for the people of the North West;
they would have to wait until the Thunder Bay Branch of the
Canadian Pacific connected the western end of Lake Superior with
Winnipeg.

If Selkirk's representative forebore to mention the possibility
of the Northern Pacific providing the looked-for connection, this
was not far from the mind of the Member for Lisgar. Dr. Schultz
proceeded to disclose that:

While it was true that the swindled bondholders had resolved not to complete the road while they were at the mercy of the American management,
yet the Legislature of the State of Minnesota had intended at their session
this winter to have solved the problem by declaring a forfeiture of the land
grant of the uncompleted portions of the road, and given it to any new
company which could have completed it.[1]

This frank acknowledgment of the plan whereby the Dutch bondholders very nearly lost the chance to make the deal which gave
them such satisfaction is only a further proof of the complicity of
the Canadian Opposition and the Northern Pacific Railroad Company. But if it was too late to win the battle of the Pembina Branch
for their American allies there was still ammunition left for a final
attack on the arch-enemy.

[1] D. of C.H.C. p. 1685.

Again Sir John Macdonald rose to speak, to deprecate the 'indecent spectacle' of an hon. gentleman, who he assumed had an interest in this railway, coming to the House as an advocate and pressing this lease in his own interests. To this Smith made an evasive retort, ending with the words:'. . . the hon. gentleman, I hope, is not my father confessor.'[1]

Macdonald continued to protest to the bitter end against giving 'to a foreign road the control of a branch of our greatest railway undertaking' for a period as long as ten years, wilfully refusing to recognize the inconsistency of his argument. To anyone who knew that Macdonald's intense desire was to see the Pacific Railway providing the east-west connection on Canadian territory his opposition to the St. Paul company might have been understandable, had he not at the same time been openly supporting as an alternative an agreement with an even more 'foreign' road, one that could not boast, as could the St. Paul and Pacific, four Canadians on its management. It is possible that Stephen held himself completely aloof at this stage, for he had little taste for political wrangling, particularly if it interfered with business. He was going to get what he wanted, and the day for reconciling those two close friends of his was not yet.

The Liberals succeeded in steering the Bill through all its stages in the Commons, but it promptly ricocheted back from the Senate with an amendment attached requiring any contract made to be laid before both Houses for one month, unless it were sooner approved of by both. This amendment was duly rejected by the Commons, who pointed out that contracts made under the C.P.R. Act of 1874 were subject only to the approval of the lower House. Once more the Bill came back from the Senate, whose insistence on the amendment was warmly applauded by Sir John Macdonald. The constitutional action of the upper House, he told the House of Commons, put a stop to their bargain with the hon. member for Selkirk to make him a rich man, and to pay him for his servile support. When the Speaker objected that the hon. gentleman could not say that an hon. member was paid for his support Macdonald amended his accusation: 'Then a reward, a gratuity.' [2]

Smith was not then in the House, but the following day he rose to a question of privilege, referring to the manner in which the Member for Kingston had alluded to him as 'most unfair' and

---

[1] D. of C.H.C., (1878) p. 1691.   [2] Loc. cit. p. 2557.

'most unjustifiable'.[1] Smith was 'spoiling for a fight', and when he went on to evoke the ghost of the 'Pacific Scandal' the leaders of the Conservative Party were not slow to pick up the gauntlet. There ensued a scene which was, to say the least, unparliamentary, and which was fortunately brought to an end by the entrance of 'Black Rod.'

ST. PAUL COMPANY REFUSED RUNNING RIGHTS

On 3 August 1878, an agreement was concluded between the Government of Canada and George Stephen respecting running powers over the Pembina Branch.[2] In October, however, the Mackenzie Government fell, and when Parliament met again the Conservatives were in office. The allusion in the Speech from the Throne, already quoted, to the establishment of railway communication with Manitoba, brought forward once more the question of the lease of the Pembina Branch. In answer to a question the Minister of Railways, Dr. Charles Tupper, replied briefly that the late Government had entered into a contract with parties connected with the St. Paul and Pacific Railway Company.[3] The actual agreement was laid before the House on 13 March 1879.

But the Pembina Branch was not to be so easily signed away. On 21 March the Minister of Railways introduced a new Bill to amend the Canadian Pacific Railway Act of 1874. Pointing out that there would be serious difficulties in putting the previous contract into operation inasmuch as the contractors still had the line in their possession for purposes of construction, Tupper proposed that an arrangement be made instead with the contractor, thus securing the operation of the line 'a year sooner than under other circumstances they could hope it to be'.[4]

The desire of the Government to make temporary provision for the operation of the Pembina Branch only until the completion of the Canadian Pacific could bring the whole system under one management was in itself wholly laudable. But the contract with Stephen had included a clause to the effect than whenever the Government was in a position to equip the Branch it could take over its operation, allowing the St. Paul company running rights. This

---

[1] D. of C.H.C. 1878, p. 2558.
[2] Sessional Papers (hereafter S.P.) 43D 1878, CO 45/498.
[3] D. of C.H.C. 1879, p. 74. [4] Loc. cit. p. 611.

was in fact disclosed by Tupper in the speech with which he introduced his new Bill. It seems obvious that the 'serious difficulties'
were somewhat exaggerated; the St. Paul and Pacific was at all
costs to be frustrated in its efforts to lease the Pembina Branch.

The new Bill received the Royal Assent on 15 May, and for
some time the Press aired the 'pros' and 'cons' of the arrangement.
Mention has already been made of the high rates charged by the
contractors who operated the line. The *Manitoba Weekly Free Press*
of 24 May was quite sure that a lease of the Branch to the St. Paul
and Pacific would have been much more advantageous to the
Province, adding:

We have always doubted the disinterestedness of the Government in their
action in the premises, and we yet doubt it.

The *Montreal Gazette*, on the other hand, declared in its issue
of 3 November that no more suicidal act could be performed than to
allow 'these St. Paul and Pacific Railway people' to get control for a
single hour of a single mile of Canadian railway. The real solution
of the problem, it continued, was to speed up construction on the
Pacific Railway:

Canadian Pacific Railway policy has been already too long dictated simply
by regard for the interests of Mr. Donald A. Smith and his associates. It
is time that the interests of Canada came to be considered in the matter.

The following chapters will present what to the *Gazette* of this
period must have been something of a phenomenon: the picture of
Mr. Donald A. Smith and his associates becoming even more
closely identified with the Canadian Pacific Railway than they had
allegedly been in the past, and that with the full concurrence of the
Conservative leaders, statesmen and railwaymen working together—
if not always in unison—to promote 'the interests of Canada'. The
man who wrought the miracle was George Stephen.

III

Canadian Pacific : the transcontinental vision

THE CONFEDERATION LINE

George Stephen to Sir John Macdonald

Causapscal,
9th July, 1880.

Private and Confidential

My dear Sir John,

Referring to your private and confidential note of the 5th. instant, to which I wired you I would send an answer on board the Mail Steamer at Rimouski, I quite understand the difficulties the Government have to contend with in dealing with the work of constructing the Pacific Railway: they have to be guided by considerations quite different from those that you or I would have to deal with were it a personal matter in which we were free to use our own best judgment. I am aware it is often impossible for a Government to adopt the best course, and it is the knowledge of that fact that makes me rather hesitate to commit myself to the enormous responsibility involved in this undertaking. You will have no difficulty, I feel sure, in finding men on the other side, more or less substantial and with greater courage—mainly because they know less of the difficulties to be encountered, but also because they will adopt measures for their own protection which I could not avail myself of.

There are two ways by which you can get the road built and operated: one by getting up a financial organization such as Allan contemplated and such as Jay Cooke & Co. got up for construction of the Northern Pacific Railway—with what result I need not remind you. A scheme of this nature involves the issue of a large amount of Bonds, just as large as an attractive prospectus will float (and you have capital material to offer for a very 'taking' prospectus): the outcome of a plan of this character is that the real responsibility is transferred from the Company to the people who may be induced to buy the Bonds, while the Company or the projectors pocket a big profit at the start out of the proceeds. This, in the rough, is I fear the method any English financial organization is likely to follow.—
The risk to the Government and to the country of allowing the matter to

be manipulated in that way is sufficiently obvious.—It would indeed be a disastrous affair to all concerned if the English public were induced to invest in a bond issue which the road could not carry—that is on which the interest could not be paid.—The other plan, and the one I should have followed, had we been able to come to terms, would have been to limit the borrowing of money from the public to the smallest possible point, and if we issued a bond at all to take care it did not much exceed $5000—(Five thousand dollars) a mile—to have looked for the return of our own capital and a legitimate profit entirely to the growth of the country and the development of the property—after the work of construction had been fully accomplished.—I could not be a party to a scheme involving a large issue of Bonds on a road which no one can now be sure will earn enough to pay working expenses.—I am more willing to risk my own means in the venture than those of the English public. It would be quite useless my going over to London; we are certain to be outbid there, and for the reasons I have given.—No English or American organization could really do the work as advantageously and at so little cost as we could, nor could they so readily develop the earning power of the property; but, while we should wait for our profit and take the risk of its coming at all, they would inevitably pocket theirs at once.

When I met Pope[1] in Montreal on Saturday he told me that the Government had *decided finally* to give no more money than twenty millions, and as I could not see my way to do the work for a less cash bonus than twenty-six and a half millions, I thought it better to end the negotiations, leaving you perfectly free to make the best bargain you could on the other side. Pope was disappointed and not very well pleased with me, but I thought and still think it was the right thing to do.—Mr. Angus has been with me all the week, and we have done little else than discuss the matter, the salmon being few and far between. We are both satisfied of our ability to construct the road without much trouble, but we are not so sure by any means about its profitable operation; but in regard to this, if we cannot operate it successfully no one else can. We think, as I explained to you at Ottawa, that we could immediately utilise the Thunder Bay branch for our Lake traffic and in this, and other ways, earn enough to secure the payment of interest upon such indebtedness as we might incur. Our experience of settling lands in Minnesota would be a great help to us in the management of the lands granted to the Road.—We are also clear on the point that the Canada Central and the Quebec roads would have to be incorporated. Nipissing is nowhere. Montreal or Quebec must be the starting point. Although I am off the notion of the thing now, should anything occur on the other side to induce you to think that taking all things into consideration, our proposal is better upon

[1] John Henry Pope, Minister of Agriculture.

the whole for the country than any offer you get in England, I might, on hearing from you, renew it and possibly in doing so reduce the land grant to some extent. Here let me say that, so far as I am able to gauge public opinion, I think most people and especially the opposition (if we may judge from the utterances of the 'Globe') would prefer limiting the grant of land and increasing the cash subsidy—that is, they would prefer giving 30 millions cash and 20 millions acres of land to 50 million acres of land without any cash; but as to this you can judge much better than anybody else.

Yours faithfully,

Geo. Stephen.[1]

This was the letter that Sir John Macdonald carried with him on his second journey to England in twelve months, his second mission undertaken with the object of raising funds for, or otherwise ensuring, the construction of the Pacific Railway.

The Conservative Party had returned to power in 1879 with a new banner labelled 'National Policy', a policy which included protection for native industries, and under which the building of the Pacific Railway became a 'national necessity'. This consciousness of nationhood was being carefully fostered, although the nation existed only precariously by virtue of the entrance into the Confederation of Manitoba and the North West Territories, three of the Maritime Provinces and, later, of British Columbia. But British Columbia had come into the union on the specific understanding that the Pacific Railway would be built by 1881. The Conservatives, who, as the Government then in power, had negotiated the agreement with British Columbia, had, as has been mentioned, made an attempt in 1872 to make good their promises, and while condemning that treaty and its commitments the Liberals, when they took office, could not deny that the ultimate completion of the railway was inevitable. Their cautious policy of building only as the resources of the country permitted without additional taxation had produced little result, and in the House of Commons in April 1877, the Opposition leaders Sir John Macdonald and Dr. Charles Tupper sponsored a Resolution: 'That this House cannot approve of the course pursued by this Government with respect to the Canadian Pacific Railway.' In a five-hour speech Tupper reviewed the history of the project since 1871, deploring the half-measures of the Liberals:

[1] Macd.P. 'Stephen' 267, Stephen to Macdonald, 9 July 1880.

. . . the moment you have declared the expediency of constructing the Pacific Railway, the moment you have gone the length that the First Minister has gone in admitting its absolute necessity, that moment you are bound to adopt every possible means in your power in order to promote the construction of that road. . . .[1]

Instead, he said, the Government had grossly overestimated the cost of construction while underestimating in the most damaging way the value of the enterprise as a commercial undertaking, thus discouraging capitalists from tendering for the construction contracts, and immigrants from settling on the lands of the North West. The Resolution was rejected by the Liberal majority, and it is doubtful whether, in the long run, the moving of it did the railway project any good. The Canadian Pacific became thereby more than ever a Conservative protégé, and even on its achieving 'national' status the stigma thus attached to it by the Liberal Party remained stronger than its appeal to national sentiment, still fairly lukewarm.

The first attempt of the Conservative Government, represented by Macdonald, Tupper (then Minister of Railways) and Sir Leonard Tilley, the Finance Minister, to obtain financial assistance in England for the Pacific Railway was unsuccessful. The Government was therefore obliged for the time being to follow the Liberal plan of proceeding with the sections most urgently needed. In December 1879, 125 miles of the located line in British Columbia, from Kamloops to the Pacific coast, were let out for construction to Andrew Onderdonk, an American contractor. This was generally referred to afterwards as the 'Onderdonk Section'.

In May 1880, a good deal of interest was aroused in Canadian business circles by the publication of the first Annual Report of the St. Paul, Minneapolis and Manitoba Railroad Company. The net earnings for the ten months that the Company had been in operation were substantial, and an appreciable sum had been realized from land grant sales and other real estate. Two conclusions presented themselves: first, that if the prairie lands south of the 49th Parallel could be turned to such account the same might be expected of those to the north of it; secondly, that there appeared to exist on the American continent a group of men who could make railway building profitable even if they started with a handicap, and who were, more-

---

[1] Journals of the Canadian House of Commons, hereafter 'J. of C. H. C.' CO 45/465, 21 April 1877. Mackenzie made a vain attempt in 1877 to interest private enterprise in the C.P.R.

over, able to command considerable sums of money for such a purpose.

On 15 June 1880, the Canadian Minister of Railways composed an official memorandum for the Privy Council, and had it endorsed by Collingwood Schreiber, who had succeeded Sandford Fleming as the Government's chief engineer. It was in this vein:

. . . the undersigned has reason to believe that owing to the great interest at present excited in relation to the North West, the value of land there, and the great success which has attended the St. Paul, Minneapolis and Manitoba Railway Company, that it would be quite practicable to obtain the construction of the line from Red River to Kamloops by an expenditure in money of $12,500,000 and 25 million acres of land. . . .

He therefore recommends that authority be given to negotiate with capitalists of undoubted means, and who shall be required to give the most ample guarantees for the construction and operation of the line on such terms as will secure at the same time the rapid settlement of the public lands and the construction of the work.[1]

The principle was duly accepted by the Privy Council, and it seems that George Stephen was at once approached on the subject of building not only the section from Red River to Kamloops but the entire line, excluding the parts already contracted for, from Lake Nipissing to the junction with the Onderdonk Section.

Anxious as they were to have the whole line built, it was important to the Government to guard against making a contract that would evoke too much criticism from the Liberal Opposition or indeed from their own party, and at the early discussions with Stephen they failed to come to terms. Then it was that Macdonald decided that he, Tupper and John Henry Pope, Minister of Agriculture, should go again to England, this time to try to find a body of capitalists— the Grand Trunk Railroad was one possibility they had in mind— who would undertake the task on more favourable terms than Stephen demanded.[2] There is no doubt that they did make genuine efforts to do so, but one can imagine that time and again Macdonald took up and re-read that frankly unbusinesslike letter of the Montreal businessman, and that during discussions with financiers who, having no interest in the Dominion other than the possibility of making a profitable investment there, spoke and acted accordingly, phrases from that letter would pass through his mind . . . 'to have

---

[1] Tupper Papers 205, 15 June 1880.
[2] E. M. Saunders, *Life and Letters of the Rt. Hon. Sir Charles Tupper*, 2 vols., New York and Toronto, 1916, vol. I, p. 286.

looked for the return of our own capital and a legitimate profit
entirely to the growth of the country and the development of the
property. . . . I am more willing to risk my own means in the venture
than those of the English public. . . . No English or American
organization could really do the work so advantageously and at so
little cost as we could . . . but, while we should wait for our profit and
take the risk of its coming at all, they would inevitably pocket theirs
at once . . . if we cannot operate it successfully no one else can. . . .'

And what of Stephen, and of the associates who would be involved
with him, should Macdonald fall back on them? Were they all
equally altruistic? Perhaps not, but to all of them, Stephen included,
fresh from their Middle Western triumph, the prospect of new and
vaster fields to conquer must have held an almost irresistible
challenge. In Stephen's mind, the Pacific Railway was a thing apart,
no mere feeder for the St. Paul road which had been an adventure in
itself but was, after all, just another successful investment. To him,
even the settlement of the West was at first only a process that made
railroading pay, but had he been thinking chiefly of the increase of
traffic that might accrue to the American road he would not have
worried himself about the necessity of incorporating the Quebec
railway system in the Canadian Pacific. Admittedly he had ideas
about using a rail connection from Sault Ste. Marie, Ontario, south
of Lake Superior and via St. Paul to Winnipeg, thus short-circuiting
the inhospitable northern shore of the Lake, and providing more
direct access to the Chicago market for western grain, but this plan,
of short duration, consisted rather in using American lines for the
benefit of Canadian. The concept of a national through line thus
triumphed over purely commercial considerations.

J. J. Hill, on the other hand, although Canadian-born, was bound
by closer ties to the St. Paul road, of which he was now general
manager. To him the Canadian Pacific was quite frankly an enterprise that could conceivably forward his own ambitions—themselves
dictated by considerable altruism—both for his own road and for the
future settlement of the American West. Kittson, another Canadian,
would follow without question where the others led; Angus was
Stephen's close friend and supporter. It would be interesting to
know just what Donald Smith thought, at this early stage, of a project which would entail working hand in glove with Macdonald. If
there was any initial opposition from this quarter it was very quickly
overcome; although it was some time before Stephen actually

effected a *rapprochement* between Macdonald and Smith, the latter fancied himself as a railway-builder and was quite determined not to be left out.

MACDONALD TURNS TO STEPHEN

The Conservative Ministers' second mission to England was no more productive than the first. Sir Henry Tyler, President of the Grand Trunk Railroad Company, would not look at their proposal unless the section from Lake Nipissing to Thunder Bay—the rock-bound route over the Laurentian Shield north of Lake Superior—could be excluded from the plan. Discussions with others were no more successful; several parties showed initial interest, but ultimately all withdrew.[1] There remained only Stephen's offer, and it was possibly with the conviction that Stephen was, after all, 'his man' that Macdonald entered into negotiations with Duncan McIntyre, of the Canada Central Railway, whom Stephen had sent to England as his representative should the need for such arise. A telegraphic correspondence with Stephen ensued, and the Premier was able to return to Canada with an air of triumph and with the news, somewhat prematurely disclosed, that a satisfactory bargain had been made.[2]

Although the main points had been agreed upon, much remained to be done in the way of settling details of the contract and of determining the composition of the syndicate which was to carry it out. The contract, moreover, was still subject to the approval first of the Privy Council, then of Parliament.

Now that the task was virtually undertaken, however, Stephen was all anxiety to set the necessary machinery in motion, and, still clinging to his recklessly altruistic motives, wrote to Macdonald on 27 September 1880:

. . . Pope spent the most of yesterday with Angus and myself and gave us in general terms a history of the negotiations on the other side. I have also seen McIntyre and the important document (which my *friends* and my *enemies* agree in affecting to think will be the ruin of us all) and I hope there will be no difficulty in our coming to terms upon all points. I want whatever arrangement is made that it shall be *fair* and *creditable* to both the Government and ourselves, and that not a day should be lost in the preparation of the contract and the act of incorporation. . . . Unless we

[1] Macdonald, in D. of C.H.C. 1880-1, vol. I, p. 39, 13 December 1880.
[2] *Montreal Gazette*, 28 September 1880.

can have the cars running over a long piece of road, west of Winnipeg, by this time next year, both the Government and the contractor will be put into discredit with the public.[1]

In London Sir John Rose, who had retired from Morton, Rose and Company in 1876, was endeavouring to persuade his old firm, in which his son Charles was a partner, to join the Canadian Pacific syndicate. His idea was that their New York house, Morton, Bliss and Company, should actually handle the business, and once the London firm was convinced, albeit somewhat reluctantly, as to the soundness of the enterprise, all efforts were directed to bringing the New York partners, Morton and Bliss, round to a similar conviction. Stephen had a two-day consultation in Montreal with Bliss, the partner chiefly concerned. The latter was by no means anxious to undertake the responsibility involved, but finally agreed to commit his firm to the extent of $5 million.[2] Early in November Stephen went to New York to consult with John S. Kennedy, another potential ally, and also to try to persuade Bliss to double his subscription, for he feared that the smaller sum betrayed a lack of confidence prejudicial to the cause. Kennedy agreed to join the syndicate, and Stephen wrote to Macdonald on 13 November that he was 'in great hopes of getting Bliss to go the $10,000,000'.[3]

A London representative of Morton, Rose and Company, Pasco du P. Grenfell, also went over to Canada to take part in the final negotiations. He acted also for the French-German house of Kohn, Reinach and Company, whose participation had been sought largely for the sake of gratifying the French element in the Dominion Parliament. Stephen would most willingly have dispensed with the French interest, whose main aim was to make a quick profit from the investment. Egged on, however, by Rose, who shared Macdonald's views on the importance of this alliance (although he wrote to the Premier: 'I am much disgusted with the French-German group. You can have no idea of all the minute and utterly unreasonable difficulties they make. . . .'[4]) Stephen set about a rather 'rough wooing' of the European company. He went over to Paris in December, and the mixture of bluntness and tact with which he approached them is revealed in a letter to Rose:

[1] Macd.P. 'Stephen' 267, Stephen to Macdonald, 27 September 1880.
[2] Macd.P 'Rose' 259.193, Rose to Macdonald, 13 September 1880.
[3] Macd.P. 'Stephen' 267, Stephen to Macdonald, 13 November 1880.
[4] Macd.P. 'Rose' 259.208, Rose to Macdonald, 7 November 1880.

... The plain way I was obliged to speak as to our own position is being *committed* irrevocably, and of our ability to carry out the work with or without any outside aid gave the elder of the two [he referred to the brothers Heine] a fit almost which Betzold [of Morton, Rose] says has culminated in an attack of gout. My speech was just a *little* plain, but it did them all great good, plus my subsequent note expressing a strong desire to carry them with us in the contract even [if] it should be decided that the French public would not take our bonds. . . .[1]

The success of these tactics contributed little to the main object in view. During the debate on the contract the leader of the Opposition, Edward Blake, disposed of the continental alliance in one sentence: 'I do not know the French house with the Dutch name.'

Among the private individuals included in the Canadian Pacific syndicate was Henry Stafford Northcote, son of Sir Stafford Northcote. In 1873 Henry—or Harry, as he was known to the family—had married Alice, the Stephens' adopted daughter. Alice Brooke's mother had been a friend of George Stephen's sister Elsie, now Mrs. Robert Meighen, and when Mrs. Brooke died while on a visit to Canada with her husband and family Mrs. Meighen had asked her brother and his wife to take care of Alice until Mr. Brooke was ready to return to England. This the Stephens gladly did; they had no family of their own—their only child had been born dead— and so attached did they become to the sixteen-year-old Alice that when the time came for her to go home she herself preferred to remain. It was then arranged that George Stephen should become her guardian. Harry Northcote came to Canada with his father in 1870 when Sir Stafford was a member of the Joint High Commission which negotiated the Treaty of Washington. They came armed with introductions from Sir John Rose, Sir Stafford having expressed a wish to meet some of 'our leading colonists'.[2] Afterwards Harry remained for a time as secretary to the British member of the claims commission. He was a welcome addition to the Stephen family, Stephen delighting to refer to 'my son-in-law'. They worked together in London over many Canadian projects until Harry's career eventually took him to other outposts of empire.

Other members of the syndicate were Duncan McIntyre, Charles Rose, R. B. Angus, J. J. Hill, N. W. Kittson and Donald A. Smith. Not all these names appeared on the contract. Kittson played his

---

[1] Macd.P. 'Stephen' 267, Stephen to Rose, 16 December 1880.
[2] Macd.P. 'Rose' 258, Northcote to Rose, 5 March 1870.

usual inconspicuous role; apart from brief references, in letters from Stephen to Macdonald in November 1880 and January 1881, to his being with them at the time, there appears to be no record of his association with the Canadian Pacific, and with this state of affairs Kittson was probably quite content.

Not so Donald Smith. Stephen had deliberately omitted his name from the contract, thinking that the document would thereby have a smoother passage through Parliament, and that his cousin might be saved from unpleasant allusions to his political life. At that time Stephen expected more opposition from the Conservative than from the Liberal side of the House. He had asked Macdonald at the outset if he had any objection to Smith's being connected with the enterprise, and the former's genial answer in the negative gave no little pleasure to Smith when his cousin passed it on.[1] Some three years later Stephen was able to stage a reconciliation, to the immense satisfaction of both Macdonald and Smith.[2] At the end of 1880, however, Smith presented something of a problem. Stephen wrote to Rose:

I have had a terrible bother with Don Smith because his name is not printed in the papers submitted to the House. It was not necessary to have it there and both Angus and I thought we were doing him a good turn in keeping it out. He has been like a baby over the thing.[3]

On the same day he wrote to Macdonald on the subject:

. . . I had to tell him that I omitted [his name] to avoid discussion in the House but rather than he should be unhappy I would let him out of the business. He is excited almost to a craze and so troublesome that I do not care if he does withdraw though his money and cooperation would be useful, so would his knowledge of and influence in the Nor West. . . .[4]

As in the case of the French alliance, Stephen's concession to political expediency proved vain. When, during the debate on the contract, Blake launched a verbal attack on Donald Smith and was interrupted by another member saying 'His name is not there', the Liberal spokesman replied, 'I know you do not see it, but it is there for all that, you know it well'. Another Liberal member, opposing the principle of building the railway by private enterprise, marvelled that the Minister of Railways, with the facilities, talent and resources

---

[1] Macd.P. 'Stephen' 267, Stephen to Macdonald, 16 December 1880.
[2] Macd.P. 'Stephen' 269, Stephen to Macdonald, 10 February 1884.
[3] Macd.P. 'Stephen' 267, Stephen to Rose, 16 December 1880.
[4] Loc. cit. Stephen to Macdonald, 16 December 1880.

he had at his disposal, 'could not have done this work as well as a dry goods merchant in Montreal, or a gentleman who had been engaged trapping muskrats in the North West'.

Such references, by both Liberals and Conservatives, in the House and in the Press, only increased Smith's agitation, for he saw in them a deliberate attempt to perpetuate the gulf fixed between him and Macdonald. Stephen was at a loss to know how to deal with him, and once in exasperation did actually offer to relieve him altogether of his interest in the project.[1] In the end, the storm blew over; although never prominent in the affairs of the Canadian Pacific Smith remained with the Company, ever giving it his most loyal, and not infrequently anonymous, support.

The fact that on this issue the Liberals chose to turn against their erstwhile supporter is typical of the politics of the period. The Liberals were using every effort to destroy, if they could, this national project of the Conservative Party, knowing that on their success depended their own chances of returning to power, and the political indiscretions of Donald Smith provided just the type of weapon that they could wield with most malicious effect. History was confuted, too, when the 'St. Paul Company' became the butt of their attacks. Stephen said the last word on the subject when he wrote to John Henry Pope:

Talk about a patriotic regard for the interests of the country—why, they would see the country at the d——l, with fiendish delight, if they could get thereby hold of the Treasury benches.[2]

THE CONTRACT: CLAUSE 15

Under the terms of the contract,[3] the Canadian Pacific Railway Company was to receive from the Government of Canada a cash subsidy of $25 million and a land grant of 25 million acres, the latter in alternate sections on either side of the railway. Both could be earned only as the work of construction proceeded. True to his original undertaking, Stephen had endeavoured, when the terms were under discussion, to ensure that these should be reasonably acceptable to both Parliament and country without setting the Company an impossible task. Nevertheless, while he desired to be as accommodating as possible, there were one or two points on which he took a firm stand. One was the vexed question of the Pembina

---

[1] Macd.P. 'Stephen' 267, Stephen to Macdonald, 23 January 1881.
[2] Loc. cit. Stephen to Pope, 10 February 1881.   [3] Appendix I.

Branch, Stephen insisting that the Company should have absolute control over this valuable feeder. Another was the need to protect the Pacific Railway from the possible incursion into its territory of rival lines, especially such as might connect with hostile American systems. A case in point was Dr. Schultz's Manitoba South-Western Railway, a local project recently granted a charter by the Provincial Government (of which Schultz was an influential member) to build from Winnipeg to the Pembina Mountains.[1] Having had experience of Schultz's dealings with the Northern Pacific, Stephen put the matter forcefully to Macdonald:

Now what do you think would be the position of the C.P.R. or of the men bound to own and operate it, if it were tapped at Winnipeg, or at any point west of that, by a line or lines running towards the U.S. boundary? What would, in such a case, be the value of the C.P.R. line from Winnipeg to Ottawa? No sane man would give one dollar for the whole line east of Winnipeg. I need not say more on this point, as it must be clear to you that *any* and *every line south* of the line of the C.P.R. running towards the boundary line must be owned and controlled by the C.P.R., otherwise the C.P.R. would be strangled. . . .[2]

Stephen's suggestion for overcoming this difficulty was for the Government to withdraw from public sale a tract of land twelve miles wide extending along the American boundary from the western border of Manitoba to the Rocky Mountains and to include this in the Canadian Pacific Company's land grant.[3] This solution was not acceptable; from then on the Government always showed reluctance to appear to be dictated to regarding the location of C.P.R. land, afraid of having to face a charge of allowing the railway to pick and choose in this valuable commodity.

The alternative was embodied in clause 15 of the C.P.R. contract, which laid down that for a period of twenty years after the signing of the contract, no line of railway should be authorized by the Dominion Government to be built south of the Canadian Pacific, from any point at or near the latter, except such line as should run south-west, or to the westward of south-west, nor to within fifteen miles of latitude 49. It was unfortunate that the provision of local rail facilities had since 1878 been a prominent issue in Manitoba

---

[1] Note: the papers of John C. Schultz are in the Provincial Archives of Manitoba, but are to remain sealed until 1972.
[2] Macd.P. 'Stephen' 267, Stephen to Macdonald, 18 October 1880.
[3] Loc. cit. Stephen to Macdonald, 13 November 1880.

provincial politics. Wherever the route of the Canadian Pacific might lie, it was clear that the main line could serve only a limited area. What the Province wanted was a honeycomb of local lines, and several charters were granted by the Legislature for the construction of such. These charters were subject to the approval of the Federal Government, and the policy of disallowance finally adopted by the latter roused a storm of opposition at Winnipeg.[1] It was some time before Macdonald, egged on by Stephen, took action openly on the question of the provincial charters, but a private understanding had been reached as early as 1881 with John Norquay, the Manitoba Premier—an understanding which Norquay, with the best of intentions, was to find it impossible to honour. His failure to do so called forth the following rebuke from Sir John Macdonald in November 1881:

. . . A good deal of disappointment is being expressed here by my colleagues, in which I must say I agree, at your allowing such reckless Railway Legislation as you did last session.

You were made aware of the reluctance with which the Syndicate undertook the building of the Railway eastwards from the Red River via the North shore of Lake Superior, and that they were only induced to accept the contract on the understanding that this Railway would not be tapped ad libitum east of Winnipeg. We shall be compelled to disallow your Acts. We who were around the Council table understood that you undertook to discourage and prevent such legislation.[2]

Probably no one could have foreseen the difficulties which Norquay was to face. Even Macdonald was slow to admit that Stephen's fears of the diversion of traffic from the North West along American lines were well-founded, and to be persuaded by him that disallowance would only mean 'national policy' applied to railways. With clause 15 safely embodied in the contract, it seemed at the end of 1880 as if further trouble from this quarter had been forestalled. Only Stephen, with his experience of American rivals, remained on the alert, and even he, at the end of 1880, had other preoccupations.

STEPHEN UNDERESTIMATES ANTI-C.P.R. FORCES

As President of the Canadian Pacific Railway Company, as finally formed, Stephen was naturally concerned with every aspect

---

[1] See James A. Jackson, *The Disallowance of Manitoba Railway Legislation in the 1880's*; Railway policy as a factor in the relations of Manitoba with the Dominion, 1878-1888, M.A. Thesis, University of Manitoba, 1945.
[2] Macd.L.B. 21.539, Macdonald to Norquay, 5 November 1881.

of the task confronting it, but three activities in particular had his personal attention: financing construction, promoting emigration to the North West and developing the Canadian Pacific both as a national and as a world-wide system. In his letters at the time of the organization of the Company there is evidence of the spirit of adventure in which Stephen approached his new commitments. The anxiety over the composition of the Company, the vexatious delays that preceded the actual signing of the contract on 21 October 1880 —these were but part of what he expected to be an exacting and even slightly perilous assignment, but no more. What they had done in Minnesota they could do again north of the boundary, on a larger scale, but with greater assistance, and unhindered by a dragging deadweight of debt. The contract itself seemed fair and straightforward. There would inevitably be a certain amount of criticism in Parliament before the Canadian Pacific Railway Bill became law, but that would be in the nature of routine; from then on it would be comparatively plain sailing, merely a case of hard work—to which he was no stranger—and of using the experience previously gained . . . so Stephen thought. The President of the new company had underestimated three forces already lining up against him, their common aim the destruction of the transcontinental project and of the Government which sponsored it: the Liberal Opposition, the established and now rival railroad companies—the Grand Trunk in Canada and the American Northern Pacific—and, lastly, the Press that those hostile forces could command, not only in Canada and the United States, but also in England. The next five years were to be for Stephen a time of constant struggle against one or all of these, and ironically, the Government which shared the enemies' fire could not declare itself the ally of the company which was making its 'national policy' a reality.

So certain was Stephen that no serious obstacle would be put in the way of the national enterprise that when Parliament met, earlier than usual, on 9 December 1880, with the discussion of the Railway Bill its main task, he was already in England, feeling his way towards some plan for systematic emigration to the North West, and sounding political acquaintances as to the possibility of the Imperial Government cooperating in such a scheme. He could take no definite action until the Company was officially incorporated, and writing to Macdonald he expressed the hope that Parliament would dispose of the contract before Christmas: 'Surely', he added, 'the

Opposition will not be foolish enough to take a line to damage us and the country too. . . .'[1]

It soon became clear that, on the contrary, the Opposition intended to use every means known to parliamentary practice to obstruct the passage of the Canadian Pacific Railway Bill. Viewed dispassionately, the protracted debate (far from being over by Christmas, it continued after recess until February) presents the picture of an academic festival of rhetoric. Not only did the usual party spokesmen play their accustomed parts; normally inconspicuous Members found themselves accorded the freedom of the floor, and such indulgence as they had not experienced since their maiden speeches. Anyone who could, without violating the Constitution, help to postpone the passing of the Bill was assured of Opposition support. It is questionable whether any single parliamentary debate ever displayed such frequent recourse to the stores of literature and mythology; from Moore on Castlereagh to Burns on Charles James Fox, from 'The Charge of the Light Brigade' to 'How doth the little busy bee', poets and playwrights past and present were called to witness to the iniquity of the Pacific Railway contract. Members evoked the Wishing Cup of Fortunatus, the Feast of Tantalus, the Lantern of Diogenes and the Sword of Damocles to illustrate their relevant or irrelevant arguments. True, one speaker was declared out of order for discoursing on the topic of the revolutionary movement of 1837, but another was scarcely restrained from taking the Members on a tour of the Pyramids and treating them to an epigrammatic history of the Jewish race.

Rudely awakened to reality, Stephen in London communicated his bewildered thoughts to Macdonald:

. . . I am literally disgusted by the conduct of the Opposition. . . . The bargain with the Syndicate was so much more favourable to the country than the terms offered by Mackenzie in /77 that I felt sure the chief opposition to the contract would come from the ministerial side of the House. I was mistaken, and confess I did not think it possible for political malignity to go so far as it has done in this discussion . . . a fair and unbiassed consideration of the whole situation must result in the conviction that the interests of the country and the company are identical and every advantage or privilege granted to the latter are necessary for the due protection of their joint interests. . . .[2]

---

[1] Macd.P. 'Stephen' 267, Stephen to Macdonald, 16 December 1880.
[2] Loc. cit. Stephen to Macdonald, 23 January 1881.

Still hopeful that once construction was commenced the Company would amply justify its existence, Stephen concluded:

We can best serve the Government and the country and ourselves by a vigorous prosecution of the work. In no other way can we so effectively silence opposition.

SETTLING THE WEST: STEPHEN'S PLAN

George Stephen's singleness of heart frequently led to over-optimism, and it is doubtful if he ever accustomed himself to the recurring vision of the path to logical conclusion being blocked by political expediency. Few English Members of Parliament would not have agreed with him that his scheme for Irish Emigration to the North West of Canada was a logical and timely suggestion for solving at least one aspect of the Irish Question, but to share Stephen's enthusiasm for it when face to face with that gentleman was one thing, and to carry 'Irish Emigration to Canada' on a metaphorical banner to a House of Commons where Politics were Ireland was quite another matter.

The idea was inevitably condemned by the Canadian Liberals. Early in the debate on the Railway Bill Edward Blake, himself an Irishman, had exclaimed:

Talk of the immigration of Irishmen to the North West. You are proposing to them to substitute the scorpion for the rod. You are proposing to those who are suffering under the tyranny of individual landlords to expose themselves to the soulless tyranny of a gigantic corporation. . . .[1]

For some time it had been Government policy in Canada as in the United States to give each intending settler on the prairie lands a quarter-section—160 acres—free of charge, with the option of purchasing adjoining lots. Not all the land in the Canadian North West was owned by the Government; the Hudson's Bay Company still held a certain amount, and certain School Lands were reserved in perpetuity. The practice of free land grants was not entirely altruistic; every settler who cultivated a lone quarter-section automatically raised the value of the adjoining acres, immigrants naturally preferring a location in an area already inhabited. As the Pacific Railway contract awarded the Company the sections alternating with the Government's free lands along the route of the main line, the established custom did not at all preclude the possibility of disposing of the railway lots.

[1] D. of C.H.C. 15 December 1880.

Stephen's plan, which finally took shape in 1883 in a memorandum which will be discussed in a later chapter was, roughly, to
provide the immigrant, at a nominal price payable over a term of
years, with a quarter-section partly cultivated, a ready-built dwelling
house, a cow and a nucleus of agricultural implements. Such a
scheme would necessarily involve a year's preparation; apart from
the making of financial arrangements, the breaking up of land and the
building of frame houses in districts where timber was not readily
available would take time. All impatience to get his scheme moving
Stephen cabled Macdonald on 22 January 1881:

When will contract be disposed of. Impossible move emigration matters
until then. This year probably lost by delay.[1]

The Premier's reply, as pencilled on the back of the telegraph form,
was 'Opposition offering continuous resistance to Bill. Expect
resolution carried next week by large majority.' The Liberals had by
this time produced a rival body of capitalists and a contract bearing
impossibly favourable terms for Canada, but although much was
made of the contrast between the 'St. Paul' syndicate and the
'Canadian' one the latter came to nothing, merely serving to prolong
the debate. Writing to Macdonald on 27 January, again on the subject
of his emigration plan, Stephen declared, 'Your obstructionists are
worse than Parnell and his co-conspirators here'.[2]

Finally, on 15 February, the Canadian Pacific Railway Bill became
law. Already Stephen had laid before W. E. Forster, Secretary of
State for Ireland, a tentative proposal for Irish emigration to
Canada.[3] All that he wanted to discover at that stage was whether or
not the Imperial Government would be disposed to co-operate, not
to the extent of an actual grant of money—this Stephen presumed
would be refused—but by granting a loan on security to the Canadian
Pacific. Stephen pointed out that besides immediate homesteaders
large numbers of men would be required in the next three years on
railway construction. Although it was said that the British Premier,
Mr. Gladstone, took the view that any attempt to transplant part of
their population would only intensify the hostility of the Irish
towards the Land Bill he was about to present to the House,
Stephen appeared to be quite content with the response to his preliminary move. He had been much encouraged by the interest shown

---

[1] Macd. P. 'Stephen' 267.   [2] Loc. cit. Stephen to Macdonald, 27 January 1881.
[3] Loc. cit. Stephen to Macdonald, 7 April and 5 May 1881, and Enclosure to
5 May.

by leading members of the Government, and was confident that the Emigration clauses of Gladstone's Land Bill would provide a satisfactory basis for operations. The Canadian High Commissioner in London, Sir Alexander Galt (A. T. Galt), was not inclined to be so optimistic, and even Sir John Rose, whom Stephen found a much more congenial colleague, but who was, nevertheless, not prone to be carried away by his own enthusiasm, wrote to Macdonald:

I am much disappointed at the lukewarmness of the Government here in reference to Emigration. The subject requires to be worked up and public opinion brought to bear on them. I have not heard a single person either side who does not say that without Emigration all the other remedies will be ineffectual. I have been doing what I could privately—Mr. Forster says he needs all the help he can [ ]. *He* does not despair but that in time it will come about.[1]

The Irish themselves tended to denounce all emigration proposals on the grounds that their America lay in the undeveloped grasslands of their own country. This standpoint was shared by the priests, in spite of the success of Bishop Ireland's experiment in Catholic colonization which was quoted as a point in favour of emigration, and it was obvious to all but confirmed optimists such as Stephen that opposition from all those quarters would not easily be overcome.

Despite these efforts to stimulate interest in his plans, Stephen was greeted on his return to Montreal in May by an accusation in the *Toronto Globe* that the Canadian Pacific had entirely neglected to encourage emigration to the North West for the coming season:

They ascribe this to the fact that Parliament did not hasten to ratify the contract before Christmas, but forget to say that the Syndicate has not advertised in Europe nor, so far as can be ascertained, done anything whatever to stimulate immigration. Their apathy in regard to their Canadian dominions is in marked contrast to their activity in bringing their Minnesota and Dakota lands to the notice of all Europe.[2]

C.P.R. FINANCIAL AND LAND POLICY

Before Stephen left London in the spring of 1881 he was joined by R. B. Angus and by J. J. C. Abbott who had been appointed Counsel to the Company, and, assisted by Sir John Rose, who played the role of 'outside adviser', they decided on the future financial policy of the Canadian Pacific.

---

[1] Macd.P. 'Rose' 259.248, Rose to Macdonald, 24 March 1881.
[2] *Weekly Globe*, 6 May 1881.

MRS. WILLIAM STEPHEN
Mother of Lord Mount Stephen, artist unknown
(In the possession of Mrs. H. G. Lafleur)

Earlier, Stephen had written to Macdonald:

My own *feeling* so far is in favour of a *moderate* financial scheme—no financial fireworks—a land grant bond rather than a bond guaranteed by the Government—but nothing will be *decided* until Angus and Abbott come over. You will be glad and surprised to hear that the Frenchmen have all come over to my view of *waiting* for results and looking to the development of the property for their profits. A quick financial coup is now quite out of their minds. In any event and independent of all financial arrangements you may rest assured of one thing. The contract will be carried out if we have to find the money ourselves.[1]

Although perfectly prepared, as was later proved, to make good this last assertion, the possibility of having to do so probably never entered Stephen's mind. The contract itself established the Canadian Pacific as a limited liability company; only five days before, in the Canadian House of Commons, in reply to a Conservative Member who had spoken in favour of generous terms for 'these gentlemen' who were risking 'their reputations and fortunes in the construction of an immense line of railway through an unpeopled country where they have got to make their business before they can get their business', Blake had pointed out:

These gentlemen expressly stipulate in this contract that they shall not be personally engaged. The only personal engagement is this single one, that they will undertake, after the Company is organized, that the Company shall deposit a million dollars for security. . . . The next minute after the organization and the deposit of the million dollars, there is an end to all personal obligation. . . .

But it was not the letter of the contract that gave Stephen confidence; it was the conviction that the work could be done, and for the sum officially estimated, $45 million. Quoting this sum in his letter to W. E. Forster, Stephen stated, as evidence of the Company's financial soundness, that $30 million was already in hand, including the Government cash subsidy of $25 million, adding, 'We can provide the remaining $15,000,000 from our own resources if we deem it necessary, or expedient, to do so'.

The authorized capital stock of the Company was $25 million, but it was at first decided to attempt no market operations until the railway had established for itself something of a reputation by the disposal of its land and by its earnings on completed sections. The

[1] Macd.P. 'Stephen' 267, Stephen to Macdonald, 23 January 1881.

past financial history of the Grand Trunk Railroad provided a precedent of unprofitable investment which Canadian railways were to find it hard to live down, and the Pacific did not intend to start by looking for trouble. When Sir John Rose wrote to Macdonald that they had practically decided to make no issue of any kind at that point but to go on with their own resources until they could show results[1] he was reporting something almost unique in the history of railway-building. It was customary for a new road to commence operations with a flourish of coupons which might or might not prove to have a sound backing but which were vastly profitable to the promoters, even should the company go bankrupt the following week.

Neither Rose nor Stephen attached great importance to the actual revenue to be gained from sales of land. As Stephen told Macdonald 'It is *settling*, not *selling* that we must aim at . . . if our lands won't sell we will give them away to settlers.'[2] The terms they proposed to offer to purchasers was $2½ an acre, with a rebate of one half on land cultivated within four years. Later a clause was introduced into the Company's land regulations whereby a percentage of land not cultivated within a prescribed period could be forfeited and revert to the Company. The main object was to get the country on either side of the railway settled—Government as well as C.P.R. sections—in order to create traffic for the road. They had no wish to deal with speculators who might buy up—and thereby lock up—large tracts of land in the hope of values rising, with no thought for anything but their own profit. While promising to co-operate in the Government's land policy, Stephen feared that this aspect was being overlooked, and wrote to Macdonald:

Don't you think . . . that it is a mistake charging more for the lands near the railway. Would it not be better to give that advantage *away* to the first comers? We say to emigrants Come now at once & take up the most favourably situated lands. That attraction properly set forth will be more potent and immediate in its effect upon emigration than anything else you can offer.[3]

According to the contract, the lands granted to the C.P.R. were to be 'fairly fit for settlement', and inevitably the Company's enemies seized upon this point with the object of retarding their disposal. Any evidence of an unfavourable nature that could be found was widely propagated. Early explorers had tended to bring back doubtful

[1] Macd.P. 'Rose' 259.248 Rose to Macdonald, 24 March 1881.
[2] Macd.P. 'Stephen' 267, Stephen to Macdonald, 5 and 8 May 1881.
[3] Loc. cit. Stephen to Macdonald, 20 December 1881.

reports about the North West lands; the original C.P.R. surveys, undertaken at the instance of the Government, had given employment to sundry naturalists and geologists whose professional jealously appears to have been proof against their ever agreeing as to the agricultural potentialities of those territories. One of the most prominent (although his fellow-naturalist, Professor Henry Hind, considered him 'more than a charlatan'[1]) was Professor John Macoun, who in 1875 had tried to convince the Prime Minister, Alexander Mackenzie, that it was possible to travel for two hundred miles in the North West without seeing an acre of bad land. All that the Liberal leader would say was 'I canna believe it'.[2] This Scottish caution was apparently shared by George Stephen's mother, Mrs. William Stephen, who on hearing of the amount of the land grant commented tersely 'I daresay a great deal of it is very wet'.[3]

Macoun, in an attempt to prove his contention, had in 1877 produced a report in which he wrote as much truth as he dared, for he hardly expected his own estimate of 200 million acres of useful land to be believed. Even a modified version was vouchsafed scant credence. Then came 1880 and the debate on the Canadian Pacific Railway Bill. Macoun was in the House, and relates how he heard Mackenzie miscalling the North West lands, quoting the adverse opinions of various explorers:

I became so excited that I called out that he had my report in his desk and why not read it also. In a minute I felt a hand on my shoulder and, on looking up, I saw one of the ushers, who invited me to keep still or else leave the building.[4]

It was a minor triumph for the Canadian Pacific when in the summer of 1884 Mackenzie took a trip over the line and changed his mind about the North West.

[1] Henry Youle Hind, *Manitoba and the North West Frauds*, Windsor, N.S. 1883. Note: A contemporary journalist once said of Hind: 'Guiteau would call him a crank' (Pres. Garfield's assassin).
[2] *Autobiography of John Macoun, M.A. Assistant Director and Naturalist to the Geological Survey of Canada, 1831-1920*, Ottawa, 1922, p. 132.
[3] Told by Mrs. Robert W. Reford to E. A. Collard. Exactly the opposite conclusion had been reached by Captain John Palliser. See Irene M. Spry, *Captain John Palliser and the Exploration of Western Canada*, The Geographical Journal, June, 1959. Palliser reported an arid 'Triangle', its base the 49th Parallel from longitude 100° to 114°W, its apex reaching to the 52nd parallel of latitude – embracing, that is, most of the prairies. Mrs. Spry comments in her footnote No. 184: 'It is noticeable that in periods of drought, like the thirties, Palliser's stock as a shrewd observer goes up, while in periods of plentiful moisture there is a tendency to feel he was short-sighted in not appreciating the agricultural potential of his Triangle'.
[4] Macoun, op. cit. pp. 158-63.

Attempts to discredit the railway lands were only intensified when in July 1881 the Company decided to make an issue of Mortgage Bonds on the security of its land grant. The Land Grant Bonds were to be redeemable at 110 in payment for lands by purchasers wishing to settle. Although they were offered only in Montreal and New York, it was an English periodical, Labouchère's *Truth*, which launched the most biting attack not only on the Company's prospects but also on the Dominion itself, which it stated to be on the verge of bankruptcy.[1] The implication was that neither the Canadian Pacific's land grant nor the cash subsidy was of value.

Declaring that the limiting of the issue to those markets was merely a ruse on the part of Montreal and New York bankers to make people believe that they had faith in the enterprise, *Truth* predicted that the Company would nevertheless be forced, before long, to appeal to the English investor. The article described British Columbia, the Province which had 'forced this contract on the country', as a barren, mountainous region which fifty railways would not galvanize into prosperity. Of Manitoba it was stated that every winter astonishing numbers of men and cattle were frozen to death there or maimed for life by frostbite, while in summer the inhabitants were driven mad by plagues of insects. The only Province worth anything at all was Ontario, and it would almost certainly annex itself before long to the United States, its best trade outlet.

Regarding the placing of the issue, *Truth* came remarkably near to a correct interpretation of Stephen's motives. One reason for making such an issue at all at this stage was to give Canadians an opportunity to show their confidence in their own national enterprise. Writing to tell Macdonald that the Bank of Montreal and J. S. Kennedy and Company had made a provisional offer for the first ten millions and were considering a further purchase, Stephen said:

I am most anxious the English people should see that Canada has faith sufficient in the enterprise to buy the bonds. Nothing will tend to give us good credit so much as letting the London folks see that they are not the only sources of financial strength in the world.[2]

Two months earlier, Stephen had given up the Presidency of the Bank of Montreal, for he felt that the Canadian Pacific would absorb all his time and energy. He had made it clear at the Annual General

---

[1] *Truth*, 1 September 1881.
[2] Macd.P. 'Stephen' 267, Stephen to Macdonald, 27 August 1881.

Meeting in June 1881 that the C.P.R. Company did not propose to borrow from the Bank, although some advantageous business might well accrue to the Bank through the enterprise.

NORTHERN PACIFIC SEEKS NORTHWARD CONNECTIONS

It was in the summer of 1881 that Stephen's suspicions regarding the intentions of the Northern Pacific Railroad became seriously aroused. While the events described above were taking place that old enemy of the St. Paul, Minneapolis and Manitoba had not been idle. Since the agreement of November 1878, the American road had been restored to more than its former strength, and in December 1880 it had successfully floated a loan for the purpose of financing an extensive construction programme. Within the next three years a new line was to be built westward from Moorhead to the Pacific Ocean, and Stephen was quick to detect any move on the part of the Northern Pacific to seek northward connections. So far as he could see danger threatened at four points. Three concerned local lines to which the Province of Manitoba had granted charters: the Manitoba South-Western controlled by Dr. Schultz, the Manitoba South-Eastern, projected by Messrs. John Haggart and Peter MacLaren, and a line to the Souris district of the Province, the charter-holder being a Toronto solicitor named Boultbee. In spite of the terms of clause 15 of the C.P.R. contract, the route planned by the South-Western brought the line within nine miles of the American boundary, while the South-Eastern planned actually to cross the boundary and run to Duluth.[1]

Sir John Macdonald was in England when, in August 1881, the Northern Pacific purchased a controlling interest in Schultz's South-Western Railway, in the hope of making a connection with its own projected Casselton branch at the boundary.[2] Boultbee's line, to which Villard of the Northern Pacific next turned his attention, still awaited a land grant from the Federal Government, and a cable from Stephen caused Macdonald to instruct Ottawa to refuse this concession. Writing to Macdonald that if Villard was allowed to carry out his plans before the Canadian Pacific had had time to establish itself the latter might as well make him a present of its line from Winnipeg to Thunder Bay and save its money on a line north

[1] Macd.P. 'J. H. Pope' 256.99, Pope to Macdonald, 18 August 1881.
[2] Macd.P. 'Stephen' 267, Stephen to Macdonald, 27 August 1881.

of Lake Superior, Stephen stressed the need for the Government to support the national line in this matter:

. . . I fear some of your colleagues are not free from the feeling that the more roads the better, a doctrine I do not object to in the least under ordinary circumstances. As you are really the author of the C.P.R. as a national through line, it will have to look to you for the protection necessary to enable it to overcome the attempts of its enemies to kill it during its infancy and time of weakness. Give the C.P.R. ten years to develop its traffic & then the Northern Pacific and every other road in the U.S. will not be able to harm our national line. . . .[1]

In a subsequent letter, Stephen explained that the C.P.R. had no wish to interfere with the South-Western so long as it kept to the terms on which the Federal Government had approved its charter— namely that it should not run to within fifteen miles of the American boundary.[2] When Villard realized that he could not gain access to Manitoba from the south-west, he turned to the South-Eastern Railway. According to Stephen, his plan was to build from Duluth to the boundary and to enter Winnipeg via the South-Eastern, there to connect with the Schultz road.[3] This scheme was foiled by the disallowance of the South-Eastern charter by the Federal Government. The South-Western Company's charter was later taken over by the Canadian Pacific.

The fourth point at which the Northern Pacific threatened to invade Canadian territory was in the Province of Quebec. The local railways there were the property of the Provincial Government, but had recently been put on the market because the latter was in financial difficulties, largely as a result of extensive railway-building. Rumour had it that the Northern Pacific hoped that by coming to the rescue of the debt-ridden Province it could make sure of a solid Quebec vote in the House of Commons against any veto of Provincial legislation in Manitoba in the interest of the Northern Pacific connection.[4] In this instance it was Macdonald who took the initiative in persuading Chapleau, the Quebec Premier, to treat instead with the C.P.R. After some negotiation, the portion of the Quebec, Montreal, Ottawa, and Occidental Railway running from Montreal via St. Jérôme and Aylmer to Ottawa was purchased by the Canadian

---

[1] Macd.P. 'Stephen' 267, Stephen to Macdonald, 27 August 1881.
[2] Ibid.
[3] Loc. cit. Stephen to Macdonald, 15 October 1881.
[4] Macd.L.B. 21.505, Macdonald to Stephen, 19 October 1881, quoting a mutual friend (unnamed).

Pacific, and the eastern section, later known as the North Shore Railway, connecting with Quebec city, was turned over to the Grand Trunk.[1] The terms of the latter agreement allowed the C.P.R. running rights over the line to Quebec. This subsequently led to friction between the two companies and the Pacific was finally persuaded by the Government to purchase the North Shore line also. Before the Q.M.O. & O. purchase, the C.P.R. had effected an amalgamation with Duncan McIntyre's Canada Central Railway, connecting Ottawa with Lake Nipissing, so that in 1882 the national line stretched, on paper at least, from Montreal to the Pacific.

NORTH OF LAKE SUPERIOR

The time allowed by the contract for the construction of the main line of the Canadian Pacific was ten years, but by the end of 1881 it became apparent to the Company that the work might be completed in half that time, particularly if it were feasible to run the line close to the north shore of Lake Superior instead of to the north of Lake Nipigon as originally planned. Although the new route would be more difficult and costly, it was thought that to be able to open the through-line to traffic by 1886 would more than compensate for the extra initial effort involved. Also, the sooner that the north-of-the-lake traffic route could be established, the greater would be the security from rival lines.

Stephen had informed Macdonald in October of this possible change in the Company's plans, finishing his letter on this facetious note:

Hill says the great advantage of finishing the whole road in five years would be that we should be getting some of the benefits on our 'first trip' here below and not having to wait till we come back with white feathers in our wings.[2]

—a reflection on the somewhat wistful tolerance with which at least one of Stephen's colleagues bore the latter's policy of waiting for profits.

What was uppermost in Stephen's mind, however, was that to hasten the completion of the lake shore line would be to silence those critics who continued to declare that the Company intended to evade this part of its task and planned instead to use a branch to the Sault

[1] Macd.L.B. 21.574, Macdonald to Stephen, 6 January 1882, and Macd.P. 'Stephen' 267, Stephen to Chapleau, 9 January 1882.
[2] Macd.P. 'Stephen' 267, Stephen to Macdonald, 29 October 1881.

for all westbound traffic. Moreover, to build a first-class line, even although it entailed expenditure out of all proportion to the distance covered, would be the most effective answer to those who suggested that if the Company, for appearances' sake, did lay a track north of the Lake, it would only be of a light and temporary nature, and all heavy freight would be routed via the Sault. Writing to Macdonald on the question of keeping traffic on the north side of the Lake, Stephen declared:

This can only be done by making the line from Nipissing in all respects a first class road capable of easy operation at high speed, and our using the most energetic measures to complete the connection with Thunder Bay in the shortest possible space of time. This new and urgent necessity on the north of the Lake division in addition to our task of reaching the Rockies by this time next year is going to tax us to the full extent of our capacity but I mean we shall do it and will trust to the full and hearty co-operation of you and your colleagues to see us through the year's work.[1]

This last remark harked back to a letter written five days earlier in which Stephen had stressed the need for the subsidy instalments earned to be promptly paid. Delay in payment was to become a serious source of friction between the railway-builders, who were constantly at work and spending money, and the Government, who dealt with official matters of this kind in season only.

Still Stephen had no immediate cause for anxiety about the finances of the Canadian Pacific. The Land Grant Bonds were selling well and the Land Department recently established at Winnipeg was doing a brisk trade. He could hardly have foreseen the combination of circumstances—in which it is even now difficult to distinguish cause from effect—which were to lead the Company into one financial crisis after another until it all but succumbed.

It is not proposed to give more than passing mention, where necessary, to the actual work of construction; from January 1882 that was in the capable hands of William C. Van Horne, an American railwayman brought north by J. J. Hill. Van Horne's energy was the more boundless because he did not have to find the money which his spectacular feats required. 'Get the work done right and send the bills to Stephen' was his attitude. Some indication of the financial commitments incurred north of Lake Superior, however, must be given. Twelve thousand men and 5,000 horses were employed on what Van Horne called 'two hundred miles of engineering impos-

---

[1] Macd.P. 'Stephen' 267, Stephen to Macdonald, 10 December 1881.

sibilities'. The total cost was $12 million, including $1,200,000 for dynamite alone. According to clause 9 of the contract, the subsidy apportioned to this part of the road (Eastern Section) was just over $15,000 a mile, with 9,600 acres of land. This could be earned only on completion and equipment of each twenty-mile stretch. It is not hard to understand, therefore, why the demands of the lake shore line on the resources of the Company, which was also engaged on construction west of Winnipeg, proved so embarrassing.

HILL AND THE CANADIAN PACIFIC

It was in the midst of these difficulties that Hill, in May 1883, left the Canadian Pacific. Although his biographer Pyle claims that Hill had all along intended to withdraw once he had helped to 'put the work on its feet',[1] no one could have said that by 1883 this had been achieved. When Stephen wrote to Macdonald in January 1881: 'Hill is a very able fellow without whom we could not easily do the work'[2] he did not seem to have expected that this help would be so soon withdrawn. Yet, while it is commonly believed that the determination of his colleagues to build north of Lake Superior instead of connecting with the St. Paul road caused a dramatic break-up of their association, with hard feelings all round, there is not yet any direct evidence that this was the case.[3]

Although evidence is not lacking to indicate that Hill and Van Horne rarely saw eye to eye, Hill remained on friendly terms with Stephen to the end of their railroading careers. Somewhat given to sweeping statements, Stephen might write to Macdonald: 'Hill has never forgiven me for building the line north of the Lake',[4] and might refer to 'our neighbour Hill who speaks well of nobody connected with the C.P.R.'[5] but he never ceased to regard Hill as a railroader of exceptional ability. More than once Stephen was disappointed in someone in whom he had placed great trust, but the fact that long after Hill's withdrawal from the Canadian Pacific the two men—whose interests did not by any means always coincide—would take counsel together over railway matters speaks volumes for the man whose spirit has taken such determined possession of St. Paul.

[1] Pyle, op. cit. vol. I, p. 302.
[2] Macd.P. 'Stephen' 267, Stephen to Macdonald, 23 January 1881.
[3] Hill's private papers will not be available until 1981.
[4] Macd.P. 'Stephen' 270, Stephen to Macdonald, 20 April 1887.
[5] Macd.P. 'Stephen' 269, Stephen to Macdonald, 2 August 1884.

It is significant, too, that in Manitoba Hill is remembered not as the man of business but as the champion of the settler. He was obsessed by the idea of developing the North West to an extent unequalled by Stephen or even Smith; he had moreover no stake in eastern Canada nor interest in Canadian politics. The most likely explanation for his deserting the C.P.R. is therefore that he saw in the St. Paul road a more satisfactory agency for the speedy fulfilment of his ambitions. When it became apparent that the American line required more than his undivided attention Hill chose to remain with it rather than with the C.P.R. He is reported to have said, many years later, 'Most men in their lives have had one great adventure; the Great Northern was mine'. The Great Northern was the system that Hill evolved from the St. Paul, Minneapolis and Manitoba; by 1893 it had been extended westward to the Pacific Ocean, finally absorbing also its old rival the Northern Pacific.

Two months after Hill's withdrawal from the Canadian Pacific, Stephen, Smith, and Angus ceased to take an active interest in the St. Paul road, but assured Hill that they would not materially reduce their holdings in the stock of the Company, 'so long at least as the policy of the company is not hostile to the C.P.R., for which we are immediately responsible'.[1]

RECAPITULATION

The position of the Canadian Pacific in the spring of 1882 was, on the face of it, highly satisfactory. From Montreal to Lake Nipissing they controlled lines traversing well-developed country. Pending the construction of the line north of Lake Superior, three lake steamers, on order at a Clyde shipyard, were to connect Prince Arthur's Landing, later Port Arthur, with Algoma Mills. From Port Arthur the 'Thunder Bay Branch', the Government-built section of the C.P.R., provided through communication to Winnipeg.

Before long, grain from the North West wheatfields would thus be transported over Canadian territory to eastern markets, and although the country north of the Lake was, from the engineer's point of view, formidable in the extreme there was promise of a considerable traffic in timber and minerals. South of Winnipeg was the well-established Pembina Branch, and the Company were building a spur to the Pembina Mountain district, reported to be rich in coalfields.

[1] Pyle, op. cit. vol. I, p. 324.

Westward, through the fertile belt, construction was proceeding apace towards the foothills of the Rocky Mountains, and prairie towns such as Brandon were springing up almost overnight with that mushroom-like growth which was characteristic of the moving frontier on either side of the 49th Parallel. The original surveys had resulted in the railway being located by way of Jasper through the Yellowhead Pass, but, at the instance of the C.P.R. Company, a Bill was introduced in Parliament in April 1882, and became law in May, authorizing a more southerly location, crossing the Rockies by the Kicking Horse Pass. At this time a practicable route had not yet been found through the Selkirk range in British Columbia, but once this difficulty was solved it only remained to join with the Onderdonk Section at Kamloops, and the transcontinental chain would be completed.

Theoretically, in a few years' time, this national road would be running like an iron backbone through the Dominion, carrying the produce not only of the North West but also of the Pacific to the shores of the Atlantic, its cars returning freighted with the manufactures of Eastern Canada, or with goods from Europe, the traffic increasing as the North West became filled with industrious immigrants. This was the nature and purpose of the Canadian Pacific as conceived by the visionaries of the fifties. This was the Dominion of Canada becoming vertebrate.

IV

Canadian Pacific: towards a workable reality

THE VULNERABLE MAIN LINE

HAD the Canadian Pacific Railway Company been only contractors for building the main line, construction could have been comparatively leisurely, and the completed 'backbone' handed over to the Government in 1891 with no thought given to its subsequent operation. According to the contract, however, the Company undertook to operate the line in perpetuity. It was therefore imperative, as soon as construction commenced, to look ahead at least to the foreseeable future. What had to be created was not just a line of railway but a commercially viable railroad system, reaching out in many directions for traffic wherewith to sustain the transcontinental road. The contract gave the Company the right to build branches, and promised land for the actual roadbed of these, but there was no financial provision for them.

In the west, as has been shown, Stephen had foreseen the possibility of traffic being drained away from the Canadian line by branch lines under rival management, and had acted accordingly. In Eastern Canada, although the main line had been extended to Montreal, and provision made for reaching Quebec city, connections with American lines were all in the hands of established and potentially hostile railway companies. Until the advent of the Canadian Pacific, the Grand Trunk Railroad had been Canada's chief transport system, and this company claimed most of Eastern Canada as its proper preserve. Had the Grand Trunk undertaken to build the Pacific Railway there would have been no cause for friction, but having declined this task it was faced with the prospect of seeing its own organization degraded to a mere local system. It soon became clear that the older road was not to accept this position.

The first openly hostile move came in the spring of 1882 when the Grand Trunk, having by a policy of aggression reduced its strongest rival in Ontario, the Great Western, to a state of helplessness, forced an amalgamation with that company, for no more apparent reason than to forestall the Canadian Pacific. The Great Western, besides its original line from Windsor to Niagara Falls, controlled the Detroit and Milwaukee Railroad from Detroit to Grand Haven on Lake Michigan, and also leased the Wellington, Grey and Bruce, running northward to Lake Huron, and the Canada Air Line from Glencoe to Buffalo. Thus every rail approach to the west through the United States lay open to the Grand Trunk. It only remained for that Company, if and when it so wished, to join hands with the Northern Pacific at Duluth to render Canada's transcontinental enterprise a Quixotic error. Of what use to blast a path yard by yard through the wilderness north of Lake Superior when westbound freight was already finding its way across Michigan and Wisconsin? The steam whistle might well sound forlorn in the Bow River Valley when the treasures of the Orient were speeding over Washington Territory, Idaho, and Montana.

Undoubtedly, when finally completed, the Canadian Pacific would offer the most direct route from coast to coast, and that without changing cars, but in 1882, with this consummation three years and millions of dollars away, what man of business, thinking only of dividends, would risk his money on the future of Canada? Only hard cash could bridge those three years and give Canada the right to call herself a nation, but hard cash in excess of what was required to complete the main line of the C.P.R. was necessary to establish a system that would be neither a reproach to its promoters nor the laughing-stock of the railway world.

To the end Stephen maintained that the resources of the Company would have been ample to finish the work according to the conditions of the contract. Even the extra commitments could have been met had the associates been able to realize their assets in a fair market. Under ordinary circumstances the Company need never have known a single financial crisis. Having the backing of the Dominion Government, not to mention a Board comprising men of noted wealth and considerable reputation as railway-builders, its credit ought to have stood second to that of no other railway enterprise. On the contrary, the years 1882 to 1885 were a time of almost continual financial stress, largely owing to the necessity of foiling attempts to rob the line of its potential traffic and to the retaliatory actions of its rivals in seeking to destroy the credit of the Canadian Pacific.

Towards the end of 1881, Stephen was planning another visit to London with the dual purpose of making a fresh effort to encourage emigration and of bringing the Land Grant Bonds to the notice of the English investor. He still did not propose to offer the Bonds on the London market, but intended, as he told Macdonald, 'to make "John Bull" buy these bonds by sending orders to this side for them at a premium'.[1] So confident was he that the merits of these securities would be duly recognized that he paid scant heed to an insidious pamphlet campaign which was being launched in the City with the object of giving the Londoner, who as a rule knew nothing of Canada, an entirely erroneous impression of the prospects of the Dominion and of its national railway. He was fully aware of what was happening; in a letter to Macdonald in December he added, almost as a post-script:

The G.T.R. and its paid ink-slingers in London are doing their best to damage the bonds and the whole enterprise.[2]

What he never believed possible was that the 'subsidised Grand Trunk scribblers', as he described them on another occasion,[3] could have more influence on the public than the more silent but solid evidence of the railway's progress displayed in more conventional media. He held firmly to his opinion that to show results in Canada and to avoid, above all, any breach with the Canadian Government, would most effectively silence opposition.

The Company was not to be without its own pamphleteer, however. The *Toronto Mail* had recently been established as a Government organ to provide a counterblast to the *Globe*, and its editor, T. C. Patteson, assumed the name of 'Mohawk' in order to reply to 'Ishmael' and 'Diogenes'—the pseudonyms of the Grand Trunk scribblers.[4] He pointed out the incongruity of decrying a security in advance of its appearance in the London market:

Only a rival corporation could have the interest to *forestall* Mr. Stephen, the president of the road, who is daily expected in London . . . the C.P.R. has possessed itself of existing roads in the Province of Ontario, and in connection with them proposes to complete a road between Toronto and Montreal, which will destroy the monopoly hitherto possessed by the Grand Trunk for the carriage of goods and passengers

[1] Macd.P. 'Stephen' 267, Stephen to Macdonald, 4 November 1881.
[2] Loc. cit. Stephen to Macdonald, 13 December 1881.
[3] Loc. cit. Stephen to Macdonald, 11 January 1882.
[4] 'Mohawk', *The C.P.R. and its assailants*, London, 1882.

from Ontario to ocean ports. Hinc illae lachrymae; that is where the shoe pinches. . . .

Quoting 'Ishmael's' denials that the lands granted to the railway had any agricultural potentialities, 'Mohawk' observed that if it had been possible to declare that the cash subsidy consisted of counterfeit coins, 'Ishmael' would have done so. Of Stephen himself 'Mohawk' wrote:

Ishmael twits him with 'obscurity' . . . his obscurity in Canada consists in the fact that in a country stretching from ocean to ocean, every business man knew his name before he dreamed of being associated with the Canadian Pacific. . . . A strong man shouldering his way through an unsympathetic world must make enemies more or less. But despite this, I never heard or read any personal abuse of Mr. Stephen. . . .

This was certainly not written with the approval of Stephen, and Patteson complained of his attitude to Macdonald:

It was all very well to belittle Joe Nelson but his 'Notes' were going everywhere. I considered the way I took to do it the only way he could be shut up, consistently with the dignity of those concerned and of the enterprise in hand. I sent 20,000 of them broadcast. . . .[1]

TRYING TO INTEREST BRITAIN

It would be misleading to imply that even the pamphlet campaign aroused any degree of general interest in Canadian affairs in England. Writing from London at the end of February 1882, Stephen complained to Macdonald of the apathy prevalent in England with regard to the Dominion. Efforts to get space in the London papers for a little publicity for the North West were met with the information that the subject was of no interest to their readers. Said Stephen bitterly:

'Jumbo' the big elephant recently bought by Barnum is a matter of ten times more interest to London than twenty colonies. . . . The fact is emigration is not popular. There is an instinctive feeling that they are losing national power when they decrease in numbers even when the emigrant goes to a British colony, and the genuine insular Britisher hates all emigration efforts and would rather have the people remain, to struggle

[1] Macd.P. 'Stephen' 267, Patteson to Macdonald, 13 February 1882. Note: Pamphleteering was a popular device at the time. Peter Mitchell, one of the fathers of Confederation, published as a pamphlet a series of letters which he wrote in support of the North West lands which he visited just before the completion of the St. Paul, Minneapolis and Manitoba Railway. (P. Mitchell, *The west and the north-west, notes of a holiday trip*, Montreal, 1880).

and sometimes starve, than to emigrate. The best evidence of this feeling is to be found in the fact that there is not a man of mark on either side, in the House of Commons, who has the courage to express the opinion they *all* hold in private that there is no permanent cure for Ireland's troubles but a wholesale transplanting of not less than one third its present population. We must rely on our own efforts to popularise the attractions of the Nor West. We shall get no help from any quarter here.[1]

The sale of 'Jumbo, the Pride of the British Heart' by the London Zoo was indeed the topic of the hour, occupying column after column even in *The Times*, and evoking such sorrow as could hardly have been equalled on the death of a national hero. *Truth* most truly described, in jingling rhyme, how 'Jumbo' eclipsed, in news value, the voting of a Land Act Committee by the House of Lords, and caused more concern than the state of Ireland or the agitation of the Land League. This was the situation in a London where Stephen was once more trying to gain serious consideration for the question of emigration to Canada. 'Jumbo' was, in fact, a force to be reckoned with. The American Ambassador, in a public speech, referred to 'the burning question of "Jumbo" '. People who would have hesitated to invest in a C.P.R. security which, they had been warned, would yield them no return whatever, sent generous cheques to 'Jumbo's' guardians in order that their idol might not lack for buns, or even oysters, on his transatlantic journey. But, ironically, it was the C.P.R.'s declared enemy who eventually put an end—an ignoble end—to the noble animal. While touring Canada with Barnum's circus, 'Jumbo' inadvertently stood in the path of a Grand Trunk freight train advancing at full speed. As the *Chicago Tribune* reported sadly, there was, in the manner of his passing, 'nothing heroic or appropriate'.

The Irish Land Act had provided for the appointment of a commission which might, from time to time and with the sanction of the Treasury, negotiate with any reputable body in Canada or in any other British oversea territory, for the advance of such sums as it might think desirable to expend in promoting emigration from Ireland. It was not until the end of 1882, however, that machinery was set in motion for carrying out these provisions of the Act. In the interval Stephen resolved to make an appeal to a different class of persons, to those who, having a little capital, were seeking more scope for their energies than could be afforded by their native land.

[1] Macd.P. 'Stephen' 267, Stephen to Macdonald, 26 February 1882.

Advertisements were inserted in newspapers and periodicals throughout the country, offering for sale to actual settlers farming and grazing lands in the fertile belt, to be paid for either in cash or in Land Grant Bonds, obtainable through the Bank of Montreal in London.

Stephen's last letter to Macdonald before sailing again for Canada still struck an optimistic note:

I am well satisfied with the result of my work on this side. I found our enemies here had directed their efforts to two points, first to make the people here believe that the North West was an uninhabitable desert, that the Government of Canada and the C.P.R. were leagued in conspiracy to palm their worthless lands off on the ignorant and unsuspecting emigrant, etc. etc. . . . This effort has 'bust' in the worst way, and I am now satisfied the interest of the people of this country of all classes will go on increasing, and that we shall have quite as many people—rich and poor— going out to the North West as we can take care of. The other point aimed at was to damage the C.P.R. Company financially. I have beaten them fairly on this point also. My strong card has been that we can build the C.P.R., if need be, without a dollar of English money; that the Company have no bonds to sell, having sold all its bonds to a syndicate who were selling them to the Canadian public much faster than was expected. If we have good luck this summer and get the line out to the Rockies this fall, there will be no difficulty in getting more English money than we shall want.[1]

FINANCIAL DEMANDS MULTIPLY

Stephen's first task on his return to Canada in April 1882, was to find the money to pay for the western section of the Quebec railroad, this purchase having been concluded in March. Until that time only $5 million worth of the Canadian Pacific's capital stock had been issued, most of this being held either by the members of the Company or by their close friends, but at the Company's meeting on 10 May, provision was made for the sale of the remaining $20 million at 25 cents on the dollar, the first option to purchase being reserved for those who had already bought of the initial issue at par. Even during construction it was decided to pay an annual dividend of 5 per cent. Later that year the authorized capital stock was increased to $100 million, but still no bond was issued on the security of the road.

[1] Macd.P. 'Stephen' 268, Stephen to Macdonald, 18 April 1882.

The payment for the Quebec railway was not the only extra expense with which the Company was faced. In Manitoba the Pembina Mountain and Souris branches had to be financed. Construction costs on the prairie section west of Winnipeg had far exceeded estimates, and much more than the Government subsidy would clearly be required. Payment of the subsidy had been adjusted in the contract to allow considerably more per mile for work done on the Eastern Section (Nipissing to Thunder Bay) than on the Central, generally referred to as the Prairie Section. The inadequacy of the allocation for work on the Eastern Section has already been mentioned; it had been expected, however, that there would be a substantial surplus of subsidy over expenses on the Prairie Section which would compensate for the deficit incurred over the lake shore line. This was why it was said in some quarters that the Company would draw the generous allowance for the prairie work and then evade the difficult task north of Lake Superior.

To add to the Company's difficulties, the Government's obligations in respect of the subsidy earned were not always promptly discharged. The estimates of work done had first to be approved by the Privy Council, and whereas railway construction was continuous, the Privy Council met only at intervals. This has been mentioned before, but it was in 1882 that the Canadian Pacific really began to feel the strain of partnership with the Government.

POLITICAL CONSIDERATIONS INTERVENE

In that General Election year Macdonald had many other preoccupations, not least of which was to avoid any appearance of favouring the Canadian Pacific at the expense of the Grand Trunk. Writing in May to Joseph Hickson, general manager of the Grand Trunk, expressing the hope that he would 'put [his] shoulder to the wheel and help [them] as of yore in the Elections', Macdonald gave the promise: 'I shall endeavour and I feel it my duty to do so to do all I properly can for the G.T.R.'[1] In an earlier letter a similar assurance had been given: 'I have, as you know, uniformly backed up the G.T.R. since 1854 and won't change my course now.'[2] It was, of course, right and proper that the Government should display complete impartiality towards rival commercial concerns, so long as only commercial issues were at stake, yet there is more than

[1] Macd.L.B. 21.740, Macdonald to Hickson, 25 May 1882.
[2] Macd.L.B. 21.671, Macdonald to Hickson, 25 February 1882.

a hint in 1882 that the just claims of the Canadian Pacific on Macdonald's attention were set aside, Macdonald being secure in the knowledge that, come what might, he could count on Stephen's loyalty. Any protest on Stephen's part would be met by the reminder that any differences between Government and Company must be kept well under cover.

With this Stephen entirely agreed. Early in 1882, before his London visit, when some minor difference over the Company's finances had been smoothed over, Stephen wrote to Macdonald observing that if the latter looked further into the matter he would find that the Company was not so far wrong as Macdonald had feared, adding:

At the same time I am thoroughly agreed with you as to the necessity of our avoiding even the appearance of anything that would give our enemies a chance of stabbing us, and misrepresenting us before the public. It is a daily surprise to me to see the lengths which blind political malignity will go to secure its ends, and we are all most anxious to keep the Government and the Company in all their dealings strictly within the letter and spirit of the law, and I hope you will not hesitate to advise us when your greater experience enables you to see danger ahead of us.[1]

At the same time Stephen did not hesitate to add, later in the same letter:

Our difficulty in getting through with the work we have laid out for this year will be very serious if the Government does not show some more consideration than their actions would indicate.

He referred there firstly to the dilatoriness of the Government in allocating the C.P.R. lands and secondly to the action of the Minister of Railways in deducting from the first instalment of the subsidy earned the price of a quantity of rails which the Company had agreed to take over from the Government but which had not, at that time, been delivered.

Regarding the actual payment of the subsidy earned, it appears that in 1882 a new condition had privately been attached. The enemies of the C.P.R. in Canada had never ceased to suggest that the Company did not intend to build the line north of Lake Superior,[2] and because of the change in location there actual construction had indeed been delayed. So great was the clamour that the Company was virtually told that unless work north of the Lake were

[1] Macd.P. 'Stephen' 267, Stephen to Macdonald, 10 January 1882.
[2] Stephen was apt to call this the Lake Superior section. (See Appendix I (i)).

speeded up the subsidy earned on the Prairie Section would not be paid.

On 1 August, during the Parliamentary recess, John Henry Pope, who was deputizing at Ottawa for the Minister of Railways, telegraphed Macdonald to the effect that the Company had agreed to start grading north of the Lake the following week, and advising that the subsidy for a further twenty-mile stretch completed on the Prairie Section be paid.[1] To this Macdonald agreed. There followed a letter from Pope to the Premier pointing out, in typical Pope terminology, the injustice being done to the railway-builders:

I received your telegram about paying the C.P.R. this time and giving them notice that no more would be paid until Council reassembles. I have paid this one today on receipt of your telegram but I have not given official notice nor do I like to do so for the reason that I have talked very sharp to Stephen Angus and McIntyre and told [ ] the only way that we could continue to pay on Western part was for them to push on the work at Thunder Bay East, and I know they have done all they could. It really would amount to destroying their summer's work to throw this Bombshell into their camp in the middle of the working season. Their expenses are now enormous—men scattered over hundreds of miles. I really do not see how this can be done without breaking everything down. I know it is for me to do as you wish in matters of this magnitude in which such important political interests are involved or get out of the way. And as I cannot see my way to push this so far as you wish do not hesitate a moment in putting someone else in my place. I assure you there will be no feeling on my part.[2]

Stephen, at this time, was on a six-week visit to the North West, but on his return to Montreal he wrote at length to Macdonald, vigorously refuting the allegations of unworthy intentions on the part of the Company, allegations which emanated not only from Opposition sources but from members of the Government also:

I am aware of the *pretention* to uneasiness on the part of the [friends] of the Government in the Press and elsewhere not excluding the Cabinet lest we should turn out a pack of rogues and 'lie down' on the Lake Superior section, having made a lot of money out of the construction of the line in the central section, leave the Government to finish the Lake Superior section and the Rocky Mountain section and so get rid of the thing. This affected apprehension is so utterly absurd that I have no

[1] Loc. cit. Pope to Macdonald, 1 August 1882.
[2] Macd.P. 'J. H. Pope' 256.163, Pope to Macdonald, 12 August 1882.

patience to notice it, and would not allude to it, even to you, but for the fact that it crops up in quarters where there is no excuse for its existence.

I take it for granted that our worst enemy will not pretend to say we have not pushed the work on the main line with energy. The *Globe* says we are building it too fast. I claim that we have been equally energetic on the eastern section and have relatively accomplished as much work—real work—though it does not 'bulk' in the public eye. You will not forget that we had to begin *de novo*. The locations and surveys of the Government were useless to us. . . .[1]

He went on to say that the whole section from Thunder Bay to Nipissing had now been surveyed, and it was hoped to have the line located that season except for a particularly bad part between Nipigon and Pic, where 'any engineering mistake . . . might cost us millions. . . . No clamor will induce us to put a spade into that section till we are sure we are right in our location of the line.' Confident that time would prove the truth of his assertions, Stephen could not prevent, nevertheless, a faint note of frustration from permeating his bold words:

. . . What is the use of boring you with all these details—there are lots of people, pretended friends, who will persist in telling you that we have no intention of building north of Lake S. up to the completion of the line, and then they will be equally vigorous in asserting and trying to make you believe that we do not mean to operate it when it is built. For such malignant wrongheadedness there is no remedy but neglect, nothing else will stop their idle talk.

His enthusiasm was quickly renewed as he went on to enlarge upon a piece of news the substance of which he had already tele-graphed to Macdonald, namely, that a practicable pass, requiring no tunnel, had at last been found through the Selkirk Mountains. The railway could thus pursue its more southerly location. The finding of the pass by Major Rogers, an American engineer with a flair for such discovery (the pass was named after him) was a momentous event for the Company and was first reported with a delightful lack of ceremony. Some considerable time after the Major had disappeared without trace into the Rockies, the butler at Stephen's new mansion on Drummond Street, Montreal, was quite put out of countenance by the arrival on the doorstep, during dinner, of a short, snappy little man with long Dundreary whiskers, 'unheralded and in a dil-apidated state', as Mary Kingsley, the unconventional African

---

[1] Macd.P. 'Stephen' 267, Stephen to Macdonald, 27 August 1882.

traveller, would have said. In vain the butler protested that Mr. Stephen could not be called from his guests; the little man stood firm. Finally the butler gave up and went to consult his master who came to the door and recognized Major Rogers. The episode ended in true biblical form with a command to the butler to array the major in suitable style and bring him down to dinner.[1]

But the finding of the Rogers Pass was but a fleeting ray of light in the gathering gloom of 1882. The letter just quoted goes on to the next sore point—the delay in the allocation of the C.P.R. lands—and ends on the same note on which it began:

The road is going to cost a great deal more money than we calculated on. The so-called Prairie section is not Prairie at all—it is a broken rolling country with a great deal of heavy work. Now the line we are building is a very different thing from the standard fixed and costing double the price of a poor Prairie road. Sandford Fleming will corroborate me in this and satisfy you that there is no surplus over the subsidy for us to bag and run away with. . . . I dare say you will hardly believe it possible we should need more money to keep us going than the subsidy provides in addition to our own capital investment, but if you could see what we are doing, it would be no surprise to you to be told that we have to find five to six millions more. When I think of all this, I cannot help feeling a little bit disgusted with those 'friends' of the Government who are all the time hinting and alleging that we intend to fail in our contract. This is an unconscionable affliction, and I am half inclined to tear it up now it is written, but in it is a faithful and frank transcript of what is in my mind. I will let it go hoping that you may find leisure to read it between now and the time we meet.

This letter is typical of the uninhibited manner in which, over a period of years, Stephen communicated his thoughts to Macdonald. Frequently he would suggest an interview, either at Ottawa or in Quebec Province, where each had a country home, Macdonald at Rivière du Loup, Stephen at Causapscal on the Matapedia River. Stephen was anxious that the Premier should be kept fully informed of Canadian Pacific developments, but it is to be feared that, to Macdonald, these continual and often lengthy outpourings assumed a gnat-like quality—especially when the shortcomings of the Government were the subject of Stephen's pestering—and were treated accordingly. In spite of his talent for business, where personalities were concerned Stephen was apt to be hasty in his conclusions. The allegations, in the letter just quoted, of anti-C.P.R. feeling on the

[1] Told by Mrs. Robert W. Reford to E. A. Collard.

Government side had their immediate origin in some remarks of Mr. Mackenzie Bowell, Minister of Customs, which had been repeated to Stephen in Winnipeg. Yet it was later to be all too clearly proved that personal or party prejudices, allied to a certain narrowness of vision, might well cause Conservative Ministers to take an anti-C.P.R. line.

The meeting referred to in this letter duly took place, but it left Stephen still uncertain of having convinced Macdonald on all points. He had forgotten, too, to bring up the subject of the Prairie Section. He therefore proceeded, 'at the risk of being voted a bore', to make this particular point all over again, referring once more to the current allegation that the Company intended to pocket the profits on the Prairie Section and then to default on the Lake Superior line:

. . . I do not care a cent for what the *Globe* and all such critics say, but I regard it as a matter of great importance that you and your colleagues in the Government should be perfectly clear on this point.

The so-called Prairie Section is not prairie at all in the sense that the Red River Valley is a Prairie. The country west of Portage la Prairie is a broken rolling country and the amount of work on our road bed is more than double what it would have been had it run along the valley. In short, the road, as we are building it, both as regards its physique and its rapidity of construction, is costing us a great deal more than the subsidy and a great deal more than we expected. We are just about even with the world at the moment, but to reach this position we have had to find 5 million more dollars from our own resources. To enable me to make up my quota I had to sell my Montreal Bank Stock.[1] I mention this to show you that there is nothing in the building of the Prairie Section for anybody to bag and lie down on, even if we were mean enough to commit a breach of contract. . . .

. . . I can stand our *enemies* saying that we are making use of the surplus afforded by the Government subsidy on the Prairie Section for the purpose of engaging in outside railway schemes designed to disturb existing interests but I cannot stand any member of the Government believing such ridiculous rubbish.[2]

DELAY IN ALLOCATING LAND GRANT

If Macdonald suffered overmuch from such reiterations, the cumulative effect on Stephen of grievances repeatedly shelved was no less devastating. This was not the treatment which a company

[1] Stephen's name did in fact disappear from the official list of shareholders of the Bank of Montreal.
[2] Macd.P. 'Stephen' 267, Stephen to Macdonald, 7 September 1882.

honestly and efficiently carrying out a contract for a project which had failed to attract a single other tender had a right to expect. The difficulties, financial and otherwise, were in themselves sufficient without the President of the Canadian Pacific having to act mendicant at the door of the other contracting party, wringing from the Government, as if in charity, the just dues laid down in the charter.

According to the contract, the C.P.R. land grant consisted of 25 million acres, made up from the odd-numbered sections in an area extending for twenty-four miles on either side of the main line for a distance of roughly 900 miles. Since the change of location, the railway belt ran almost due west from Winnipeg to the foothills of the Rockies. This gives the impression that the Company knew exactly where its lands lay. One has a mental picture of the prairies diced into neat 640 acre sections, Government lands alternating with railway, with here and there a square marked with a flaming torch to indicate that this plot was consecrated to the cause of education. In actual fact, much of the territory had never even been surveyed, and it would have been quite impossible to indicate to the holder of a Land Grant Bond the exact location of that portion of the Dominion of Canada represented by his coupon.

When it came to selling land to settlers the position became even more acute. But besides the imminent prospect of delay in land sales, should all homesteads within the surveyed area be taken up, there was the danger that at some more distant date it would be discovered that the Company had induced the public to invest in property which did not even exist. Stephen had calculated that, when the Government sections, Hudson's Bay and school lands had been subtracted, there remained in the railway belt no more than 5 million acres fairly fit for settlement. Obviously the balance of the Company's land grant would have to be located elsewhere, and Stephen's fear was that, with the large sales being negotiated with the numbers of colonization companies to which the current land boom had given rise, the Government would not have sufficient land left, in a suitable locality, to fulfil its contract with the Canadian Pacific.

The pressing need for working capital resulting from excessive construction expenses and the improbability of providing it by a long-term land policy of selling only for immediate settlement were, moreover, by the summer of 1882 making it clear to the Company that it could no longer avoid selling a quantity of its land in large blocks. To minimize the undesirable effects of such a step a company was

formed of men known to be friendly towards the C.P.R. which agreed
to purchase from the railway company $13½ million worth of Land
Grant Bonds and 5 million acres of land, consisting of six sections
out of every ten in the Company's town and village sites.[1] The
active members of the Canada North West Land Company were
Edmund B. Osler,[2] President of the Ontario and Quebec Railway
Company (later amalgamated with the C.P.R.) and William Bain
Scarth of Toronto, a son of James Scarth of Binscarth, Orkney, who
had emigrated to Canada in 1855. Scarth, who was appointed
general manager, had previously been manager of the Scottish,
Ontario and Manitoba Land Company. He was an active Conservative,
very much in the confidence of Macdonald,[3] and later represented
Winnipeg. The financial agents of the Land Company were John
Kennedy Tod and Oliver Northcote of New York, and among their
English associates was the Duke of Manchester who made large
investments in the North West lands. There was no stipulation, in
the agreement with the C.P.R., about the location of settlers, but in
practice this was actively encouraged.[4]

The formation of the land Company was reported with variations
in England. On 8 June 1882, the City column of *The Times* printed
a letter from Alexander Begg, the C.P.R. Land Agent in England,
correcting the impression that the railway company had disposed of
the greater part of their land grant to land corporations. At first the
demand, both in Canada and in England, for shares in the Land
Company was so great that Stephen refrained from buying any himself. Later, when the Grand Trunk had released its 'scribblers' on
the new enterprise with such effect that the value of the shares fell
sharply, Stephen, in order to support the market, bought a considerable block, incurring great personal loss thereby.[5] To help
the Land Company out of its difficulties, in December 1883, the
C.P.R. consented to resume roughly half of the Bonds and land of
which the Land Company had relieved them.

At intervals throughout the summer of 1882 Stephen laboured to
impress upon the Prime Minister the urgency of having the lands
located. The subject inevitably cropped up in the long letter he wrote
on his return from the North West in August:

[1] *The Times*, 8 June and 25 July 1882. See also James B. Hedges, *Building the Canadian West*, The Land and Colonization Policies of the C.P.R., New York, 1939, p. 74.
[2] See Harvey Cushing, *The Life of Sir William Osler*, Oxford, 1940, pp. 124-5.
[3] See Macd.P. 'Scarth.'   [4] Hedges, op. cit. p. 75.
[5] Lord Mount Stephen to Robert Meighen, 27 September 1901.

. . . The fact is the lands are not there to anything like the extent talked about. At any rate you will agree with me that the Government having made a contract to give the Company 25 million acres, provision ought to be made for carrying out the contract. The delay in giving us the lands we have already earned and which we were promised should be given on June 1st has been a great loss and embarrassment to us already, and I do hope you will take this matter into your own most serious consideration and promptly dispose of it in a way that will be fair and just to all concerned. We cannot build and equip the C.P.R. without money, and money can only come from the resources we have at command . . . we shall need every acre of the grant to enable us to find the money requisite to finish our contract, and I look to you to help us in this matter. Delay will be fatal to us, we cannot wait. . . .[1]

On receiving an encouraging response from Macdonald, Stephen went a step further and prepared a memorandum setting forth a possible solution to the problem.[2] On the assumption that 20 million acres would have to be found outside the railway belt, he proposed that part of the deficiency be made up from odd-numbered sections to the south of the line, between the railway belt and the boundary—this after satisfying the Manitoba South-Western Railway land grant—and from even-numbered sections in the same tract, if necessary, or in the railway belt. The remainder could be located along branch lines projected north of the railway belt, although it seemed to Stephen that the grants already made to colonization companies might have absorbed most of the available land. In any case, to make up the total C.P.R. grant would exhaust it all, and it was imperative that this land should immediately be reserved. In a covering letter Stephen wrote:

. . . Let me say here that I feel much relieved at finding you so thoroughly appreciate the necessity and importance of prompt action in this land matter. It would be terrible blow to us if our enemies could create a feeling in the public mind that the lands were not there to give us, unless we took worthless lands. . . .

Two weeks later he ventured to express the hope that Macdonald would let him know when he and the Deputy Minister of the Interior, Lindsay Russell, could meet representatives of the Company to discuss land matters.[3] On 4 October, after some communication

---

[1] Macd.P. 'Stephen' 267, Stephen to Macdonald, 27 August 1882.
[2] Loc. cit. Stephen to Macdonald, 8 September 1882.
[3] Loc. cit. Stephen to Macdonald, 22 September 1882.

between Stephen and Russell,[1] J. J. C. Abbott, Counsel to the Canadian Pacific, submitted to Macdonald an official application, based on Stephen's memorandum, with a map indicating the tracts which the Company desired to have reserved.[2] Stephen also wrote again privately to Macdonald:

. . . I hope there is nothing in our application which we are not justified in asking and which it would be unwise or impolitic for the Government to accede to.

The important thing for us now is to get a patent for all the land earned up to this time, say 500 miles at 15,500 acres per mile. The demand on us for money is something appalling. $400,000 went to Winnipeg last week and one million more has to be there on 10th. These demands are quite enough to scare timid folks, but I have no fear as long as you stand by us and trust us. . . .[3]

Before the application reached the Privy Council, however, Sir Charles Tupper, Minister of Railways, went out with Stephen to the North West to review the situation. Finding that the quantity of lands obtainable south of the railway belt was even less than had been calculated, Stephen proposed taking a solid tract along the main line, including both odd and even sections, from Brandon, Manitoba, to the Rockies.

A good deal of credence had been accorded the view of Sir A. T. Galt, Canadian High Commissioner in London, that the land bordering the C.P.R. between Moose Jaw and Medicine Hat was worthless for agricultural purposes. This was corroborated by C. J. Brydges, Land Commissioner of the Hudson's Bay Company, both men thereby incurring a displeasure that in the case of Galt, at least, amounted to little short of hatred on the part of Stephen. After inspecting the region for himself Tupper was inclined to disagree, and telegraphed Macdonald to this effect, adding that if Stephen would modify his proposal, and accept a solid tract west of Regina only, he would advise acceptance of his proposition.[4] When Stephen himself wrote to Macdonald on the subject the latter, armed with Tupper's new intelligence, replied:

I don't think it would do at all to propose to Parliament to give the C.P.R. the even-numbered lots along the line of the railway. It would intensify the

[1] Loc. cit. Stephen to Macdonald, 25 September 1882. See also Macd.P. 'Railways,' 9, Stephen to Russell, 25 September 1882.
[2] Macd.P. 'Stephen' 267, Abbott to Macdonald, 4 October 1882.
[3] Loc. cit. Stephen to Macdonald, 5 October 1882.
[4] Loc. cit. Tupper to Macdonald, 16 October 1882.

cry of monopoly and do Government and Company much harm. . . .
There will be quite sufficient row about the conveyance to you of the best
lands south of the line. Let us go by degrees in what we do. . . .[1]

'FAIRLY FIT FOR SETTLEMENT'

On 24 October the Privy Council, after considering a report from
the Minister of the Interior and hearing Stephen's views, issued
an Order in Council reserving the odd-numbered sections between
Regina and the Rockies from sale, and allotting to the Canadian
Pacific certain lands to the south of the railway belt. This was a step
in the right direction but was a disappointment to Stephen, who had
looked on his offer to accept a solid tract along the railway belt as a
practical solution worthy of more general approval. In ironical mood
he wrote to Macdonald:

. . . I supposed from what took place when I was before the Council at
Ottawa the other day that you and your colleagues would regard my
proposal as a most favourable one for the Government, especially
politically, as it embraced a section of country which so 'high authorities'
as the High Commissioner and the Land Commissioner of the Hudson's
Bay Company had with *sorrow* on their lips but *gladness* in their hearts,
pronounced to be worthless and if I mistake not had even told you that
they did not believe the C.P.R. would take a foot of such lands. . . .[2]

Apart from denying it the even-numbered sections on the main
line, the Government had withheld from the Company part of the
lands south of the railway belt which Stephen understood were to be
awarded it. Following fresh representations by Charles Drinkwater,
Secretary to the C.P.R., to the Secretary of the Interior, a further
reservation was made in southern Manitoba early in 1883. Even then
the total land grant was not provided for.

On March 3 the *Toronto Globe*, taking advantage of the situation
to level an attack at both Company and Government, published a
garbled version attributing all difficulties to the abandoning of the
Yellowhead route in favour of that by the Kicking Horse Pass:

. . . the C.P.R. Company has declined to receive more than 5,000,000
acres out of the 11,000,000 in the odd-numbered sections in the 40-mile
belt between Winnipeg and Fort Calgary. . . . This is a most unfortunate occurrence for the country, and all the damage that will ensue
from it is the direct consequence of the gross blunder made by the
Dominion Government two years ago when the southern diversion of the

[1] Macd.L.B. 22.7, Macdonald to Stephen, 20 October 1882.
[2] Macd.P. 'Stephen' 267, Stephen to Macdonald, 28 October 1882.

main line was sanctioned. . . . Intending immigrants will surely put the worst construction possible on the matter.

For several months the *Globe* harped on this congenial string, reverberations being heard at other receptive points, and there was unfortunately just sufficient truth in its outpourings to gain credence for the whole. It was not true, as was stated on 24 July, that much of the land along the main line was unfit for settlement, but it could not be denied that in the general confusion it was sometimes difficult for an intending settler to secure a homestead, let alone pre-emption rights, with the result that he turned away to find a location south of the boundary. On 8 August the *Globe* published, over the initials 'W.M.' an article emphasizing the uninviting appearance of the much-maligned land east of Medicine Hat, and calculated to discourage intending immigrants by suggesting that the demeanour of the Indians, recently deprived of their all-purpose staple by the disappearance of the buffalo, portended their going on the warpath at any moment.[1]

A protest from the *Montreal Herald* merely called forth an even more damaging rejoinder from the imperturbable *Globe*. With an air of virtuous innocence the latter pointed out that it had neither said nor insinuated that the Canadian Pacific was responsible for the Indians being armed or for their being dissatisfied. The *Globe* was full of admiration for the great energy displayed by the Company in constructing its line with such unparalleled speed, although it doubted, indeed, whether the settlement of the North West had been helped thereby. It did not blame the Syndicate in the least for building the road so near the frontier and through so many miles of the great alkali desert; it was for them to do whatever promised to be most profitable. Only the Government was at fault for failing to guard the public interest in the location of the road.[2] A later article declared:

[1] 'W.M.' was thought to have been William McDougall, Lieutenant Governor Designate of the North West Territories in 1869. It was commonly believed that the building of transcontinental railways cut across the migration routes of the buffalo. A different explanation is given in W. M. Davidson, *Life of Louis Riel*, serialized in *The Albertan* (later published in book form), chapter 17, 29 November 1951: 'When Sitting Bull . . . crossed the boundary to escape the American Army, he organized his forces on Canadian soil and continued to menace the enemy from that base. Officers of the American army conceived the strategy of starving the enemy by destroying his food supply . . . accomplished by stretching troops in a thin screen across the boundary . . . through Montana to the Rocky Mountains and blocking the spring migration into Canada.' cf. F. G. Roe, *The Extermination of the Buffalo*, Canadian Historical Review, vol. XV, March 1934.   [2] *Globe*, 13 August 1883.

. . . And if we have said, as we now repeat, that the price which the country is bound to pay for the prairie section of the road is two or three times more than it will cost, and that their franchises are immensely valuable, this is calculated not to break down but to build up the credit of the Company.[1]

Three weeks later the *Globe* was still criticizing the Canadian Pacific for running its line through land unfit for settlement and then demanding that the Government should give it its land grant elsewhere, even going so far as to indicate on maps where that land should be selected. (One wonders where the *Globe* got its information.) This drew forth a letter from Stephen, published on 12 September. (Appendix II). Without mentioning why it had proved impossible to take all of the land grant in the railway belt, he categorically denied the truth of the *Globe's* statements as to the nature of the land there and the refusal of the Company to accept any of it from the Government.

This was, said the *Globe*, 'on the whole a reassuring letter'. The paper regretted that Mr. Stephen's testimony to the value of the lands was not endorsed by all those who had travelled over the region in question, but if the railway company was determined to accept the lands as being in general 'fairly fit for settlement' the *Globe* was not disposed to press the matter further.

CREDIT VALLEY BONDS AS SECURITY FOR CONSTRUCTION

It had occurred to Stephen, facing the critical summer of 1882, that there was a perfectly legitimate way by which the financial position of the Company could be eased without recourse to the stock market. What was required was a lump sum to ensure continuance of the work during that season; after that he believed they would be 'out of the wood'.[2] To slow down construction was unthinkable; once the line reached the foothills of the Rockies immigration would surely increase, and the investing public would see that the Canadian Pacific was no mere road on paper.

The contract had demanded that the Company should deposit with the Government the sum of $1 million in cash, or in approved securities, as security for the construction of the road, as well as $5 million worth of Land Grant Bonds, the latter to be retained for ten years after completion of the work, as a guarantee for the operation

---

[1] *Globe*, 17 August 1883.
[2] Macd.P. 'Stephen' 267, Stephen to Macdonald, 8 May 1882.

of the railway. The former deposit had been made in cash, but in a postscript to a letter written to Macdonald on 12 May 1882, Stephen mentioned that he had in mind to ask the Finance Minister, Sir Leonard Tilley, to allow him to substitute equivalent securities. It did not enter Stephen's head that there could be the least objection to his proposal, and in his calculations for the season's work he counted on the million dollars as being available. The subject was not mentioned again until two months later, when a communication from Alexander Campbell, Minister of Justice, stating that he had looked into the question of the deposit and had decided that the statute would not admit of the proposed substitution, caused Stephen to pen an indignant protest to the Premier:

Here is a note I got last night from Campbell. Surely the view he takes is a very technical one. A security to which he takes no exception, as a security, considering it perfectly good if offered by anybody except the C.P.R., cannot be otherwise than a good security for the performance of any contract. Supposing we fail in our contract—a thing not very likely to happen—the Government will have these bonds to fall back upon, which to it is as good as the money. I have never taken into account the possibility of our not being able to substitute any other good security for the cash, and have made my arrangements accordingly. If this resource fails me I shall be very much put about, in short it will be a great injury to us and to our credit. We have so many enemies that we dare not try to borrow even temporarily. If we did, they would get an opportunity of damaging us and the work we are engaged in. After this season—next year—we shall be operating some 1700 miles of road in all and showing our friends and enemies that we are not a 'scheme on paper.' Then we can use our credit if need be. . . .[1]

The following November found Stephen in Ottawa, still agitating for the repayment of the cash deposit. Much discouraged by the attitude of the Finance Minister, to whom he had made the fullest statements of the needs of the Company, he again approached Macdonald:

. . . Sir Leonard . . . seems to be unable to appreciate the fact that the mere construction of the road is only a part of the work we have to provide for, and I dare say would treat my statement that when we have finished this year's work in the Nor West and got fully paid for all the road built we shall have at least 14 millions of our own money invested in the property, as so much talk for effect. I am sure you do not think I would

[1] Macd.P. 'Stephen' 267, Stephen to Macdonald, 8 July 1882.

come up here and haggle over this matter if we did not really need the money. . . .[1]

Finally, on 1 December, the Company received repayment of the million dollars, in lieu of which Debentures of the Credit Valley Railway Company of rather more than equal value—the property of Stephen himself—were deposited as security for the construction of the Canadian Pacific.   Stephen's interest in the Credit Valley dated back to 1880 when, in the process of extricating his friend George Laidlaw from various financial difficulties, he had acquired a large personal interest in the Company. He had written to Macdonald at the time:

. . . As a friend of Laidlaw you will be glad to hear that I have succeeded in getting him and the Credit Valley Railway out of all their troubles, and putting *both* in an independent position. . . .[2]

As Laidlaw himself was later to say, he did not want the Credit Valley any more than he wanted Barnum's white elephant. On the whole, the elephant might have been less trouble. Before long the results of Stephen's well-intentioned actions—the getting of the bonds and the parting with them—were to prove more than enough to embitter one whose altruism was continually subject to misconstruction.

NEW ASSOCIATES AND FRESH EXPEDIENTS

The day-to-day struggle to meet the costs of construction and equipment of the railway had by the end of 1882 left Stephen convinced that some new expedient was necessary to ease the incessant strain. Although he himself remained as confident as ever of the final success of the enterprise, the constant setbacks were telling on the faith of his colleagues. Before leaving London in April he had realized that the French members were losing interest, while Morton, Rose and Company were not to be relied upon to go out of their way to be helpful. Sir John Rose was as active as ever in his capacity as liaison between the Canadian Government—including the High Commissioner's Office—the Canadian Pacific and the Hudson's Bay Company, but Stephen suspected that he was no longer in the intimate councils of his late firm, and that his son Charles had practically transferred his allegiance to the Grand Trunk. It was impera-

[1] Macd.P. 'Stephen' 267, Stephen to Macdonald, 18 November 1882.
[2] Loc. cit. Stephen to Macdonald, 23 January 1881.

tive, therefore, to consolidate the Canadian 'wing', reinforcing it, if need be, by the infusion of new blood.

Since the summer of 1881, Stephen and Duncan McIntyre had been on the Board of the Ontario and Quebec Railway, of which Edmund B. Osler was President. This Company was building a line from Montreal to Toronto which would eventually seek connections with the Credit Valley and the Toronto, Grey and Bruce Railways in Ontario, and at the Quebec end with the Atlantic and North Western. The last-named was only sixty miles long, but it possessed an invaluable asset in a bridge over the St. Lawrence. In May 1882, the Canadian Pacific entered into negotiations for the control of this line and bridge, hoping thereby to gain access to the rail systems south of the river.

Earlier in 1882 the Ontario and Quebec had assumed certain financial responsibilities in respect of the Credit Valley, and although it was not until 1884 that these various systems were finally consolidated it was obvious that in such a coalition lay the answer to the problem raised by the amalgamation of the Grand Trunk with the Great Western. Yet even after the subsequent leasing of the Ontario and Quebec by the Canadian Pacific, the former line continued to maintain its own distinct identity; although the two companies had several directors in common—a by no means uncommon coincidence in Canada at that time—their sources of income remained entirely separate.

Having thus taken preliminary steps towards safeguarding the future of the national line, Stephen next proceeded with a scheme he had in mind for ensuring its continued rapid construction. He had given a hint of what was afoot when, at the end of November 1882, he wrote to Macdonald on the matter of the Government's accepting his Credit Valley Debentures in place of the cash deposit:

. . . Our pinch is *now*. After New Year we shall have plenty of funds from other sources. I think we have at last found a 'bridge to cross the stream'. . . .[1]

The contest was between the Canadian Pacific and all the roads in Canada and the United States running through Chicago for the trade of the Canadian North West. Stephen's purpose was to disarm an important section of those who might be drawn into opposition by making them his allies.

---

[1] Macd.P. 'Stephen' 267, Stephen to Macdonald, 21 November 1882.

8

Already he had a foothold in New York, and the credit of the Company there, in spite of the influence of the Northern Pacific, stood fairly high. It has been mentioned that in December 1882, the authorized capital stock of the Canadian Pacific was increased from $25 million to $100 million. In the second week of that month Stephen and R. B. Angus repaired to New York. Stephen was due to sail for England a few days later, but the intervening time was profitably spent. On the eve of his departure he wrote to Macdonald:

I have been at work here night and day and have left myself only time to say goodbye. I start with a light heart having added greatly to our *achieving power* since I came here as will soon be seen when we come before the public in January. The C.P.R. will be built without a dollar of money from London. Angus remains here for a few days to tie up the ends. . . .[1]

When the news of the New York negotiations became public it was found that two organizations had been formed: the North American Railway Contracting Company[2] and a body generally known thereafter as the Stock Syndicate. The former was essentially a temporary creation, its broad purpose being to ensure construction of the Canadian Pacific through the medium of contractors who would receive payment partly in cash and partly in the stock of the railway. The Company thereby secured the participation of leading financial firms such as Drexel, Morgan and Company, Winslow, Lanier and Company, Kuhn, Loeb and Company and Seligman and Company of New York, William L. Scott of Erie, Pennsylvania, and Boissevain and Company and Oyens and Company of Amsterdam. In practice, the Canadian Pacific management was to continue to superintend the work of construction.

The Stock Syndicate was composed of a number of American capitalists headed by W. L. Scott of Erie, Pennsylvania, and under a contract drawn up on 29 December they agreed to take $30 million worth of Canadian Pacific stock at an average of $52\frac{1}{2}$ cents on the dollar. In January 1883, the New York Stock Exchange gave an official quotation for the entire issue, and the Syndicate was able to dispose of its holdings, in shares of $100, at a favourable price.

In England, meanwhile, Stephen was hard at work finding prospective purchasers for the new issue, none of which was offered on

---

[1] Macd.P. 'Stephen' 267, Stephen to Macdonald, 13 December 1882.
[2] See Sessional Paper 31 k, 1884, Memorandum by Secretary of Canadian Pacific Railway Company to Deputy Minister of Railways.

the London market. He wrote optimistically to Macdonald, saying that he had sent applications to New York for over $3 million worth on behalf of friends in London and in Scotland. His latest information was that the stock was proving so popular in New York that all allotments would have to be cut. He added:

I have never had misgivings about eventual success in spite of all opposition but sometimes it has taken some courage to keep weak-kneed associates from wilting. The new people I brought in with us before I sailed from New York made me certain of the outcome. My trouble and danger was from old associates losing pluck. Thank heaven that is all over now. . . .[1]

Having achieved this much in England, Stephen next proceeded to Holland to seek the co-operation of his friends there. On January 19 he cabled Macdonald from Paris:

Success Amsterdam and London complete in spite of Trunk's most determined efforts to decry and discredit Company and defame us personally.[2]

There was no time for letter-writing then, but Sir John Rose stepped into the breach and kept the Canadian Premier fully informed of all developments. The Grand Trunk 'scribblers' were as busy as ever, and Rose enclosed what he termed 'elegant extracts' in his letters. The London market was, he said, practically shut against the Canadian Pacific, but there were a few independent thinkers who were willing to take up and hold some of the stock at least until the effects of the hostile misrepresentations had passed away. These, with their New York and Amsterdam colleagues, were calculated to supply all the funds necessary for the completion of the railway.[3]

On 1 February, when success seemed indeed to be assured, Rose cabled the good news to Macdonald,[4] supplementing his brief message with a letter giving a detailed history of the whole New York transactions:

I must at the outset say that the result is almost wholly due to the untiring efforts of our friend Stephen, whose zeal, energy, confidence in himself and the enterprise, seem to inspire everybody else with the like confidence. . . . In order to carry out these arrangements, which have taken much time and anxious effort, it was indispensably necessary to enlarge

---

[1] Macd.P. 'Stephen' 267, Stephen to Macdonald, 4 January 1883.
[2] It was at this time that Stephen adopted the telegraphic signature 'Dufftown'. In 1890 it was changed to 'Estevan'.
[3] Macd.P. 'Rose' 259.346, Rose to Macdonald, 18 January 1883.
[4] Loc. cit. 259.349, Rose to Macdonald, 1 February 1883.

the circle of interested parties and to give them participation in all the advantages which might flow from the original contract. Even then it required faith sufficient to 'remove mountains' to induce capitalists to look at it. . . .[1]

As in a prairie mirage distance is momentarily annihilated, so the completed Pacific Railway seemed suddenly to lie at the very feet of its stout-hearted President. The following months were to prove that what he saw was indeed nothing more than a mirage.

HOSTILE PRESS

Such was his elation at the successful outcome of the financial negotiations described above that even the persistent hostility of the railway's enemies failed to depress Stephen at this time. On 27 January he cabled Macdonald:

Enemy in his last ditch. Ground of attack today's papers that the enterprise will never pay because of the exceptionally low rates charged by the Company compared with similar roads. All going well.

Five days later he wrote in similar vein:

. . . Hickson's hired scribblers under the leadership of Abbott [2] keep pegging away at the C.P.R., the Government and the country but to very little purpose, and everything is in the most flourishing condition. . . . Abbott tells his friends confidentially that Hickson has now such complete control of the Press and of Parliament that he can do anything he likes with both. . . . I am not afraid of the Dominion Legislature doing anything to cripple the C.P.R. in its efforts to secure for itself as the national highway the traffic to and from Old Canada to New Canada, though it may be necessary to present the real question properly before the public mind.

We are at a general disadvantage in having the newspapers in Canada nearly all, on both sides, if not against us certainly not against our *enemy*. I say *enemy* because no other word expresses their opposition. . . . All their efforts now are directed to the creation of a feeling that the road can *never* pay and investors will lose their money, but I can meet all that with ease. The general feeling among investors is most favourable. The fact that we have secured our money without *asking* the British public to aid us has been a tower of strength to us and correspondingly discomfitted Abbott and his clique. . . .[3]

The support of the Canadian papers was achieved by the Grand

[1] Macd.P. 'Rose' 259.351, Rose to Macdonald, 1 February 1883.
[2] William Abbott, a shareholder of the Grand Trunk Railroad, once its Secretary; later expelled by the Stock Exchange.
[3] Macd.P. 'Stephen' 267, Stephen to Macdonald, 1 February 1883.

Trunk by the simple expedient of judiciously distributing advertising patronage. The *Toronto Globe*, besides favouring the Grand Trunk,[1] was also the chief mouthpiece of the Liberal Party which continued, when occasion offered, to express disapproval in the House of the actions of the Canadian Pacific Company. A year earlier, in February 1882, the Liberals had carried a motion demanding annual and detailed reports of all the Company's activities. These were duly furnished, laid on the Table and subsequently published as Sessional Papers.

In London, the *Daily News* and later the *Standard* printed in their city columns whatever came from the 'poisoned' pens of such as William Abbott and the pamphleteer Joe Nelson, supplemented by extracts carefully selected from the Canadian papers by the enemies of the Canadian Pacific. The financial periodicals varied from support of the Grand Trunk to impartiality or indifference. The *Financier* and *Money Market Review* tended to be anti-C.P.R., and *Fairplay* was liable to oppose either or both of the rival railway companies. The *Railway Times*, while quick to defend the Canadian Pacific against false allegations, adopted and firmly persevered in the attitude that the sooner the two companies decided to sink their differences and come to some amicable arrangement regarding spheres of influence, the better it would be for all concerned.

Diverse disengaged journalists volunteered, from time to time, to conduct a 'C.P.R. organ' (to be financed, of course, by the Company) but even if the Pacific could have afforded to compete with the Trunk in this field Stephen was not inclined to favour such an expedient. He did, during his visit to England in the winter of 1882-3, assist in launching the *Canada Gazette*, a London publication devoted to Canadian interests, and especially to supplying authoritative information about the North West. There was, he found, evidence of a growing curiosity about the Dominion which the daily papers could not satisfy, having no space to spare for such topics, and so little was actually known about Canada that unfavourable reports were all too readily believed. The Editor of the new paper was Thomas Skinner, Chairman of the Canada North West Land Company and a member of the Royal Commission on Crofter Immigration. Founder of the Stock Exchange Year Book, he was an unofficial financial adviser to the Canadian Government.

---

[1] Cf. its attitude when the G.T.R. was new. See Creighton, op. cit. (*The Young Politician*) p. 250.

INDISCREET HIGH COMMISSIONER

Soon after Stephen's arrival in London in December 1882, he prompted Macdonald to have the High Commissioner, Sir A. T. Galt, contradict a statement in the *Daily News* to the effect that recent surveys showed a belt of land 300 miles wide across Canada to be worthless land.[1] Galt's perfunctory response in relaying the Premier's message to the *News* without personal comment only served to intensify Stephen's distrust of the High Commissioner. For his part, Galt considered that it was for Stephen and Rose to deal with the Grand Trunk's attacks themselves, although, at the same time, he was of the opinion that it was 'absolute lunacy' to continue a struggle which must, he thought, eventually end in coalition. He particularly resented the tendency of the Press to identify the Dominion Government with the railway controversies. Writing in this vein to Macdonald, Galt concluded:

One thing I am sure of, and that is that the Canadian Pacific will never be finished without coming to London for money, and that it is bumptious folly for Stephen to neglect—as he has done—every means of conciliating this market.[2]

The New York negotiations had given rise to rumours which it was impossible to demolish until the truth could appropriately be disclosed. So, too, had certain plans for connections in Eastern Canada with American lines. It was probably while Stephen was in New York that he concluded an agreement with William K. Vanderbilt for an exchange of traffic with the Michigan Central Railway. In addition to controlling a line from Chicago to Detroit, the American railway magnate had acquired the Canada Southern, which connected at St. Thomas with the Credit Valley. Thus the Canadian Pacific secured an outlet, over friendly lines, to the great grain centre of the Middle West. Coming at the same time as Stephen's decision to increase the number of his associates, this arrangement led to the belief in some quarters that Vanderbilt was a member also of the Stock Syndicate. At all events, Stephen began to detect signs of a tactical success, nor was he as blind as Galt imagined to the advantage of following it up. He wrote to Macdonald regarding the possibility of the London market losing faith in the Grand Trunk:

[1] Macd.P. 'Stephen' 267, Cable, Stephen to Macdonald, 27 December 1882.
[2] Macd.P. 'Galt' 220, Galt to Macdonald, 9 January 1883.

. . . When our power of controlling traffic at its sources in the east (Quebec and Ontario) is a little better understood you will see a great tumble in G.T.R. securities. The development of the Ontario and Quebec line with its connections in the east and with the Vanderbilt system in the west is already beginning to scare the operators here. I am working quietly at this and cultivating the most friendly relations with the Stock Exchange men at present supporting G.T.R. and have no doubt of being able by and bye to convert them from bulls to bears. . . .[1]

As the Stock Syndicate was a purely C.P.R. matter, no one enlightened the High Commissioner in advance of any public statement. Galt hastened to report to the Prime Minister the information that had come his way, remarking that if men such as Vanderbilt were indeed in the Syndicate Stephen ought to have no more financial trouble:

I have not heard what concessions he has made to these people to get them in—but Vanderbilt's name suggests American connections that may scarcely be acceptable in Canada. In any case it looks as if the control of the C.P.R. had gone into American hands, and it may so happen that the objection to Manitoba R.R. charters to the frontier will disappear. I hope you will look closely after the North Superior section.

If I am correctly advised the Northern Pacific is in the new combination, which is clearly going to head off the G.T. in various ways. . . .[2]

Sir John Rose was not to be envied in his role of unofficial peacemaker. Nor was Galt the only object of Stephen's displeasure at this time. In C. F. Brydges' last report to the Hudson's Bay Company he had made some slighting reference to the Canada North West Land Company, which had been formed to dispose of Canadian Pacific land. Donald A. Smith, who was on the Hudson's Bay Board, shared his cousin's opinion of the Land Commissioner. Rose wrote to Macdonald that although Brydges had not been entirely blameless he considered the bitterness of Stephen and Smith went too far:

. . . The former has become very imperious and intolerant of opposition, and I am afraid he will make enemies where conciliation would be more politic. His earnestness and force of character are invaluable qualities, considering the gigantic work he has on hand, but it is no easy matter to hold an even balance between *his* views and those of *more cautious men*. . . .

---

[1] Macd.P. 'Stephen' 267, Stephen to Macdonald, 18 February 1883.
[2] Macd.P. 'Galt' 220, Galt to Macdonald, 13 January 1883.

I think Stephen is wrong in attributing to Galt intentional or malevolent misrepresentation about North West. He may have been indiscreet in expressing his opinions. . . . I am trying to bring them together—but how it may result I know not. . . .[1]

Unfortunately, mere indiscretion on the part of Canada's official representative was dangerous enough. Certainly, on the subject of the Stock Syndicate, his reactions were singularly akin to those of the *Globe*, which once more launched out into an attack on the C.P.R. contract. In order to secure Canadian control of the great national work, said the *Globe* of 25 January, the people's representatives had consented to enter into one of the hardest bargains in history. Gone was the strength of that argument when the Philistines of Wall Street were allowed to make sport of the stock of that enterprise, and gone, certainly, was all guarantee of Canadian control. In London this note was echoed by the *Financier*, which pronounced it 'a serious matter' for the control of the Canadian Pacific to pass into American hands. The *Railway Times* of 21 April rose up in indignation on the Company's behalf:

Who, pray, ever said that the Canadian Pacific was to pass into American hands? . . . To trade upon our deeprooted distrust of American railroaders and to argue therefrom that the door of the English moneymarket will be barred against the Canadian Pacific is neither more nor less than an unadulterated libel, as scandalous as it is unjust. . . .

CREDIT VALLEY BILL; GRAND TRUNK ATTACK

In the absence of positive statements, criticism of the new financial arrangements tended to wilt, and attention was once more directed to C.P.R. activities in Ontario and Quebec. There, for all to see, was Canadian Pacific freight being despatched from Montreal to Manitoba via Brockville and the Vanderbilt system. So far the C.P.R. had taken no definite step towards incorporating the Ontario and Quebec, or the Credit Valley, but on 21 February 1883, the latter Company petitioned Parliament for power to amalgamate with, or lease its line to, either the Ontario and Quebec or the Canada Southern, Vanderbilt's satellite.

On 5 March, the day on which the Credit Valley Bill was read for the first time, Blake tabled a motion that the C.P.R. Company be asked to furnish a detailed account of all its financial transactions up to date, including those relating to the recent issue of stock and to

[1] Macd.P. 'Rose' 259.335, Rose to Macdonald, 4 January 1883.

the acquisition of the lines of the Canada Central and Quebec, Montreal, Ottawa, and Occidental Railways. He also desired information regarding its interest, if any, in the Credit Valley and Ontario and Quebec. Blake's suspicions had been aroused by the fact that, in its routine annual report to Parliament, the Company had been found to be in possession of a large block of Credit Valley stock. This was the stock, the property of Stephen himself, which had been substituted for the cash deposit. Being extremely reluctant to have the general public know to what extent he and his immediate colleagues were obliged to aid the Company from their private resources, Stephen had suppressed the intelligence that the securities were his own; to have it known would have been as harmful to the Company's credit as to have Blake's version believed.

Introducing his motion, Blake observed that the Canadian Pacific, instead of concentrating its resources on the main line—the work contracted for—appeared to have been devoting a large portion of the Government subsidy to extensions and branches not included in its contract. He drew attention to the fact that of the large block of stock recently issued, only a fraction had been applied for in London. Disregarding the fact that no issue had been made in England, he proceeded to account for this phenomenon thus:

It was because the course pursued is one which has aroused the hostility of the other great railway corporation which this country possesses—the Grand Trunk Railway Company. . . .

Even Macdonald was a little alarmed at the turn of events; he had no desire to see the Canadian Pacific involved in open warfare with the older road. In answer to his queries, however, Rose wrote from London:

I don't think Stephen will run amuck against the Grand Trunk. His own difficulties are yet considerable, and I am daily imploring him not to make enemies. . . .[1]

On the contrary, Stephen was in much too optimistic a mood to consider it necessary to take up arms against the Grand Trunk. He wrote to Macdonald:

. . . It is too bad of Blake . . . to act and speak as if from a G.T.R. brief. His words aggravate my difficulties but nothing more and we are sure to succeed in raising the position of the C.P.R. to one of high credit here, though to do so needs time and temper too. . . . The G.T.R.

[1] Macd.P. 'Rose' 259.363, Rose to Macdonald, 14 March 1883.

people here are in a blue fright about the Ontario and Quebec and Credit
V. connection with the Vanderbilt systems, and although nothing has
been said by us publicly about it a *whisper* has got abroad and the consequence is a very dull weak market for G.T.R. securities. . . .[1]

It was the Grand Trunk which, driven to desperation by the
prospect of losing, after all, its Canadian monopoly, declared war.
At its half-yearly meeting on 29 March, the President, Sir Henry
Tyler, chose to make his address an open attack on the Canadian
Pacific:

. . . The C.P.R. is a gigantic undertaking, and possibly those who are
carrying it out have hardly realised the task which they have undertaken;
and I say so because from what I know of their proceedings, they do not
seem to have found it enough for them. They have come into our territory
in different directions, and have acquired lines of railway, and entered
upon schemes of aggression. . . . But, gentlemen, we have never had
any feelings against them. We should have been delighed to work harmoniously with them, if only they had contented themselves with
making the C.P.R., and had come, as I think they ought to have come, to
us to assist them to do it, to exchange traffic with us, and to work with us
harmoniously. . . . The last thing we hear is that they are going to make
a connection with Mr. Vanderbilt, and that they are going to compete
with us for traffic between Montreal and the West. . . . They say, on the
other hand, that we are doing a great deal of harm to them, and that we
are keeping them out of the markets in London and other places. Well, we
as a Board have never taken any steps of the sort. I am addressing a great
number of shareholders and the representatives of a vast and powerful
company, having a very important influence upon the money market of
this metropolis. I venture to say, that if anybody from Canada attacks
our united system, it is not necessary that they should meet with any
opposition from this Board. . . .[2]

Mr. William Abbott then rose to assure the shareholders that if he
saw a raid being made upon the Company's property by parties in
Canada desiring to obtain money in England for aggressive purposes,
he should not hesitate to raise his voice and wield his pen to prevent
the money being got in London or anywhere else. He remembered
that when the Charter was granted they all rejoiced that money was
to be found in Canada to develop the enormous territory north of
Lake Superior, and unite British Columbia with Canada. But what
was the result? They shirked the line north of Lake Superior, and

[1] Macd.P. 'Stephen' 267, Stephen to Macdonald, 22 March 1883.
[2] *Railway Times*, 31 March 1883.

bought up competing lines to worry this company. If the Grand Trunk only let it be known that the purse-strings of England were closed to Canada, the great Syndicate would be brought to their senses and they would hear no more of such aggressive schemes.

'Whoever dares these boots displace must meet the great Bombastes face to face', mocked the *Railway Times*. To Stephen it was clear that however great his contempt for Abbott, and even if he did consider Sir Henry Tyler to be, as he told Macdonald, 'nothing but a bottle of stale ginger pop', such a public challenge could not be left unanswered. On 5 April he addressed a circular letter to the shareholders of the Grand Trunk Railroad, painstakingly setting forth the purpose and position of the Canadian Pacific, and pointing out the injustice of the Grand Trunk's attacks (Appendix III).

STEPHEN-TYLER PEACE PACT REPUDIATED

Whatever may have been its effect on the shareholders, this reply probably had less influence upon the G.T.R. Board than had certain intelligence 'judiciously communicated' to it regarding the C.P.R.'s intended new system from Montreal westward.[1] Through Sir John Rose, the directors of the Grand Trunk announced their willingness to discuss peace terms. As Stephen had foreseen, even they were at the mercy of Stock Exchange operators who were indifferent as to which Company carried the traffic of the Canadian West; to them the enterprise with the better prospects was the one to be supported, and if rumours concerning the C.P.R.'s new connections proved to be true, the outlook for that line certainly appeared promising.

For some days negotiations went on, applauded by the *Railway Times*, deplored by the *Globe*, and regarded by Rose—who took no active part in the discussions, preferring to retain the role of mutual friend and counsellor—as a hopeful sign, even if he were not exactly sanguine about the eventual agreement of the parties concerned.[2] The result was the despatch of a joint cablegram from Tyler and Stephen to their respective general managers in Canada, Hickson and Van Horne, instructing them to prepare a conditional agreement whereby the Canadian Pacific, on ceding to the Grand Trunk its prospective properties in Ontario, would be afforded liberal traffic facilities on

[1] Macd.P. 'Rose' 259.385, Rose to Macdonald, 11 April 1883.
[2] Macd.P. 'Rose' 259.378, Rose to Macdonald, 10 April 1883 and 259.385, Rose to Macdonald, 11 April 1883.

all the lines of that Company, the intention being 'to avoid competition and work together in all respects for mutual benefit'.[1]

Writing to Macdonald, Rose sought to account for the unexpectedly co-operative frame of mind in which 'our impulsive friend Stephen' met the Grand Trunk proposals. His explanation was that the latter had finally been convinced that there was a limit to the financial burdens which Donald Smith and his other friends would assume in connection with the Canadian Pacific and affiliated schemes.[2] Several months earlier, however, Stephen had assured the Prime Minister that despite all that the Grand Trunk had done to discredit and injure the Canadian Pacific, he was determined that in any and all matters that might come under discussion by the two companies the C.P.R. would be governed purely by business considerations.[3] More than once Stephen was to show a preference for obtaining running rights over a line over acquiring or building it himself if the former course appeared more economic. At this juncture, moreover, secure in his recent tactical victory, he could afford to be magnanimous.

It was his colleagues across the Atlantic who proved uncooperative. It was not clear who took the initiative; some say Van Horne, others Vanderbilt. Probably it was those who were closely connected with the Ontario and Quebec. Be that as it may, the joint cablegram evoked a very definite refusal to countenance such a seemingly Utopian acheme. (When the *Railway Times* learned the nature of the agreement, even that paper commented that it had 'only moral philosophy to recommend it'.)[4] On 16 April, Stephen wrote to Tyler:

I regret to inform you that our united attempts to harmonise the interests of the Grand Trunk and Canadian Pacific Railways have proved, I fear, for the present, at all events, impracticable. Since the dispatch of our joint cablegram to the two general managers, I have been in active cable correspondence with my colleagues, both in Canada and New York. A message received today seems to convey what I fear must be regarded as the conclusion at which they have arrived, and which, I regret to say, is adverse to the proposed arrangement and its practicability at the present time. I am still without a reply to a further message I have sent in answer, but, as I can hardly entertain the hope that it will alter the case, I

---

[1] *Railway Times*, 21 April 1883.
[2] Macd.P. 'Rose' 259.381, Rose to Macdonald, 11 April 1883.
[3] Macd.P. 'Stephen' 267, Stephen to Macdonald, 2 September 1882.
[4] *Railway Times*, 21 April 1883.

think it right to lose no time in communicating with you. It would serve no good purpose to enter into the details of all the objections which have been encountered, beyond stating that the control of the Ontario and Quebec, contrary to my expectations, cannot be surrendered to the Grand Trunk Railway. In the meantime I may assure you that it will be my endeavour to maintain the most friendly relations with your company in every way consistent with the interests of the C.P.R.[1]

The immediate sequel to the breakdown of negotiations with the Grand Trunk was the C.P.R.'s application to Parliament on 20 April for leave to present a petition for an Act empowering them to lease the lines of the Credit Valley and Ontario and Quebec Companies, and part of the Atlantic and North Western, including the bridge at Montreal. In spite of a certain amount of opposition, particularly while the Bill was before the Select Committee on Railways, it became law on 25 May. As the chief argument against the measure was that it might merely be a device for strengthening the hand of the Canadian Pacific in forcing the Grand Trunk into a coalition, an amendment had been added, at the suggestion of J. J. C. Abbott, Counsel to the Company, to the effect that if the Canadian Pacific ever amalgamated with the Grand Trunk, the authority to lease the lines in question should lapse.

In May 1883, the C.P.R. Company seemed for the moment to have its difficulties under control. The stock was quoted in New York at 63, and Stephen wrote to Macdonald from London:

. . . Our G.T.R. friends are very quiet now and anxious that we should let them alone. . . . Abbott and I are *quite* friendly. . . . Daily we grow stronger here and increase in the confidence of the public. I feel quite confident a few months more will finally establish us financially and leave me free to attend to the settlement of the lands. . . .[2]

[1] *Railway Times*, 21 April 1883.
[2] Macd.P. 'Stephen' 267, Stephen to Macdonald, 14 May 1883.

V

An uphill struggle

EMIGRATION AND THE IRISH QUESTION

ALTHOUGH the quotation with which the previous chapter ended would seem to indicate that from the time of his arrival in England in December 1882, to his departure in May 1883, Stephen had been entirely preoccupied with the financial interests of the Canadian Pacific, this was very far from being the case. As a result of his efforts during that time, his scheme for assisted Irish emigration to Canada very nearly came to fruition. Whatever—or whoever—may have been the ultimate cause of its rejection (by almost common consent the answer was 'Mr. Gladstone') this did not come about through lack of attention on the part of its originator.

Stephen was not the only advocate of emigration as an answer to the Irish Question, but he had perhaps the best opportunity of any-one of putting his theories into wholesale practice. He had the land, and could quickly create the necessary machinery; what was required was an initial capital sum with which to set the machinery in motion.

Under the Arrears Act of 1882, the British Government had appropriated a sum of £100,000 towards the emigration of Irish peasants from the distressed districts, but on condition that only £5 a head should be allotted. The management of the fund was to be largely in the hands of local Boards of Guardians, who were em-powered to borrow further sums as required. This took care of the traffic from the Irish end; what was lacking was an agency to under-take full responsibility for the emigrants at the receiving end.

Stephen's first idea was to make the North West Land Company the agency for dealing with the emigrants in Canada. When in Winnipeg with Sir Charles Tupper he had discussed with Scarth, the general manager, the possibility of co-operating with the Imperial Government in carrying out the emigration provisions of the Arrears Act,[1] and one of Stephen's first acts, after the successful

[1] Macd.P. 'Scarth' 261, Scarth to Macdonald, 6 February 1883.

launching of the new issue of the Company's stock, was to approach Lord Derby, Secretary of State for the Colonies, on the subject.[1]

Before he could secure an interview with the latter, an opportunity offered to address the general public. Taking his cue from Sir George Trevelyan, Chief Secretary for Ireland in succession to W. E. Forster, who in the House of Commons on 27 February had described the miserable plight of the poorest class of Irish farmers, condemned in many cases to extract a precarious living from two or three acres or less of arable land, Stephen wrote to *The Times* on 1 March:

. . . Assuming that these unfortunate people are really farmers accustomed to work at the cultivation of the land, and that they are able and willing to work at it, I would suggest that 10,000 of them, with their families, say 50,000 in all, be sent out to the Canadian North-West and landed there during the months of May and June, at the expense of the Government. If that were done, I think I am safe in saying that every family could be provided with 160 acres of the very best quality of farming land, free of cost, and that arrangements could be made with the railway, land, and colonization companies interested in the settlement of the country, by which each farmer would be advanced the capital necessary to build a small house and to give him a start in his new life.

Within the next few days, Stephen had evolved a more definite proposal which he duly submitted, in the form of a memorandum, severally to the Colonial Secretary, the Lord Lieutenant of Ireland, and the Canadian Prime Minister.[2] To the last Stephen wrote of his plan:

It has fascinated every member of the Government I have seen but I am not yet sure about the G.O.M. He is on principle opposed to state aided emigration but expediency may in this case override principle as it often does.

The late and present Irish Secretary are enthusiastic and Lord Derby has written me today to come and see him on Monday. The Conservatives will not oppose it and Mr. O'Connor Power tells me the Irish party will support [ ] as an alternative measure. . .[3]

At the Colonial Office interview Lord Derby expressed the opinion that emigration was the only real remedy for Irish ills, and

---

[1] Macd.P. 'Stephen' 267, Stephen to Macdonald, 18 February 1883.
[2] Confidential Print, Misc. No. 49, CO 812/26. At Appendix IV.
[3] Macd.P. 'Railways' 9, Stephen to Macdonald, 15 March 1883. Also Stephen to Spencer, 16 March 1883, in Irish State Papers: File on Assisted Emigration 1883-9, hereafter 'Irish File'.

pronounced Stephen's scheme practical and simple.[1] Although he could not say what view the Treasury might take, he promised to use his good offices in that direction.[2] He questioned Stephen closely regarding the security for the repayment of the loan and the latter got the impression that the Colonial Secretary was satisfied with his answers. Stephen, for his part, stressed the necessity for the Government to give a definite assurance of co-operation before further steps could be taken towards setting the scheme in motion. He found Lord Spencer (the Lord-Lieutenant) and Trevelyan more enthusiastic, and confided to Macdonald his hopes that the former would be able to persuade Gladstone to share his point of view.

Meanwhile, with the aid of Sir John Rose, Stephen was trying to crystallize a plan for pooling the lands of the C.P.R., North West Land and Hudson's Bay Companies. The general idea was to form a separate company to deal with emigration on behalf of all three, co-opting such prominent public figures as could be induced to participate.

It was early decided that, should the Government agree to make a loan, the company should ask for it to be paid in instalments, in respect of each batch of emigrants actually despatched from Ireland, and for whom provision would by then have been made in the North West. Thus there could be no question of receiving money for services not performed, and should the scheme break down the advances would immediately cease.[3]

By March 1883, it had become apparent that the Canadian North West, chiefly because of its connection with the vexed question of Ireland, had at last attained a certain news value in England. A *Times* leader declaring emigration to be 'the only permanent remedy' gave Stephen another opportunity to address a letter to that forum of public opinion, urging that no time be lost in coming to a decision as to how that emigration should be carried out.[4]

A month later *The Times* published in full Stephen's memorandum,[5] and the editor asked Sir John Rose to write an article reporting recent developments in the negotiations. Rose[6] chose instead to respond with a private letter which could be used as the

---

[1] Irish File, Stephen to Trevelyan, 20 March 1883.
[2] Macd.P. 'Stephen' 267, Stephen to Macdonald, 22 March 1883.
[3] Irish File, Stephen to Hamilton, 7 April 1883.
[4] *The Times*, 21 March 1883.
[5] *The Times*, 26 April 1883.
[6] Macd.P. 'Rose' 259.410, Rose to Macdonald, 16 May 1883.

basis for another leader. On 16 May the first leader faithfully repro-
duced Rose's information and arguments, devoting a whole column
to the topic. The Nor' West had arrived. Referring to a favourite
Parnellite contention that the 'pinch of hunger' policy had been
devised to enable the Government to carry out a wholesale deport-
ation, the leader pointed out that, on the contrary, it seemed that it
was the Government which displayed most hesitation in proceeding
with such a plan. The chiefs of the Irish Executive were believed to
have warmly approved of the Canadian Emigration scheme; 'the
project, however, still hangs fire, and there is much reason to attribute the delay to the distaste shown, on many occasions, by the
Prime Minister for any measure of State-assisted emigration'.

Early in April, the Lord-Lieutenant had suggested to Stephen
that a small experiment might be tried that spring, and that if it were
successful, the Government might take the appropriate steps to continue on a larger scale.[1] But Stephen insisted that unless legislation
were actually taken during the current session, thus guaranteeing
Government co-operation, it would not be worth while to establish
the machinery required to ensure the efficient operation of the proposed organization. Once official sanction were assured they would
readily agree to prove, by the results of a modest experiment, the
merits of their scheme.[2]

Referring to Stephen's scheme in the House on 10 April,
Trevelyan gave the impression that the Government had approved it
in principle, but were 'determined not to spoil by hurry the success
of their operations'. Taking it that this meant that the Government
were committed to his project, Stephen cabled Macdonald accordingly[3] and wrote privately to the Chief Secretary for Ireland asking
for an assurance that the necessary legislation would be passed that
session.[4]

Meanwhile Lord Spencer's secretary, R. G. C. Hamilton, had on
behalf of the Lord-Lieutenant prepared a memorandum giving the
latter's views on Stephen's proposal. On 14 April he sent copies to
the Treasury and Colonial Office. While believing that only by
emigration could a permanent improvement be effected in the state

---

[1] Macd.P. 'Rose' 259.385, Rose to Macdonald, 11 April 1883.
[2] Irish File, Stephen to Hamilton, 7 April 1883. Also Hamilton to Treasury, 15 April
1883, in Confidential Print North American 111, CO 807/40. (Memo on Mr. Stephen's
Scheme of Irish Emigration to Canada.)
[3] Macd.P. 'Stephen' 267, Stephen to Macdonald, 11 April 1883.
[4] Irish File, Stephen to Trevelyan, 11 April 1883.

9

of the congested districts, Lord Spencer stipulated that in the event of the scheme being approved, two conditions should be attached, namely, that the emigrants should proceed from the distressed areas only, and, secondly, that the holdings vacated should not be let to new tenants but should be consolidated with neighbouring holdings. In view of Stephen's reaction to the idea of making a preliminary experiment, the Lord-Lieutenant stressed the need for early action if legislation were to be taken that session. He thought that Stephen's plan was the best that could be adopted, and although, from the point of view of the Treasury, the advance of £1 million for ten years without interest might appear a serious matter, the advantages accruing would, if the scheme succeeded, be considerable. If the organization visualized by Stephen could be set up there would, in fact, be very little pecuniary risk involved, whereas there were, in the plan, 'the elements of a great success'.[1]

The permanent secretary at the Colonial Office, Sir Robert Herbert, had with Sir John Rose made a tour of the Canadian North West the previous summer and was, as a result, both well-informed and sympathetic to the idea of large-scale emigration. After discussing the memorandum with Lord Derby, he replied that the Colonial Secretary, who had received oral explanations from Mr. Stephen, was disposed to favour the proposed arrangements, but that before approaching the Governor-General of Canada on the subject it was desirable to establish that Her Majesty's Government had agreed to the principle of the scheme.[2] It all depended, therefore, on the Treasury.

No immediate decision was forthcoming from that Department, and in the interval the correspondence between the Irish Government and the Colonial Office was referred unofficially to the Canadian High Commissioner. Galt had himself taken up the question of emigration and had made his own contribution to the collection of memoranda on the subject.[3] He regarded Stephen's scheme as a move in the right direction, but thought it would be advisable to leaven the Irish mass by the inclusion of an English and Scottish element.[4] On hearing from the Colonial Office he took it upon himself to find out what the Canadian Government's reaction would be.[5] He received

[1] CO 807/40, Hamilton to Treasury, 14 April 1883.
[2] CO 807/40, Colonial Office to Irish Government, 28 April 1883.
[3] Confidential Print, Misc. No. 60, CO 812/31.
[4] Macd.P. 'Galt' 220, Galt to Macdonald, 20 April 1883.
[5] Macd.P. 129, 'Railways' 9, Galt to Macdonald, 30 April 1883.

the reply that the latter would be pleased to know that the Pacific Railway, Hudson's Bay or North West Land Companies would, jointly or severally, undertake the task, and that the Government would grant free homesteads on which security to the extent of $500 each might be taken by the party assisting the immigrant. Galt duly reported this to the Colonial Office.[1]

STEPHEN'S SCHEME FALLS THROUGH

On 9 May the Oracle spoke. The Treasury Minute, a copy of which was forwarded by the Irish Government to the Colonial Office, stated that the First Lord of the Treasury and the Chancellor of the Exchequer considered that Mr. Stephen's proposals might be entertained, as modified by the Irish Government, but with the following proviso:

That the engagements to be entered into by Her Majesty's Government should be with the Dominion Government, and not directly with the company or companies concerned. The Dominion Government would be at liberty to employ what agency they might think desirable, but they would be responsible, throughout the transactions, for the treatment of the emigrants in accordance with the conditions laid down in the scheme, and would have to secure the repayment of whatever sums Her Majesty's Government might advance to them under the proposed agreement.

On that condition, the Treasury would consider lending to the Canadian Government £1 million in instalments as the work proceeded, without interest, for ten years from the date of each instalment.[2]

Taking it for granted that this meant merely that the Canadian Government was asked to guarantee the repayment of the loan by the emigration company, Stephen cabled Macdonald in this sense and received the reply:

Parliament near prorogation. No legislation possible this session. Government favourably inclined. Await details.[3]

Stephen took this to be an encouraging sign and proceed to press for provisional sanction to the proposal, subject to its later ratification by Parliament. If this were agreed to, and the Imperial Government would thereupon obtain the necessary authority for the loan,

---

[1] CO 384/146, 'Emigration: Canada' 7363, Galt to Colonial Office.
[2] CO 807/40 Irish Government to Colonial Office, 10 May 1883.
[3] Macd.P. 'Stephen' 267, Stephen to Macdonald, 11 May and Macdonald to Stephen, 12 May 1883.

Stephen was willing to risk making preparations for a small emigration from Ireland the following spring. On 17 May a cable was despatched from the Colonial Office to the Governor-General:

Irish Emigration. Government cannot engage with companies, but will advance up to 1,000,000 £ repayable without interest in ten years, provided Dominion Government engages to secure repayment and becomes responsible for treatment of emigrants according to condition of Stephen's scheme. Can Government obtain concurrence of Parliament, or undertake without it secure repayment?[1]

The Canadian Government understood from this that it was being asked to undertake a responsibility which would involve it too deeply in actual dealings with Irish settlers who were liable to make political capital out of any misfortune that might befall them. Although Sir John Rose had also cabled Macdonald, advising him that no risk would be attached to guaranteeing the advances to the emigration company, which would itself manage the mortgages and relieve the Government of the embarrassment of dealing directly with the emigrants, Lord Derby received the reply that there were insuperable objections to the Canadian Government becoming either directly or indirectly the creditor of the settlers.[2]

Not only Stephen but the Irish Government also had read a different meaning into the Treasury's proviso. But although the latter tried to have the point clarified,[3] no official move was made by the Treasury towards reassuring the Canadian Government.

On receiving a cable containing the text of the Governor-General's reply to the Colonial Office, Rose again cabled Macdonald asking him to keep the question in abeyance, if possible, until Stephen, who was sailing that day, should arrive in Canada.[4] Stephen was firm in his conviction that the loan should be made direct to the emigration company, and he and Macdonald resolved to stand by the Canadian Government's decision, confident that the British Government, impressed by the need for an emigration scheme such as Stephen had offered, would in time modify its terms.[5] Sir Charles Tupper, who in June replaced Galt as High Commissioner in London, agreed with this view, as did Sir Robert Herbert.

---

[1] CO 807/40 Colonial Office to Governor-General, 17 May 1883.
[2] Loc. cit. Governor-General to Colonial Office, 19 May 1883.
[3] See CO 384/146, 'Emigration: Canada' 9744, Irish Government to Colonial Office, 6 June 1883, and CO 807/40 Colonial Office to Governor-General, 14 and 16 June 1883.
[4] Macd.P. 'Rose' 259.433, Rose to Macdonald, 24 May 1883.
[5] Macd.L.B. 22.218, Macdonald to Tupper, 25 July 1883.

Lord Lorne, the retiring Governor-General, was worried lest the obduracy of Macdonald and Stephen should harm rather than help the project, and Stephen wrote to Macdonald of a visit paid by His Excellency to Causapscal, Stephen's country home, where they had discussed the subject:

He is very full of my Irish project and seems concerned lest you and I do something that will put a stop to further negotiations, and made me promise to write you and urge the advisability of pursuing a course that will keep the matter open and so strengthen the hands of those members of the Imperial Government who are supposed to favour the scheme. I told His Excellency that as nothing *can* now be done during the present session of Parliament to obtain the powers necessary before they can deal with the scheme, I thought the best course for us to follow on this side was to stand firm and refuse to deal with them except on the basis of my *very* liberal proposal.

That I was sure if they really had the belief they professed in the potency of emigration as Ireland's remedy, they would come to our terms this winter before Parliament met again. In short as nothing can be done this year it would be folly giving ourselves away before the time had come for a real effort to be made. . . .[1]

He had made a point of seeing Tupper before he sailed for England and had briefed him, he told Macdonald, in these terms:

. . . I urged him to avoid appearing too anxious about these Irish settlers (they are a doubtful lot at best) otherwise Gladstone would try to force the Government into a position of responsibility that would be or might be exceedingly inconvenient.

You will not misunderstand me. I am very anxious to get these emigrants, just as anxious as His Excellency, but I feel quite sure we shall get them and on our own terms by waiting towards the end of this year, when I am again in London and I hope aided by Lord Lorne himself. . . . I am confident a little firmness on the part of yourself and your new High Commissioner will accomplish all we desire. . . .

I have now done all I promised to His Excellency I would do, and I leave you to handle Lord Derby in such a way as to impress him with the view we take here that the offer made to the Government was an extraordinary liberal one. . . .

Sir John Rose, writing from London, described Gladstone as being 'very wrongheaded on the subject of Emigration', and said it seemed hopeless for the present to try to combat his influence.[2]

[1] Macd.P. 'Stephen' 267, Stephen to Macdonald, 20 June 1883.
[2] Macd.P. 'Rose' 259.438, Rose to Macdonald, 22 June 1883.

Macdonald adjured the High Commissioner to hold firmly to the Canadian Government's position, but added that he would welcome any move towards extending Stephen's scheme to include emigrants from other parts of the British Isles:

Entre nous, we don't want the Western Irish emigration. They are bad settlers and thoroughly disloyal. It won't do for us to have a little Ireland in the North West. I look forward with considerable apprehension to Fenian intrigues between our Irish and Yankee Irish. . . .[1]

As far as the Imperial Government was concerned, the question was considered to be still open, although it would be more accurate to say that complete deadlock had been attained. In the House of Lords on 31 July, Lord Emly asked for an explanation of the delay in coming to terms with Mr. Stephen, adding that 'it did seem to him the most short-sighted policy of the Government to higgle over the proposals made to them, and to run the risk of their being withdrawn'. Replying for the Government, Lord Derby declared that there was no question of higgling with Mr. Stephen, 'a person upon whom we can perfectly rely, and with whom we should have no hesitation in dealing'; the Government had assented in principle to his proposal but with one important modification. The latter was not thought unreasonable in view of the fact that, while it would benefit Ireland to have its surplus population removed, it would at the same time be equally beneficial to Canada to have a large area thus settled. The Canadian Government, however, did not appear to have seen the matter in that light, and had so far refused to incur responsibility for the repayment. Some negotiations had taken place, but the Canadians did not seem disposed to give way.

Later that year Lord Lorne wrote to Macdonald that there was little hope just then of State aid to emigration.[2] In March 1884, the question was again raised in the House of Lords, when the Earl of Carnarvon, who was personally acquainted with Stephen as well as having first-hand knowledge of the North West, moved for the production of the correspondence between Stephen and the Secretary of State for the Colonies. In an extremely evasive reply to Lord Carnarvon's speech, in which the latter had incidentally drawn attention to the congested state of the English labour market as illustrating the need for considering a general scheme of state-aided emigration, Lord Derby ignored the fact that what Canada wanted

---

[1] Macd.L.B. 22.218, Macdonald to Tupper, 25 July 1883.
[2] Tupper Papers 263, Macdonald to Tupper, 22 November 1883.

was farmers, working on their own account, and spoke at length of the undesirability of flooding the Dominion with immigrants who would inevitably, he said, cause a lowering of wage-levels and be altogether most unpopular. Stephen's scheme fell through, he declared, because the Canadian Government absolutely declined to guarantee repayment of the sum proposed to be spent, and other securities were not deemed sufficient. Lord Derby concluded by saying that it would be inconvenient to give the inter-Departmental correspondence, but such correspondence as could be given would be produced. This turned out to be only the exchanges between the Colonial Office and the Governor-General.[1]

There the matter remained. The *Globe* made much of what it represented as the failure of the C.P.R. Company to obtain a loan of a million pounds sterling, free of interest, which, suggested that paper, it would have been very convenient to get in advance of expenditure.[2]

PROVINCIAL RAILWAY DEMANDS

The refusal of the Imperial Government to accept the security of the three Canadian companies for a loan in aid of emigration—security represented by the value of their North West lands—was followed on the part of the *Globe* by the campaign, already referred to, during the summer of 1883 to try to show that these lands were in fact an extension of the Great American Desert. Nevertheless, and in spite of the breakdown of the plan for assisted emigration, independent settlers had shown their confidence in the North West by arriving that year in their thousands. During August 1883, the Prairie Section of the Canadian Pacific was completed to the Rocky Mountains, and work was progressing on the north shore of Lake Superior as fast as was humanly possible. For the establishment of its 'Ontario division' the Company lacked only the formal approval of its shareholders.

In more ways than one, it was the very success of the enterprise which led to its near failure. Apart from the reaction of the Company's enemies, who were the more determined that the Canadian Pacific should not succeed, there were the natural results of the Company's own policy to be met. It had wanted settlers; it had wanted freight traffic; but in getting both it came under an obligation to provide

---

[1] *Accounts and Papers* 8, vol. 54, 1884.   [2] *Globe*, 13 August 1883, *inter alia*.

adequate rolling stock and grain elevators. In order to compete successfully with the millers of Minnesota and with rival lires, facilities had to be made available at the appropriate seasons to move grain by the C.P.R. route, and at rates which compared favourably with those of its rivals. What was apt to be expected of the completed portions of the Canadian Pacific was the service of an old-established system. The Company was only too anxious to satisfy the public, but it all meant money, money in excess of what the contract allowed for, and money which, moreover, would not be immediately returned.

Other demands made upon the Company while the road was yet in its infancy were of a particularly ironical nature. It has been shown that the chief purpose of the national line was to bind together the provinces of the Dominion. Already, with a similar end in view, the Intercolonial Railway had been built from Quebec to Halifax for the benefit of the Maritime Provinces, in accordance with a Confederation pledge; now the Western Provinces were to be united by 'bands of steel' to the centre of Old Canada.

During the 1880's, however, instead of a growing unity, there became apparent a tendency on the part of certain provinces to claim a greater measure of local autonomy, and, paradoxically, the Canadian Pacific, the symbol of their union, was used as a lever by which concessions might be forced out of the Federal Government. This was not to any extent a concerted effort, but the individual claims served as harassing tactics. Manitoba, still crying out for a network of local railways, was unwilling to wait until the Canadian Pacific should be in a position to provide all the necessary branch lines. When the C.P.R. purchased from the Northern Pacific the charter of the Manitoba South-Western, it was expected to complete the line forthwith, whether it were profitable or not. The Dominion Government was as anxious for this as was the Provincial Legislature, and the matter was constantly referred to in Macdonald's correspondence with Stephen. Macdonald's anxiety did not extend to ensuring that the Manitoba South-Western's land grant was promptly allotted.

In Quebec Province, the demand was for the C.P.R. terminus to be at Quebec city, instead of at Montreal. Here the French element heartily applauded the attempts of the Federal Government to persuade the C.P.R. to purchase from the Grand Trunk the North Shore Railway from Montreal to Quebec. The Maritimes, for their part, wanted the transcontinental line to be extended to one of the Atlantic ports, and eventually the persuasions of the Federal Government involved the Company in the construction of the Short Line to St. John, New Brunswick—destined to cause much worry in the process. Stephen would at this stage have preferred a direct connection between Montreal and Portland, Maine, by which freight from the West might more quickly reach the Atlantic. In the early days speed meant more than national sentiment, expecially when the latter barely existed except to clothe opportunists with a cloak of would-be virtue.

All this created a disturbing element in Parliament and country, adding to the anxieties of both Government and railway Company. When at last financial exigencies, born of unforeseen vicissitudes, forced the Canadian Pacific to appeal to the Government for help, members of the dissatisfied communities tried to edge in some condition for the benefit of their own localities in return for their political support. Macdonald might well fear for his Party when aid to the Canadian Pacific was on the tapis, and his reluctance to bring in legislation for that purpose is understandable. Yet the C.P.R. was but an agency then for carrying out the National Policy in railways. To stand by the one was to stand by the other. It would have ill become the statesmen to whom the Canadian Pacific owed its origin to show less faith in the enterprise than was displayed by those to whom they had delegated the task of making the Confederation line a reality.

While Macdonald tried to please everybody, the C.P.R. seemed to please nobody. The Company had contracted to build and operate a line from Nipissing to the Pacific coast; it was therefore criticized for branching out in certain directions for its own protection—that was not in the bond. Yet because its system did not at the same time become an all-embracing octopus it was held to have failed in its national mission.

Although Stephen admitted to Macdonald that one of the difficulties he had to contend with was loss of faith in the future of the C.P.R. on the part of old associates, this was not a fact that he desired to have publicly known. It was unfortunate that Hill's withdrawal in May 1883, for reasons already hazarded, was followed later that year by that of J. S. Kennedy. The Canadian Pacific was only one of Kennedy's many interests, and as American railway affairs became precariously involved towards the end of 1883 he no

doubt felt he had his hands full south of the boundary. His withdrawal did not mean the severing of all links with the New York
house, but it gave an unfortunate impression, and signalled the
beginning of the end of the C.P.R.'s favour on Wall Street.

A less defensible defection was the retiral, the following year, of
Duncan McIntyre. He alone appears to have relinquished his
position on the C.P.R. Board—he remained an investor—because
the constant strain attached to the management of the railway during
this period proved too much for him.[1] There remained in active
control Stephen, Smith (in 1883 his name was officially inscribed on
the list of directors), Angus, and Van Horne who replaced McIntyre
as Vice-President.

MARKET SLUMP : STEPHEN DEVISES DIVIDEND GUARANTEE

In spite of the gloomy prognostications of the *Globe*, Stephen in
September 1883 still found reason to be confident in the future of
the Canadian Pacific. Recent unfavourable trends on Wall Street had
not escaped his notice, but the prospect of entering the London
market seemed to him less remote since his moral victory over the
Grand Trunk. His philosophic resolution that the C.P.R. should be
built without a dollar of English money was liable to be cast aside
when opportunity made philosophy superfluous. Writing in optimistic vein to Macdonald on 20 September, he concluded:

Meantime the break in N.Y. market in Northern Pacific securities
operates somewhat against us in that mercurial market. I shall be very
glad when I get to England and have the bulk of the stock held there.[2]

To provide for that winter's construction, which included some of
the heaviest and most costly work in the Rockies and north of Lake
Superior, a further issue of stock was contemplated. Within the
next month, however, the state of the money markets worsened, and
as in 1873 an uncertainty which demanded of the investor the utmost
prudence and caution rendered the selling of railway securities well-
nigh impossible. Speculators were taking advantage of the situation,
and Stephen was afraid lest C.P.R. shareholders, in the panic of the
moment, should be intimidated into sacrificing what they might be
persuaded was worthless property. Acting on the advice of friends
of the Company in Europe and the United States, Stephen devised a

[1] Macd.P. 'Stephen' 269, Stephen to Macdonald, 31 March 1884.
[2] Macd.P. 'Stephen' 267, Stephen to Macdonald, 20 September 1883.

plan whereby not only would the outstanding stock be made more secure, but the unsold portion would be rendered marketable also.

On 24 October he submitted to the Minister of Railways and Canals, for whom John Henry Pope was acting, a proposition whereby on the Company depositing with the Government money and securities sufficient to cover the cost, the Government should guarantee to pay a minimum annual dividend for ten years of 3 per cent on all the Company's stock, the Company to supplement this during construction by 2 per cent, and afterwards by such amount as earnings warranted.[1] It was, in effect, a proposal to buy an annuity; the Government was asked merely to act as depositary for the fund.

Stephen proposed to constitute the dividend fund in the following way: the Company to pay immediately $15,000,145 in cash, and a further sum of $5 million on or before 1 February 1884. Within seven years a final instalment of $4,527,000 would complete the total necessary to produce 3 per cent annually on $100 million of stock. He suggested that as part payment the Government should withhold the postal subsidy due to the Company (this he estimated to amount to about $3 million) and that as security for the two latter payments the Government should accept Land Grant Bonds, and also create a charge upon the $5 million worth of these Bonds already held by the Government as security for the operation of the road. Thus although the full price of the annuity would have to be paid, most of it in advance (it was proposed that the Government should allow interest at 4 per cent on the cash held) it was hoped that the $45 million of unsold stock would be more readily convertible into working capital, while that already issued would become a stable 5 per cent security. It was not necessary to put the matter before Parliament, and after discussion in Council the guarantee was agreed to. On 29 October Stephen wrote to Macdonald:

I am off to New York this afternoon to get Tilley's 15 millions.[2]

PRESS ATTACKS ON GOVERNMENT AND C.P.R.

Meanwhile the *Globe* was denouncing with its customary venom what it termed 'simply a scheme for raising money on the Government's credit'. This of course it was, but it ultimately rested on the credit of the Company. According to the *Globe*, this was of no account.

[1] S.P. No. 31, 1884, CO 45/565, Stephen to the Hon. Minister of Railways and Canals, 24 October 1883. Compare C.P.R. Contract, Clause 9(d).

[2] Macd.P. 'Stephen' 267, Stephen to Macdonald, 29 October 1883.

The paper staged an interview with a member of the rival C.P.R. Syndicate of 1881, and reported him as saying:

The fact that they have had to seek such a guarantee is pretty good evidence they have very little faith in the future of their enterprise, and this will do more to injure the prospects of our North West country than all the Opposition Press (against whose articles the Tories are constantly protesting) have ever said or can say. 'What if the Company should fail to provide for the guaranteed dividend?' was asked. 'In that event,' was the answer, 'the Government would probably have to take the road off their hands and complete it. Perhaps that is what the Company desire. With the guarantee they will be able to dispose of their stock, and the whole enterprise may soon be found in the hands of parties other than the members of the present Company. It is unfortunate that the Company have by their conduct excited suspicions regarding their ultimate intentions. It looks as if they wished to avoid the risks involved in operating the road after it is completed. . . .'[1]

An official cable had been despatched on 27 October to Morton, Rose and Company in London with the bare information that the Canadian Government had passed an Order-in-Council guaranteeing absolutely for ten years a minimum dividend of 3 per cent on the $100 million capital stock of the Company, and this intelligence was relayed to the Press there. Unfortunately it was instantly taken for granted in some quarters that the guarantee took the place of the cash subsidy, as provided for in Clause 9(b) of the contract (Appendix I) and was thus worth a great deal more to the Company.[2] Unable directly to assail the apparently enviable position of the Canadian Pacific, the *Standard* proceed to undermine it by attacking the financial state of the Dominion, which it described as 'weak and precarious' owing to extravagant expenditure on unremunerative public works.[3] In order to give the most unfavourable impression possible of the value of the Government's guarantee an ominous picture was presented of 'commercial distrust and unsoundness, banking embarrassments and distressed manufactures'.

The *Globe*, tumbling to the fact that a rise in C.P.R. stock to 68 in the first week of November was probably the result of a misapprehension, foresaw the undoubted reaction which would follow publication of full details, but hinted that the whole truth was being intentionally withheld. Already, the *Globe* alleged, the whole opera-

---

[1] *Globe*, 31 October 1883.   [2] *Railway Times*, 3 November 1883.
[3] *Standard*, 2 November 1883. See also *Montreal Herald*, 19 November 1883 (contradiction).

tion was regarded with suspicion in New York, a Wall Street paper having applied to it 'a slang name descriptive of something close akin to fraud'.[1] In a later issue the paper advised the Government and the Company to make known the full truth, saying:

They may be assured that already there is widespread suspicion that the real purpose of the arrangement is to enable them and their associates to realize the profits on the prairie section of the road and to escape with them.[2]

Where the Canadian Pacific was concerned, the *Globe* had an almost supernaturally keen nose for trouble. Any uncertainty in the Company's proceedings was exploited to the full, so that it mattered little what the final outcome was; the *Globe* had anticipated it with its own version. It has been seen, in the matter of financing the St. Paul railway, that Stephen took little account of how his actions might be interpreted by the public or Press; business considerations alone weighed with him. By these again he was guided when he decided to have the guarantee arrangement modified. It was not then imperative to issue the entire $45 million worth of remaining stock and, in spite of the guarantee, risk considerable loss thereby owing to the uncertain state of the market. Whether Stephen was unable to raise the $15 million necessary to fulfil the Company's part of the bargain with the Government, or was simply persuaded, on second thoughts, that such a large advance outlay was unwise, is not clear. At all events, regardless of the effect this might have on public opinion, he decided to issue only $10 million worth immediately, thus requiring the Government to guarantee only $65 million instead of the full amount of authorized stock. This would entail a reduced deposit of $8,561,733 on a total of $15,942,645. The virtual 'option' on a guarantee of the remaining $35 million would be secured by the Company's handing over certificates for this stock to the Government to be available for issue with guarantee on the Company's making payment of the appropriate sum.

These modified proposals were embodied in a fresh application to the Department of Railways on 5 November, and were duly agreed to in Council.[3] On 9 November, Stephen telegraphed Macdonald from New York to the effect that the cash deposit had been credited to the Government's account at the Bank of Montreal,[4] and the

[1] *Globe*, 1 November 1883.   [2] *Globe*, 5 November 1883.
[3] S.P. 31, 1884, CO 45/565, Stephen to Hon. Minister of Railways and Canals, 5 November 1883.
[4] Macd.P. 'Stephen' 267, Stephen to Macdonald, 9 November 1883.

following day the final agreement was signed. As the Company no longer had direct control of the $35 million of unissued stock, it was obliged to cancel the contract with the North American Railway Contracting Company. As it happened the arrangements in connection with that corporation had not been completely carried out; no stock had been transferred, and expenditure had continued to pass through the C.P.R.'s books. The latter was thus again responsible for the entire work of construction.

A full and authoritative statement regarding the guarantee was issued by Stephen in New York and telegraphed to London. Both *Standard* and *Globe* made much of the fact that the details proved the arrangement to be less favourable than earlier conclusions had promised.[1] The *Globe* accused the Government of exceeding its powers as well as its duty, making out that it assumed all the risk:

The Company, it is admitted, are in such a position that without the Government guarantee they could do nothing more. They therefore have nothing to lose by the failure of this new device for raising money should it fail. But the Government of Canada—that is, in such a case as this, Canada itself—has much to lose, and already it has lost not a little. . . .

While the *Globe* wilfully failed to see that the guarantee was providing money for the completion of the road, alleging that it would only enable stockholders to sell at a higher price, Stephen congratulated himself on having forestalled such action. After ten days of adverse press comment he could still write optimistically, if not complacently, to Macdonald:

Having secured holders of the stock in their investment all my concern now is to finish the road by the spring of 1886 and place the Company in a position to do its great work of settling up the Nor West efficiently and creditably to the Government and to itself without caring much what the result may be to me personally even if I should lose all the money I have put into it, though that is hardly possible. . . .[2]

Once again Stephen had underestimated the power of the forces against him. It soon became clear that the same influences were at work in New York as had in the past served to close the London market against the Canadian Pacific. The *Wall-street Daily News* of 17 November, referring to the railway as 'a Northwest wild-cat', declared:

---

[1] *Standard*, 13 November 1883; *Globe*, 13, 14, 15 and 21 November 1883.
[2] Macd.P. 'Stephen' 267, Stephen to Macdonald, 23 November 1883.

There is one stock on the list whose pretensions deserve to be thoroughly exposed. The Canadian Pacific is masquerading around as a 5 per cent security. It is a dead skin, and any investor who buys the stock on the humbugging pretences made for it will lose every cent. . . .

Echoing the phrases of the Grand Trunk 'scribblers' of some months before, it represented the Canadian Pacific as running through 'an unbroken wilderness in the frozen regions of the North, edging on the Arctic circle, with termini at Ottawa and some place in the wilds of British Columbia', adding that even if the Government gave them half of Western Canada to build the line, no such railroad as the C.P.R. could earn working expenses in that generation.

For some time rumours had been current of a Grand Trunk/ Northern Pacific alliance. Early in August Sir Henry Tyler had sailed for Canada, reportedly with that purpose in view. Three months later, the St. Paul *Pioneer Press* reported that a connection between the two lines at Detroit was to be effected by means of subsidiary lines, which would also provide an outlet to New York, while the Grand Trunk was planning to build an extension to Duluth to facilitate business with the Northern Pacific and with a view to penetrating eventually into the Canadian North West.[1] It is debatable whether the bankruptcy of the Northern Pacific, occurring at the end of 1883, had less unfortunate repercussions on the fortunes of the Canadian Pacific as a North American railway security than the alliance which it interrupted might have produced.

Meanwhile Sir John Macdonald, writing to Tupper, the High Commissioner, about recent events, asked whether he and Sir John Rose could get for him reliable evidence of anti-C.P.R. action on the part of the Grand Trunk which could be used, if necessary, in the House the following Session:

. . . Armed with that I could throw out a hint . . . that would make Hickson tremble to his boots. Canada has power not only to see through its Government that her interests are not imperilled by the ambition or jealousy of any Railway Company but has also a *locus standi* as a creditor. The G.T.R. owes her 3½ millions sterling with 30 years interest which she for the purpose of building up a Canadian Railway for Canadian Commerce has [subordinated] to other claims. It has now become an American line with its termini at Chicago and Portland. The Canadian local transport business has been made secondary to the through or Foreign traffic and Canada must legislate or enforce its debt. A

[1] Quoted in *Railway Times*, 17 November 1883.

threat of that kind judiciously used at the right time would soon bring these people to their bearings.[1]

This threat was never carried out; the older road was, with its officials, too useful politically. Moreover it became politic to remain on good terms with Hickson and so avoid a charge of favouritism towards the Canadian Pacific. In November 1883, however, the Prime Minister was inclined to be more optimistic than the C.P.R. President about the future of the road. He ended the letter just quoted:

Geo. Stephen—for the first time—seemed depressed notwithstanding his enormous pluck but we have assured him of thorough backing and with a 10 years Guarantee of 3 per cent., the stock ought to find ready sale at 70 or more in the English market.

COMPANY'S POSITION WORSENS

The utter failure of the guarantee to achieve its purpose in raising the market value of Canadian Pacific stock marked a distinct turning-point in the Company's career. Having sunk $8 million of ready money in a well-considered attempt to improve its position, Stephen found the C.P.R. less favourably situated in December 1883 than it had been two months previously. Instead of making a new issue of stock, he pledged the $1 million worth covered by the guarantee in New York for a loan of $5 million.

From that time, the Company was on the defensive. Its enemies had been enabled, as if according to plan, to launch one attack, and were standing by confident that ere long an opportunity would offer to deal an even more telling blow. They had predicted trouble for the Canadian Pacific and it had come; it only remained to force the stock out of the New York market and bring about the long-awaited appeal to London. The vultures of 'Tokenhouse Yard' would do the rest.

Stephen was bewildered; for one of his undertakings to be so maliciously assailed was a new experience; financial ability was of no avail when matched against the unscrupulous wiles of politicians and rival railwaymen who were thinking only of the day and would see no further than the desirability of destroying this obstacle blocking the immediate path to their respective goals. The downfall of the Canadian Pacific would assuredly have meant a Liberal triumph, but

[1] Tupper Papers, 263, Macdonald to Tupper, 22 November 1883. See Creighton, op. cit. (*The Young Politician*), pp. 250–253 for early G.T.R. history.

GEORGE STEPHEN
by Robert Harris
(In the possession of Mrs. Aubrey Geddes)

information that might be required by the Government in its deliberations. On 15 January he submitted an official statement of the affairs of the Company to the Minister of Railways, with suggestions as to how relief might be afforded. In the first place he asked for a temporary advance of $22½ million, to enable the Company to maintain its rapid construction of the line. His next proposal was that the stipulation for cash and bond deposits as security for the construction and operation of the road should be abandoned, such progress having been made as to render these safeguards anomalous. A further request was that in future the cash subsidy should be paid on estimates, and not withheld until each twenty-mile portion had been completed. Finally, he suggested that payment of the second instalment of the guarantee fund, due that month, should be postponed until November 1888, when it would actually be required by the Government for payment of dividends.

As security for the repayment of the loan of $22½ million (which, after an initial sum for clearing the Company's floating debts, would be paid out as the work proceeded), and for the guarantee obligations Stephen proposed mortgaging, first, the lands so far unappropriated, and secondly the Company's main line and property, including the Pembina Branch and the lines east of Callander, 'with such remedies for the enforcement, both of interest and principal, as may be deemed expedient'.[1]

Two months previously Stephen had calculated that the total cost of the work yet to be done to complete the contract would amount to $25,100,000—$11,600,000 to close the 290 mile gap between the summit of the Rockies and Kamloops, where the Onderdonk Section began, and $13½ million for 45½ miles north of Lake Superior. He had written to Macdonald:

With the subsidy in cash and Land Grant Bonds and other resources at our command there would not be the least difficulty in financing for this sum as well as for all other wants of the Company if we had not such a malignant crowd of enemies to fight. . . .[2]

Only the Government, appreciating the true value of the Company's assets, was in a position to give the Canadian Pacific the credit it deserved.

A searching inquiry into the Company's affairs by the Government engineer and the Deputy Minister of Inland Revenue found

[1] S.P. 31c, 1884, CO 45/565.
[2] Macd.P. 'Stephen' 267, Stephen to Macdonald, 19 November 1883.

everything in order. The former, Collingwood Schreiber, then recommended that the Company's application be submitted to Parliament, but on condition that the Government's lien on the road should extend to all branches, and that a default of six months in payment of interest or principal on the charge created should give to the Government the right to take possession of the railway and all its property.

With these conditions incorporated the proposals were placed before Parliament substantially as Stephen had framed them, but omitting the request for the return of the Land Grant Bond deposit. It seemed that the Company was paying a high price for relief; in case of default the Government would fall heir to a property worth many times the value of the advance. In ordinary circumstances no financial house would have required such stringent terms of security, but this was no ordinary proposition. The Government of Canada was not in business as a money-lender; its action had to face a political test. It was a matter of policy in which actual figures had little part. As Stephen afterwards explained to the Canadian Pacific shareholders:

Less care in preparing the provisions for enforcing payment of the loan and interest would have exposed the Government and Company to criticism even more virulent (if that were possible) than that which they received.[1]

Even Stephen, never dreaming that this measure would not dispose, once for all, of the Company's financial difficulties, did not foresee the danger of tying up the C.P.R.'s resources so thoroughly. Moreover, despite the need to preclude rejection of the Bill, the terms themselves revealed a regrettably poor estimation of the Company's assets. Well might Stephen confide to Tupper:

The one thing I am anxious about is lest anything should be said in the House that our enemies could twist into a statement that the C.P.R. had exhausted its resources. My contention is that the resources of the Company are ample for all its purposes if these resources are only fairly dealt with. . . . This should be insisted on. . . .[2]

As usual, opposition began before the details of the proposals were even decided upon, let alone published. On 11 January Rose cabled Macdonald:

[1] *Railway Times*, 19 April 1884.
[2] Tupper Papers 270, Stephen to Tupper, 9 January 1884.

Of vital importance that first intimation any measure be authoritatively and accurately cabled here. Party preparing garbled adverse reports. . . .[1]

The first official announcement—although no particulars were then divulged—came in Lord Lansdowne's speech at the opening of Parliament on 17 January. It was not until 1 February that Sir Charles Tupper introduced the resolutions in the House, yet on 19 January the *Globe* was ready with a lengthy comment on the expected measure, under the headlines: 'The Developments Looked on as a Dodge to Escape Personal Responsibility. Directors Shirking Liability.' Attributing the 'sudden and complete collapse' of the Canadian Pacific entirely to its efforts to monopolize the trade of the North West, the *Globe* declared:

It is very doubtful indeed whether the country should involve itself any further to help a Company which has failed so completely to fulfil the promises made on its behalf, or entrust the continuance of the work to men who have brought themselves to such a position of helplessness when the more difficult portions of their undertaking may be said to have been only entered upon. It may be better to sacrifice the millions they have been paid as profit on the Prairie Section than to proceed further under the same reckless management. . . .

If Parliament did pass the Bill, it said, it ought to insist that, as a condition, Manitoba ought to be freed from the ban imposed by clause 15 of the C.P.R. Contract, and the Canadian Pacific's monopoly there abolished.

MANITOBA'S GRIEVANCES

The train of events leading from the inclusion of clause 15 of the contract culminated in what was known as the Disallowance Agitation. Although the full storm did not break until three years later, it was in December 1883 that an organization was formed which, backed by certain Provincial politicians and their allies among the Canadian Pacific's railroad rivals, was instrumental in bringing the agitation to a head.

Local meetings during the autumn of 1883 were the prelude to a conference held at Winnipeg on 19 and 20 December, from which emerged an association calling itself the Manitoba and North West Farmers' Protective Union and flourishing a Declaration of Rights. The members claimed, on behalf of Manitoba and other prairie

---

[1] Macd.P. 'Rose' 259.528, Rose to Macdonald, 11 January 1884.

provinces, equality of privilege with the older provinces as regards both railway legislation and the disposal of their public lands; they considered as indispensable a newly-projected railway line intended to run north to Hudson's Bay, there to connect, when the Bay was navigable, with Atlantic steamers; they complained that the prairie farmers suffered from a heavy duty on agricultural implements, imposed for the benefit of eastern manufacturers; lastly, they claimed that the C.P.R.'s freight rates were excessive, and that the Ogilvies, having a monopoly of elevators, kept down the price of wheat. What the Province wanted was more railway competition, in other words unrestricted entrance for the Grand Trunk and Northern Pacific.

Regarding the alleged elevator monopoly, Stephen assured Macdonald that anyone might build elevators at any station of the C.P.R. on precisely the same terms as Ogilvie; it was just possible that W. W. Ogilvie had created an impression in the minds of other buyers that it was useless to compete with him.[1] As to the Hudson's Bay Railway—in Stephen's opinion it was an impossibility, but, he wrote:

. . . So far as the C.P.R. is concerned I have no objection to a line to the Hudson's Bay, or for that matter to the North Pole if the promoters will put their own money into the enterprise. It would be a fatal blunder for the Province of Manitoba to become mixed up with the finance of that or any other railway. . . .[2]

Manitoba at the end of 1883 was a fertile territory in which to sow seeds of discord. The collapse of the land boom, after a period of wild and wholesale speculating, had followed a crop failure which at that early stage had more than monetary significance. It is probable, then, that at first the Farmers' Union received genuine support from settlers in southern Manitoba, the area chiefly affected. Before long, however, it became clear that there was more behind the organization than the desire to remedy local conditions. The temporary disappointments of the farmers had been exploited in order to gain support for more remote objects. At the second convention of the Union in March 1884, the introduction of an anti-immigration resolution, and talk of secession from the Confederation, opened the eyes of many settlers to the implications, and gradually only a nucleus of disappointed speculators and political agitators remained

[1] Macd.P. 'Stephen' 267, Stephen to Macdonald, 6 December 1883.
[2] Macd.P. 'Stephen' 269, Stephen to Macdonald, 5 January 1884.

members.[1] Liberal sympathies became, in fact, a condition of membership.[2]

Although an effort was made by the 'Blake Grits' to have clause 15 abolished as a condition of the concessions contained in the C.P.R. relief Bill of 1884, this came to nothing. Macdonald had not expected trouble from this quarter; some years before he had come to an understanding with 'Honest John' Norquay the Provincial Premier, that Manitoba should not oppose the Dominion's railway policy.[3] As will be seen, Norquay found it no easy task to ensure this in face of increasingly violent opposition in his own Legislature.

As it happened, the agitation only served to postpone local railway-building in Manitoba. Reports cabled to London with the object of affecting the market for Canadian Pacifics not only achieved that aim but resulted also in the complete failure on Stephen's part to raise the money to build the Manitoba South-Western.[4]

ROUGH PASSAGE FOR RAILWAY RELIEF BILL

While these troubles were brewing in the West, the debate on Lord Lansdowne's Address was proceeding at Ottawa. To a long diatribe by Blake on 18 January, accusing the Government of encouraging the Canadian Pacific to engage in activities outside the contract, the Prime Minister scathingly replied:

. . . The remarks of the hon. gentleman show that he is not able to grasp the grand idea involved in the construction of this railway. . . .

The trend of the debate boded ill for the railway Bill. Stephen returned to Montreal. He wrote to Macdonald before leaving the capital:

I am going down in the morning and you may be sure I will do all I can to keep things moving, and in life, till relief arrives, but you must not blame me if I fail. I do not, at the moment, see how we are to get the money to keep the work going, but I will know better what I can do when I get to Montreal and consult with my colleagues. If I find we cannot go on I suppose the only thing to do will be to put in a Receiver. If that is to be done the quicker it is done the better. . . .

---

[1] Jackson, op. cit. p. 52.
[2] Oral evidence: James Robinson, Mather, Manitoba. Confirmed by testimony of John Dobbyn, Souris Valley, to Select Committee on Colonization, J. of C.H.C. 1885, CO 45/569, Appendix 3.   [3] See above, chapter III, p. (75) n. 2.
[4] Macd.P. 'Stephen' 269, Stephen to Macdonald (Cable) 13 May 1884, and 14 June, 1884. See also *Winnipeg Times*, 12 June 1885.

I am getting so wearied and worn out with this business that almost any change would be a relief to me.

Whatever happens I shall always feel grateful for the readiness which you have throughout shown to help us in every possible way.[1]

Two days later, in what appeared to be an attempt to draw a parallel with the 'Pacific Scandal' of 1872, the *Globe* printed a leader which harked back to Macdonald's 1880 negotiations for the building of the railway. It reminded its readers that the public had never been enlightened about what proposal Mr. Stephen and his friends had made before Macdonald went to England. Rumour had it that Mr. Stephen, when he found that Macdonald and his colleagues were in his power, had refused to adhere to the original proposal, and had wrung from them the present terms, so much more unfavourable to Canada. What—asked the *Globe*—had induced the Premier to repel the advances of European capitalists, and to agree to such terms as Mr. Stephen and his friends chose to dictate? 'Even then, few thought, that the inducements were either patriotic or pure. . . .'

Stephen in Montreal had more to think about than the barbed innuendoes of the *Globe*. He wrote to Tupper:

. . . It is not a little disappointing that we should be maligned and branded as scoundrels by the very people whose interests we have been supporting at enormous *loss* to ourselves individually but so it is, and we must put up with it. . . . Had I supposed it would take to 1st March before help could reach us I would not have made the attempt to carry on. . . . I am regularly at my wits end to know how to work through till we can get relief. . . . Everything coming from the Government in payment for work done goes to the Bank of Montreal in payment of the $3,500,000 we owe the Bank, and cannot be diverted to pay wages and supplies. . . .[2]

When at last the details of the Bill were made known, they were hailed by the *Globe* as being worse than anyone could have foreseen:

Not only are the Company not to put a dollar of their own money into the Canadian Pacific Railway proper, but they are to keep the millions they have already taken out of it and give no value in return, and they are to have the control of all those additional millions, spend them as they please, and make what profit out of it they can. . . . No man in Canada can be so stupid as to believe that the security is worth anything or that one dollar of this thirty millions will ever return to the Treasury. . . .[3]

[1] Macd.P. 'Stephen' 269, Stephen to Macdonald, 22 January 1884.
[2] Tupper Papers 271, Stephen to Tupper, 24 January 1884.
[3] *Globe*, 1 February 1884.

Provincial opposition was invited by an attempt to show that the burden would fall mainly on Ontario; and what, asked the *Globe*, were Quebec or the Maritimes to gain by the opening up of the North West?

Addressing the House on 5 February, Sir Charles Tupper (who was still nominally Minister of Railways) declared that if the last dollar received from every source were deducted from the amount so far expended on the Canadian Pacific, there would still remain a large balance representing the contributions of the Company. While recognizing that the Syndicate no longer existed, that the Railway was now the property of the Company,

'. . . I cannot forget,' he said, 'that there would have been no C.P.R. Company, there would have been no such gigantic progress as there now is if these gentlemen had not had the courage, the energy or the enterprise to risk their own money to the extent of $10,000,000 before asking the people of this country to put a single dollar into the purchase of stock. . . .'

He was not there, however, to support the interests of individuals; these gentlemen had entered into the contract of their own accord, risking the possibility of profit or loss. The resolutions before the House must stand on the broader foundation of the interests of Canada itself.

To the 'Blake Grits' this was a vain appeal. Once again the old arguments were brought forward, as though they had never been successfully contradicted, and new angles of attack were adopted in keeping with more recent trends. The pointers set by the *Globe* were faithfully followed. Now that the Canadian Pacific was on its knees asking for more money, why—asked a member from the eastern seaboard—did the Government not demand that the winter port be made in the Maritime Provinces? 'Are we called upon to uphold this monopoly creator?' echoed a voice of Ontario. The people of the North West were spoon-fed, contributed the Conservative representative of Cardwell, a Liberal member adding: 'Well, this Company are not spoon-fed; I believe the Government feed them with a shovel.' That the Government should take the part of the C.P.R. Company was described as an outrage and a betrayal of the interests of the people. 'The watch-dogs of the flock are ranging the hills with the wolves', declared the Member for North Norfolk, 'the flock is scattered without a protector'. To which Members responded with a reassuring 'Bow-wow!'

The Grand Trunk, meanwhile, was threatening to organize an even more intensive attack on the C.P.R. unless the latter would concede to it the Ontario and Quebec.[1] This the Pacific refused to do, while Macdonald, in answer to a direct demand from Hickson that no aid should be granted to the C.P.R. unless it could be guaranteed that the latter would not go out of its legitimate way to damage the Grand Trunk, asked for a more explicit statement of the alleged damage. This was not forthcoming.[2]

The Canadian Pacific's new connections in Eastern Canada were constantly referred to at this time by the railway's opponents. In his speech in the House on 5 February, Blake once more brought up the question of the Credit Valley, saying that it appeared that $484,000 of the C.P.R. Company's money had been spent on Credit Valley Bonds, now held by the Government as security for the construction of the line. Some days later the *Toronto Mail* published a letter from George Laidlaw, moderately-worded but making no bones of the fact that the early history of the Grand Trunk had been a tale of jealously-guarded monopoly, of the strangling of lesser enterprises such as his own Credit Valley. It was after a vain attempt to raise money in London in face of concerted Grand Trunk opposition that Laidlaw had turned for help to George Stephen, who, before the formation of the C.P.R. Company, undertook to take over and finish the Credit Valley. Said Laidlaw:

He did not want the Credit Valley any more than he wants Barnum's white elephant. But out of regard to those in England and Scotland who, at his instance, invested in the undertaking, and on account of a very friendly interest in myself and regard for my desperate struggles and condition, he undertook the job, and then and there sent his man of business to this city, paid all my personal debts—a large amount—took over my securities and interest in the C.V.R., arranged a syndicate, settled the affairs of the C.V.R. as best he could, and completed and equipped the line. . . .[3]

Three days later, in a speech already quoted, the Member for North Norfolk delivered in the House a merciless attack on Stephen's integrity, taking advantage of the obscurity which for most people still surrounded the subject to revive the question of the financing

[1] Macd.P. 129, 'Railways' 9, Stephen to Macdonald, 14 February 1884. See also *Railway Times*, 1 March 1884.

[2] 'Grand Trunk Railroad—Correspondence between the Company and the Dominion Government regarding the Canadian Pacific loans' (pamphlet).

[3] *Toronto Mail*, 16 February 1884.

of the St. Paul, Minneapolis and Manitoba Railroad. This was, of course, before the Farley lawsuit had run its course, before the charges against Hill and his associates had been disproved. The effect of such a speech as the following can therefore be imagined:

. . . A member of this Company was once President of the Bank of Montreal—a responsible position. When in that position he took $8,000,000 from the chest of the Bank of Montreal, without the consent or knowledge of the directors of that Bank—at least he is reported to have done so. . . . He is reported to have invested that money . . . in the St. Paul and Minneapolis Railway, and, through collusion with the Receiver of that road, it is said he procured a report as to the condition of its affairs which was sent to Holland . . . which report induced the Dutch bondholders and stockholders to part with their interest in the road at less than it was worth, thus enabling them through this collusion to buy the road at less than its value. And having used the Receiver as his tool, he forgot the old adage that there should be honour among thieves. He is charged with having forgotten to give the Receiver his share of the plunder, and the Receiver is said to have brought suit in the United States Court at St. Paul. The Court refused to entertain the suit on the ground that it would not degrade itself by giving a decision as to how plunder should be divided among the different members of a gang. This is one of the gentlemen the Government wish to aid to the extent of this loan, one of the gentlemen upon whose figures we are asked to make up our opinion. . . .

By a miracle of Party discipline, the Bill was passed in the Commons on 28 February. It went to the Senate with a Conservative amendment providing against any future amalgamation of the Canadian Pacific or any of its branches or leased lines with the Grand Trunk, and after what seemed to Stephen an interminable delay the Bill became law on 8 March. It was only just in time. The Bank of Montreal had refused a request from the Minister of Railways for further temporary accommodation for the Canadian Pacific.

The debate had in itself done more damage than could readily be repaired. Returning to Montreal from New York after discharging the Company's debts, Stephen wrote to Macdonald:

. . . The Yankees are all happy now, having got their money from the C.P.R., but somehow the stock both in New York and London is *dead*—nothing doing in it. . . .[1]

---

[1] Macd.P. 'Stephen' 269, Stephen to Macdonald, 21 March 1884.

VI

Crisis and completion

IN April 1884, Canadian Pacifics stood at 48. Yet at the opening of navigation that spring the C.P.R. had an all-Canadian route open from the St. Lawrence to the Rocky Mountains: from Montreal to Toronto by the Ontario and Quebec, thence to Owen Sound by the Toronto, Grey and Bruce to connect with the new steamers plying to Port Arthur, and finally on to Calgary by Canadian Pacific proper. Already the Company controlled the alternative route from Montreal to Lake Nipissing via the Quebec, Montreal, Ottawa and Occidental Railway and the Canada Central. It remained only to complete the line north of Lake Superior and to meet Onderdonk at Kamloops in British Columbia.

'But what then?' asked the London *Standard*, and supplied an answer from New York's *Bradstreet's Journal*

The Company will have to run an unprofitable road, and to pay interest to the amount of at least $1,500,000 a year. . . . In this state of matters it will be very difficult for the Company to avoid another crisis in its affairs. The penalty of forfeiture of all its property for default in the payment of interest will hang over it. From what source will it obtain the means of repaying loans to the amount of $30,000,000 by the year 1891? That it will be able to sell its stock is very improbable, and that it will be able to realise upon its lands fast enough to meet this demand is extremely doubtful. . . .[1]

It was, indeed, this burden of interest to be paid which troubled Stephen more than any physical problem of construction. He had no doubt of being able to restore the credit of the Company once the finished road was in a position to demonstrate its merits to the world, but in the interval he could not fail to see that the effect on the public mind of such heavy commitments as the loan entailed was enough to discourage investment in the enterprise.

[1] *Standard*, 26 February 1884.

Barely a month had passed since the loan Act became law when the *Globe* launched a new campaign with the object of hastening another crisis for the Canadian Pacific. A visit which Stephen paid to Macdonald in Ottawa towards the end of March was the signal for the *Globe* to announce that the C.P.R. Company had applied to the Government for a further loan of $5 million or, failing that, had asked the Government to waive its lien upon the road and allow the recent loan to go unsecured.[1] The interview, it stated, had been a very stormy one, Macdonald flatly refusing to entertain the suggestions, declaring that he had already been almost ruined politically by his efforts to comply with the Company's demands. If the *Globe's* object was to cause a breach between Government and Company the result must have been disappointing. On Stephen's writing to the Premier: 'My dear Sir John—Can you suggest any way of stopping such things as the enclosed from yesterday's Globe?'[2] a public denial was made in the House by Sir Hector Langevin. No such application, said Langevin, had been made by the C.P.R. Company.

In April, Stephen paid a flying visit to London, partly to raise money for the building of the Manitoba South-Western but also hoping by his personal influence to revive public confidence in the Canadian Pacific. In the event he failed completely to interest investors in railway-building in Manitoba, now notorious as a hotbed of sedition,[3] while he found the task of inspiring new faith in Canadian Pacifics an uphill struggle indeed. The speeches in the recent debate had done their devastating work well. He wrote to Macdonald:

People here cannot understand a great political party having recourse to such tactics for merely political objects, and believe there must be truth in the damaging statements made upon the floor of Parliament. . . .[4]

In London, the railway was regarded as just another American fiasco—unfortunately precedent was not lacking—and Stephen himself was no longer deferred to as the Oracle upon sound investment. It may have seemed to some that his meteoric career had been but the fortune of circumstance, and that now his luck was turning. And was it not hinted that the Dominion itself was heading for economic catastrophe?

Undeterred by the snub so recently administered, the *Globe* seized on the report that Stephen had been unable to raise money

[1] *Globe*, 2 April 1884.
[2] Macd.P. 'Stephen' 269, Stephen to Macdonald, 3 April 1884.
[3] Loc. cit. Stephen to Macdonald, 14 June 1884.
[4] Loc. cit. Stephen to Macdonald, 26 April 1884.

for the Manitoba South-Western, and observed that it must be very damaging for the C.P.R. Company to have it known that it was incapable of raising 'for a road so greatly favoured the small amount that is necessary'. Not only had the President failed to finance the Manitoba South-Western, it added, but he had also experienced a similar setback in connection with other projects, and as a result a new demand was to be made at once upon the Government.[1]

STEPHEN'S ANXIETIES

Back in Montreal, Stephen was physically exhausted. He had done his utmost in London to 'inspire confidence where alarm more or less existed',[2] knowing that to show the slightest sign of the apprehension he himself felt would be fatal. Only to Macdonald would he admit the fears he was almost afraid to admit to himself; to the rest of the world his confidence had to appear unshaken. On 18 June he wrote to the Prime Minister:

. . . I am going down to the Matapedia tonight to try and get a little rest for 8 or 10 days as after the 1st July I shall have to be on guard here *alone*. We are so harassed to find money to keep things moving that my efficiency for work is not improving and I must make an effort during the next 10 days to get myself into condition. If I could only see my way clear to the end of the year I should feel at ease. . . .[3]

The remainder of the letter, and the more official one which he also addressed to Macdonald that day, give some indication of just how much Stephen had on his mind at this juncture. There were two telegrams too, but these were as rays of light in the gloom, passing on the good news of a request from London for a substantial quantity of Bonds, and of a report from the North West of flourishing crops on the experimental farms west of Moose Jaw; to the latter Stephen added the wry comment: 'This is pretty good for the *Globe's* alkali desert.'

The semi-official letter pointed out that by an oversight $1,004,000 worth of Land Grant Bonds, representing subsidy earned by the Company as at 1 January, which the Bank of Montreal had held as security for advances to the Canadian Pacific, had by order of the Finance Minister been returned to the Bank after these debts had

---

[1] *Globe*, 27 and 30 May 1884.
[2] Macd.P. 'Stephen' 269, Stephen to Macdonald, 26 April 1884.
[3] Both letters and telegrams in loc. cit., 18 June 1884.

been paid but on account of the Government. In other words, these Bonds, which Stephen had hoped to turn into cash with which to pay the August dividend, were tied up as though they had never been earned along with the unearned portion of the land subsidy. There appeared to be some difficulty about cancelling the order to the Bank, but in the personal letter Stephen stressed the need to find some way out—if need be to hand back to the Company instead part of the Bond deposit held as security for the operation of the line. Any temporary adjustment would be welcome which would at least provide the Company with a source of ready money. Stephen thought that if he could cable London that the dividend was provided for it would do more than anything else to stimulate English interest in the stock.

He mentioned another source of anxiety. According to the recent Act, instalments of subsidy and loan could be earned on estimates, instead of on completion of each twenty-mile stretch of road. But still there was an enormous discrepancy between the estimates of the Government engineer and the amount actually spent. At the time of writing Schreiber had gone with Van Horne to see for himself how the Lake Superior section was swallowing up the Company's resources, and Stephen wrote:

. . . I trust the result of Schreiber and Van Horne's visit to Lake Superior will be that we shall be able to get our *full* payment for work done at the end of each month. It is simply impossible for us to go on if we have to finance for the work of construction as well as for all our other wants. Our inability to pay our way from day to day is doing the Company no end of harm. . . .

But the most pressing need of the moment was the provision of an elevator at Port Arthur. This would cost $300,000, but with the country looking forward to one of the best harvests it had known the Canadian Pacific could not afford to economise in this direction if the money could possibly be found. As Stephen said:

. . . If the C.P.R. is not in shape to handle the crop there will be such a howl in the North West that we should all have to leave the country. If I had the money myself I would advance it in a moment for this purpose, but my capacity in that way is exhausted. I mentioned this matter to Pope yesterday and asked him to consider whether the money coming to us from Section B. could not be used for this purpose in the meantime: the completion of Section B. could wait while the Elevator can't. . . .

LONDON AGENTS WAVER: APPROACH TO BARINGS

Ten days later Canadian Pacifics were at 39, and Morton, Rose and Company cabled that it was impossible to sustain the market. Stephen's reply was: 'Let market rip—but let us always show fullest confidence personally in success enterprise.'[1]

Stephen's growing contempt for the Company's London agents was frequently evident in his letters to Macdonald during the summer of 1884. When the payment of the August dividend became an immediate issue he wrote:

We have at last got the bonds and now I must stir round and get them turned into money within the next few days and that will not be so easy a matter in the present state of distrust of everything. I have been in cable communication with Morton Rose & Co. on the subject and they seem to be perfectly *cowed* and unable to help in any way. We must get into connection with a stronger and more courageous firm over there without delay. . . . I wish we had a firm like Barings to represent us in London. Such a connection would solve all our difficulties. . . .[2]

Stephen had reason to fear that not only were their agents unable to help but they were also unwilling to do so. His suspicion that Charles Rose was more inclined to promote the interests of the Grand Trunk was regretfully confirmed by Sir John Rose in a letter to Macdonald:

It is painful to see how much animosity is shewn to Canadian interests— not confined to outsiders, but displayed, I grieve to say, by those of our own household. . . .[3]

The August dividend was met from other sources. By the middle of the month Stephen had made up his mind that the time had come to approach Baring Brothers. Hitherto he had been inclined to think that the Canadian Pacific had nothing but hostility to expect from either Barings or Glyns, on account of their connection with the Grand Trunk. But by 1884, Stephen may have guessed that their connection with the Grand Trunk was as much a source of regret to Baring Brothers as it was to himself; more important, in any event, was the fact that Barings and Glyn, Mills and Company were the joint agents of the Canadian Government. As such, Stephen considered that they could hardly fail to recognize the importance of supporting the national railway.[4]

---

[1] Macd.P. 'Stephen' 269, Stephen to Macdonald, 28 June 1884.
[2] Loc. cit. Stephen to Macdonald, 19 July 1884.
[3] Macd.P. 'Rose' 259.573, Rose to Macdonald, 24 July 1884.
[4] Macd.P. 'Stephen' 269, Stephen to Macdonald, 19 August 1884.

MRS. GEORGE STEPHEN
artist unknown
(In the possession of Mrs. Aubrey Geddes)

It so happened that a near connection of the London Barings, Alexander Baring, was a member of the firm of J. Kennedy Tod, the C.P.R. agents in New York. It was therefore arranged that this young man should go over to London at the end of August for the purpose of persuading Baring Brothers to take up the Canadian Pacific account. Macdonald had at first objected to this move as being unfriendly to the elder Rose, but Stephen convinced him that, judging from recent communications from both Sir John Rose and his late firm, the latter would be only too glad to be free of all connection with the C.P.R.[1]

Alexander Baring therefore set out for London armed with a letter from Macdonald, worded according to a draft by Stephen, indicating that it would be a great satisfaction to him if Baring Brothers could see their way to accepting the proposals about to be made to them.[2] Towards the end of September, Baring cabled that those members of the firm whom he had approached were inclined to entertain his proposal, but as all the partners were not on the spot no definite conclusion could yet be arrived at.[3] A week later, Stephen reported to Macdonald that Alexander Baring's latest communication to his firm in New York was that every transatlantic enterprise was viewed with distrust in London, 'Erie, Wabash, G.T.R. and the like' having 'done their work'.[4] With older roads setting an unprofitable example, what hope was there for the Canadian Pacific?

Shortly afterwards, both Stephen and Macdonald went over to London, but whether or not they had any further contact with Baring Brothers at this time, no immediate help was forthcoming for the Canadian Pacific.

Stephen had been particularly anxious that Barings should assist the Company to pay off the $5 million loan negotiated in New York in November 1883, for which $10 million worth of guaranteed stock had been pledged as security.[5] The loan was due to be repaid in November 1884. When that time came Stephen and some of his close associates, having borrowed the wherewithal on their personal securities, discharged the loan and purchased between them the $10 million of stock.[6]

[1] Macd.P. 'Stephen' 269, Stephen to Macdonald, 22 August 1884.
[2] Macd.L.B. 23.59, Macdonald to Baring Brothers and Company.
[3] Macd.P. 'Stephen' 269, Stephen to Macdonald, 24 September 1884.
[4] Loc. cit. Stephen to Macdonald, 1 October 1884.
[5] Loc. cit. Stephen to Macdonald, 24 September 1884.
[6] Loc cit. Stephen to Macdonald, 29 December 1884.

11

NORTH SHORE RAILWAY: A POLITICAL PAWN

On 8 July 1884, John Henry Pope, Deputy Minister of Railways, wrote thus to the Prime Minister:

I enclose, herewith, Mr. Schreiber's confidential report on the work north of Lake Superior, which will speak for itself. I think there is no doubt, from what he says, that they have not received all the pay they should have received for the work already done; however, we will soon be able to figure that out. Of course, we must keep ourselves safe whatever happens. . . . .

Stephen is going to call upon you, and I think it might be as well were you to talk over the North Shore Railway. His impression is, that it does not pay nor never will, and I am inclined to agree with him, and, for that reason, cannot say very much; but, from a political point of view, I suppose that it is necessary that the Pacific should reach Quebec. Stephen, however, would much prefer making arrangements with the Grand Trunk for traffic over it to Quebec and letting the Grand Trunk run the chance of paying the interest. Apart from political effect, I would say that is correct, and if they were reasonable at all in that part of the world, they would say that that is all they have a right to expect, but reason does not seem to be their strong point, it is expenditure of money they want, whether it pays or not, and that must be considered from a political point of view. . . .[1]

Stephen had a warm regard for this Minister whom he always affectionately referred to as the 'old man', and Pope in these days was a staunch ally. Stephen wrote of him to Macdonald, shortly after the above letter was penned:

. . . It . . . does me no end of good to have a full and free talk with him every now and then. His judgment is so clear and sound and his courage so great that I find him a most valuable counsellor in helping me over what Burns called 'stops and styles'.[2]

Even during the anxious days of January 1884, Stephen found time to write to Macdonald solely on the topic of Pope's health, or rather illhealth, for the 'old man', living a bachelor existence in Ottawa and immersed in work, paid scant heed to it himself. In later days, too, when as Minister of Railways Pope allowed political considerations frankly to outweigh all others, even to the extent of forfeiting Stephen's confidence, the latter found himself torn between disappointment at this betrayal and concern for the manner in which Pope wantonly spent his last remaining resources of strength.

[1] Macd.P. 'Pope' 256.263, Pope to Macdonald, 8 July 1884.
[2] Macd.P. 'Stephen' 269, Stephen to Macdonald, 30 July 1884.

Regarding the North Shore Railway—the portion of the old Quebec Government road from Montreal to Quebec which was held by the Grand Trunk—Stephen had told Macdonald in April that in its present circumstances it was useless for the Canadian Pacific to consider taking it over.[1] The Company had suffered enough discredit through acquiring necessary and profitable lines without inviting criticism by the purchase of a road which could only be run at a loss. The Government was ready, for the sake of gratifying the demands of the Province, to subsidize an additional line to Quebec city, but Stephen would not commit the C.P.R. Company to its construction, preferring to make traffic arrangements with the Trunk on the North Shore.

Provincial claims remained a source of anxiety to both Government and railway company. Manitoba was still at simmering point; in July 1884, Macdonald had actually been apprised of a plot for an armed rising. While not unaware of the possibility of a white or half-breed revolt inciting the Indians to take the warpath, the Prime Minister was not inclined to attach much importance to the agitation of the Farmers' Union, with which he had little patience.[2] Stephen, more sorrowful than angry, wrote to Macdonald:

. . . It is sad to think there should be any ground for supposing any disloyalty existed in that country. The men who lead and form public opinion there are yet all too new to the country to love it but I hope this will soon cease to be the case. When a man has a farm of his own and is prospering he will become conservative and loyal. The idlers and scalawags can never be trusted. . . .[3]

Stephen was trying to persuade the Government to substitute a cash subsidy equivalent to a dollar an acre—a very conservative figure—for the Land Grant of the Manitoba South-Western. Both he and the Minister of the Interior, Sir David Macpherson, were anxious that the line should be completed in time to deal with the next year's crop, but Stephen failed to see how a land subsidy could be converted into working capital. He wrote to Macdonald in September:

You will be glad to hear that wheat is some ten cents a bushel higher in our own side the line than it is in Dakotah. I want to see the Dakotah people flocking back to our side and this will do it if we can keep it up. . . .[4]

[1] Macd.P. 'Stephen' 269, Stephen to Macdonald, 26 April 1884.
[2] Macd.L.B. 22.458, Macdonald to Norquay, 1 July 1884.
[3] Macd.P. 'Stephen' 269, Stephen to Macdonald, 2 August 1884.
[4] Loc. cit. Stephen to Macdonald, 19 September 1884.

He seemed to have forgotten that south of the boundary was a railroad which was paying him handsome dividends, instead of draining away both his fortune and his reputation, as was the Canadian national enterprise.

Towards the end of July 1884, Sir John Macdonald wrote to Sir Charles Tupper complaining of illhealth and saying:

. . . I would leave the Government tomorrow if it were not that I really think George Stephen would throw up the sponge if I did. He was so worried and sleepless that his wife became alarmed and had him sent off to the seaside. . . .[1]

But on the same day he also wrote to Stephen with a proposal which, at that point, must have seemed unduly ambitious. He asked him to consider establishing a Government-subsidized steamship service on the Pacific, connecting with the railroad. A Japanese shipping Company, the Mitsu Bishi, had already made overtures to the Canadian Government regarding such a project, and Macdonald thought that some form of collaboration might be arranged between them and the Canadian Pacific.[2]

Stephen evinced no surprise at the suggestion, but his first reaction was, typically, to offer support to another company which might provide the desired service and with which he might then arrange a 'running agreement'. He was in no haste to monopolize the Pacific, just as later he hesitated to involve the C.P.R. in establishing an Atlantic service of its own. To Macdonald he replied:

. . . The Allans have had the matter under consideration for some time and And: Allan goes over to the other side very soon to discuss the question with his friends in L'pool and Glasgow. . . . I will stir Allan up by giving him a hint that others have their eyes on the subject. . . .[3]

Although reports began to appear in the Press that a Pacific steamship service was to be established in conjunction with the C.P.R. as soon as the road was open from coast to coast, the project was inevitably postponed in face of another financial crisis which was looming up ahead of the Canadian Pacific.

[1] Macd.L.B. 23.35, Macdonald to Tupper, 28 July 1884.
[2] Macd.L.B. 23.29, Macdonald to Stephen, 28 July 1884.
[3] Macd.P. 'Stephen' 269, Stephen to Macdonald, 30 July 1884.

C.P.R.'S ONTARIO AND QUEBEC RAILWAY ISSUE FAILS

Ever since the passing of the C.P.R. Loan Act in March, two things had caused Stephen particular anxiety: the repayment of the loan and the restoration of the Company's credit. He had, therefore, devoted himself to the preparation of a scheme whereby the Company might be cleared of its obligations and placed on an independent and sound financial basis.

When he had consented to the mortgaging of practically all its resources in order to obtain the advance of $22½ million it had not seemed possible that this sum, paid out as construction progressed, after the floating debts of $7½ million had been cleared, should not together with the balance of subsidy cover all expenditure. He no longer looked upon the $35 million worth of unissued stock as likely to help at this stage; nor had he now any great faith in the unearned land grant. Only time would render these securities marketable with any degree of profit. What he contemplated now that construction was so far and safely advanced was the step he had in the early days so firmly avoided—the issue of a Bond on the security of the railway itself. This would involve fresh legislation to free the property from the Government lien. As always, Stephen confided to Macdonald what was in his mind, but sensing alarm on the latter's part at the prospect of bringing in further C.P.R. legislation, he had assured him that there was no immediate need to pursue the matter: 'We'll cross that bridge when we come to it.'[1]

Towards the end of that year both Macdonald and Stephen went over to London, the former on Government business, the latter to arrange for the issue, through Morton, Rose and Company, of Debenture Stock of the Ontario and Quebec Railway, the interest being guaranteed by its lessor, the Canadian Pacific. This was the first time that a security connected with the C.P.R. had been offered directly on the London market. Stephen did not expect a great response, but hoped that applications for $200,000 or $300,000 might be received as a token of public recognition of the merits of this valuable line. Even the Grand Trunk had shown, by its repeated attempts to gain control of the Ontario and Quebec, that this was too sound an enterprise to be happily left in rival hands.

When the Ontario and Quebec featured as a five per cent security on the London market, nevertheless, it was portrayed by the *Standard*

---

[1] Macd .P. 'Stephen' 269, Stephen to Macdonald, 22 July 1884.

as a property with a doubtful financial history which its owners had
only too thankfully unloaded on 'their other undertaking, the
Canadian Pacific'.[1] William Abbott published a new circular,
referred to by the *Railway Times* as 'the old piece, by special desire',
in which he endeavoured to show the worthlessness of the Canadian
Pacific guarantee.[2]

It so happened that a message from Mr. Bliss of New York to
the London firm, telling them not to make the issue at all, arrived
too late, after the stock had been advertised. Stephen was inclined to
think that this had discouraged Morton, Rose and Company—
already unwilling—from actively procuring applications.[3] At all
events, the issue was a complete failure.

'THE EDGE OF A PRECIPICE'

Stephen, meanwhile, had received a disturbing communication
from Montreal. Once more there had been delay in payment of the
Government subsidy, either through Schreiber's latest estimate not
being ready, or because the Finance Minister was not in a position to
meet the demands upon his Department.[4] The margin upon which
the Company worked was at all times so fine that any hitch might
render the possibility of collapse only a week or two distant. Appealing to Macdonald to cable Ottawa to expedite matters, Stephen
added: 'Do not let *anyone* have a *hint* that we are in such straits.'[5]
Six days later he again begged Macdonald to cable John Henry Pope,
suggesting that he might assure the latter that his—i.e. the Canadian
Government's—'financial arrangements here had been completed
for all the money required'.[6]

Stephen was particularly perturbed at this time because both he
and Donald Smith were owing the Bank of Montreal. They had
obtained a loan for C.P.R. purposes on the security of their own
Toronto, Grey and Bruce Railway Bonds, hoping to make a sale of
Land Grant Bonds in Glasgow and thus clear the debt. It had
proved impossible to dispose of the Land Grant Bonds and the
repayment of the loan was already overdue. Stephen wrote to
Macdonald:

---

[1] *Standard*, 4 December 1884.   [2] *Railway Times*, 13 December 1884.
[3] Macd.P. 'Stephen' 269, Stephen to Macdonald, 15 December 1884.
[4] Loc. cit. Stephen to Macdonald, 11 November 1884.
[5] Ibid.   [6] Loc. cit. Stephen to Macdonald, 17 November 1884.

. . . It worries me almost beyond bearing to be in default personally. The real trouble is that the position of the Company is affected by the apprehension that the property will fall into the hands of the Government, which nothing will cure but the substitution of a mortgage bond for the present Government lien. . . .[1]

Early in December Macdonald and Stephen were back in Canada, the former repairing to Ottawa, the latter to Montreal. On 10 December Stephen wrote:

. . . I have been hard at work since we parted trying to gather back into hand all the loose threads of this worrying web on which I have been working so long and I can see that we need not look for any further relief, at least to any considerable amount, from Schreiber's estimate of the value of the work to be done and I must set about at once the work of devising some plan which will at the same time provide for the repayment of the loan from the Government, and also provide the capital required to carry on the business till May 1886 when the road will be in full operation and earning enough to pay its way. I cannot tell you how sorry I am for your sake as much as my own that all this could not have been postponed for another year. But the credit of the Company both at home and abroad is at the moment gone and the ability of Smith and myself to sustain it is about exhausted: the position must be faced or failure must ensue . . . and yet I feel it ought not to be so, considering the position and splendid prospects ahead of the C.P.R. . . .[2]

The next few weeks saw Stephen once more on pilgrimage to Ottawa, where consultations on ways and means were again in progress. Macdonald, dreading the task of bringing up the subject in Council, let alone in Parliament, sought to postpone the evil hour. For Stephen anything would have been preferable to the prolonged suspense. He wrote to Macdonald:

. . . I feel like a man walking on the edge of a precipice, with less "nerve" than is comfortable or even safe in such a case. No trouble about waiting till a convenient time to break the disagreeable subject to all concerned, except that the uncertainty makes me all but unfit to struggle with the difficulties that come up from day to day. . . . On Saturday we got a telegram from Port Arthur that the men had struck, and would go off the work if we did not send them their pay. We sent a man up . . . and hope to gain time till our next estimate comes. . . .[3]

[1] Macd.P. 'Stephen' 269, Stephen to Macdonald, 24 December 1884.
[2] Loc. cit. Stephen to Macdonald, 10 December 1884.
[3] Loc. cit. Stephen to Macdonald, 29 December 1884.

STEPHEN AGAIN SEEKS GOVERNMENT AID

Early in January 1885, Stephen submitted a statement of the Company's affairs to the Minister of Finance, and to Macdonald and to Sir Hector Langevin, Minister of Public Works, he sent a rough outline of his proposal for relief, as a basis for discussion in Council. He planned to cancel the $35 million worth of unissued stock, and to issue instead $30 million worth of 4 per cent Bonds, secured by a first mortgage on the main line of the Canadian Pacific, principal and interest to be guaranteed by the Government. From the proceeds of these Bonds he would allocate $16 million for part payment of the previous year's Government loan, and the remainder would be devoted to meeting expenditure incurred outside of the contract, the balance of subsidy and loan being still sufficient for the bare fulfilment of the contract work. The balance of the loan— $14 million—would be paid in Land Grant Bonds. Stephen pointed out that from January to November 1884, $8 million had been spent on work not specifically contracted for, yet essential to the enterprise.

Stephen's immediate worry, apart from satisfying some of the 'smaller' creditors who could ill afford to wait indefinitely for their money, was to provide for the Company's share of the February dividend.[1] Already the *Standard* had published a report that the Company was no longer to supplement the guaranteed dividend of $1\frac{1}{2}$ per cent half-yearly during construction, and Canadian Pacifics had automatically dropped several points.[2] Stephen was besieged with cables from London which he could not answer until the payment of the usual dividend was assured. In a few days the Company's books had to be closed, preparatory to the declaration of the dividend, and there was no time to lose, if the downward trend of the stock were to be arrested. In submitting his proposals he expressed the hope that the Privy Council might see fit to make an advance on supplies, as provided for in the contract, keeping back the corresponding sum out of the monthly estimates.[3]

In Council, Macdonald met with the expected opposition. The Ministers of Justice, Customs, and Marine and Fisheries—Campbell, Bowell and McLelan—were against any further aid to the Canadian Pacific. McLelan even threatened to resign if any such step were

---

[1] Macd.P. 'Stephen' 269, Stephen to Macdonald, 9 and 17 January 1885.
[2] *Standard*, 16 January 1885.
[3] Macd.P. 'Stephen' 269, Stephen to Macdonald, 17 January 1885.

agreed upon.[1] Sir Leonard Tilley, too, the Minister of Finance, was but lukewarm in his support, and like Macdonald saw no need for haste in dealing with the question.

The wholehearted support of the Government would have meant much to Stephen at this time, weary as he was of the whole concern, yet conscious that as the guardian of other people's property he must persist in the role of suppliant. He had ceased entirely to care about what financial failure might mean to him personally. 'Were it only my own interests that were at stake', he wrote to Macdonald, 'I would at once give up the whole thing. The loss of the money would be a gain to me otherwise.'[2]

A few days before the Council meeting, Macdonald had received a confidential cable from Sir John Rose:

Unscrupulous and apparently organized attacks credit Pacific Company. Object breaking down. See no means counteracting except avowed determination Government stand by as national undertaking. Present condition things doing much injury general credit Government itself.[3]

Six days later, probably in answer to a cable from Macdonald, he cabled again, appealing to the Prime Minister even if legislation were impossible at least to find some way to help the Company to meet its February dividend. The Company's books had closed in London on the 14th without the usual announcement of the amount of the dividend being made, and this was interpreted as implying that the Canadian Pacific was bankrupt.[4] The *Railway Times* announced on the 17th that Canadian Pacific stock had been heavily sold on 'gratuitously unfounded rumours' of the Company's inability to pay its share of the dividend. It seemed that the rumours were to prove only too well founded. An offer by Macdonald to advance the amount of the supplementary dividend if legislation could thereby be postponed until 1886 was rejected by Stephen as impossible.[5]

The lack of vision on the part of Canada's Ministers at this time sorely tried Stephen's patience, at no time very strong. 'What alarms me', he told Macdonald, 'is the apprehension that the Patient will die while the Doctors are deliberating on the remedy to be

[1] Tupper Papers 310, Macdonald to Tupper, 24 January 1885.
[2] Macd.P. 'Stephen' 269, Stephen to Macdonald, 24 January, 1885.
[3] Macd.P. 'Rose' 259.594, Rose to Macdonald, 10 January 1885.
[4] Loc. cit. 259.598, Rose to Macdonald, 16 January 1885.
[5] Macd.L.B. 23.101, Macdonald to Stephen, 20 January 1885 and Macd.P. 'Stephen' 269, Stephen to Macdonald, same date.

applied.'[1] He was particularly impatient at the attitude of the Minister of Finance, of whom he wrote to Macdonald:

. . . Between ourselves, he does not even now understand in the least the legislation of last session or the objects it had in view. If the settlement of this business is to be left to him to arrange it will never be done. He simply cannot do it, and feels quite cheery at the prospect of the Government getting a cheap property.

I won't weary you with all he said. I kept my temper because of the interests involved. It is clear as noonday Sir John, unless you, yourself, *say* what is to be done nothing but disaster will result. The question is too big for some of our friends, and nothing but your own authority and influence will carry anything that will accomplish the object. . . .[2]

A week later he wrote in the same vein, having just telegraphed New York to advertise the closing of the books there, and being apprehensive of the consequences of not having announced a supplementary dividend:

. . . I endeavoured, but I fear vainly, to impress Sir Leonard with the importance of this matter to the Company, especially in view of its issuing a bond. He seemed, notwithstanding all my efforts to explain the matter, to think there was still plenty of time and would not listen to any statement to the contrary from me, and I could do nothing but hold my tongue. . . . The C.P.R. after all the battering it has had will only gain public confidence now as it begins to show actual results—earnings. That it would soon do if it only once had a fair start. Tilley told me the other day that he had no faith in its ability to pay its way for years to come. . . . I could not help saying that if he held such opinions I could not blame others for their adverse opinions.

In the face of what we have shown the road to do since August last it is rather hard to bear this coming from such a source. I know quite well that he has no knowledge of the business and that his opinion is the outcome of *timidity* more than anything else, still all the same it makes my work an uphill one. . . .[3]

'OLD TOMORROW'

Stephen was pinning his faith to Macdonald, but it seemed that Macdonald was either not fully convinced of the urgency of the situation, or else preferred that the Canadian Pacific rather than the Conservative Government should be sacrificed. Writing to Tupper

---

[1] Macd.P. 'Stephen' 269, Stephen to Macdonald, 17 January 1885.
[2] Ibid.   [3] Loc. cit. Stephen to Macdonald, 24 January 1885.

of the Privy Council's reactions to Stephen's proposals, he quoted a former editor of the *Montreal Gazette*, Tom White, as having told him that they could not be carried. The Press, he added, were 'already alarmed' and 'beginning to sound the tocsin'. He continued:

I myself fear that *The Week* is right when it says that however docile our majority we dare not ask for another loan. The thing is hung up until next week. How it will end I don't know. . . .[1]

The Week represented the opinions of Goldwin Smith, who, although a friend of both Macdonald and Stephen, was immovably convinced that the transcontinental railroad was a concept contrary to the natural law that decreed the North American continent to be one and indivisible. Why those opinions should have meant so much to the leader whose dearest wish it had been to see the railroad built is inexplicable except in terms bitterly critical of a great statesman. For six months the question of relief for the Canadian Pacific hung fire while the Prime Minister known as 'Old Tomorrow' devoted himself to the passing of a measure of peculiarly Conservative interest concerning the franchise.

On 26 January Stephen wrote Macdonald enclosing a telegram from the C.P.R.'s New York agents stating that the Governing Committee of the Stock Exchange threatened to suspend the official quotation of the stock unless the exact amount of the dividend to be paid were published. Stephen wrote:

In the 'fix' in which the enclosed message from our agents in New York placed me this p.m. I had no alternative but to act at once, and feeling that in the event of disaster happening it would make very little difference to me personally if $650,000 more were added to my commitments on behalf of the Company,—in either case it would be ruin—Smith and I decided to borrow the money for the Company and to declare the usual dividend. Default now would have weakened us in selling bonds. . . . I have taken a big risk in this case but hope it is the last time I shall have to do such a thankless service for the Company. . . .[2]

A week or two later, Stephen and Smith endorsed a five months' note for $1 million—the Bank of Montreal advancing the money— to provide the Company with current funds.[3] Outside the Company, only Macdonald was told of this. Stephen had sensed, while moving about among the Members at Ottawa, that it was thought in some

---

[1] Tupper Papers 310, Macdonald to Tupper, 24 January 1885.
[2] Macd.P. 'Stephen' 269, Stephen to Macdonald, 26 January 1885.
[3] Loc. cit., Stephen to Macdonald, 9 February 1885.

quarters that he and his associates had not done all they might to save the C.P.R., and he was anxious that Macdonald should be under no misapprehension on that score. He told him:

I venture to say that there is not a business man in all Canada, knowing the facts, but would say we were a couple of fools for our pains. But as long as we are able to save and protect the Company against its enemies who seem bent on its destruction, we shall not grudge any risks or loss that may occur. Personal interests have become quite a secondary affair with either of us. . . .

Not all his old associates were as loyal as Donald Smith. In a postscript to his letter to Macdonald of 24 January, Stephen wrote:

You will be *sorry* to hear that McIntyre's firm has sent us another missive to say if we do not pay the 5 or 6 thou. dollars we owe them forthwith they will lead the claim to their lawyers for suit. This is 'bad form' but do not take any notice of it.

Dutifully, the *Globe* continued sounding the tocsin. Why, it asked on 5 March, did the members of the Company not use some of their own money to complete their contract, instead of running to the Government for aid? (On the previous day, Macdonald had denied in the House that any application for aid had been received.) The C.P.R. Company, the *Globe* pursued, had received from the Government in the first place more money than was required to complete the whole line from Callander to the Pacific; they had made enormous profits out of the construction company; they had been drawing handsome dividends. 'If Mr. Stephen and his associates have the amount of faith in the country and the Pacific Railway that they affect to have, let them invest the profits on their stock transactions in paying off the present floating debt of the Company. . . .'

In 1883 Stephen had taken up residence in the last and most splendid of his Montreal homes. The mansion on Drummond Street had taken three years to build, materials, furnishings and craftmanship having been imported from distant lands: oak from England, mahogany from Cuba, marble and onyx from Italy, satin-wood from the Orient, stained glass from Austria and skilled wood-carvers from Scotland. It was typical of the owner that it was situated not in lofty grandeur on the Mountain, surveying the hub of the Dominion from afar, but in the very heart of the busy thoroughfares, unobtrusive but inexpressibly solid. The drawing shows it as it was when first built.

From time to time references had been made by the enemies of the Canadian Pacific to the money that must have been spent on this house. During the debate in Parliament on the C.P.R. Loan Bill in 1884 such remarks were heard as 'Let them build the railway before they build palaces'.

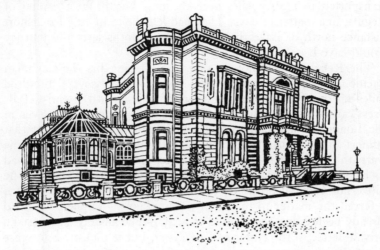

In 1885, when Treasury officers, after assessing all Stephen's cash assets and securities, went to Drummond Street to make an inventory, someone who was present afterwards recalled the occasion thus:

. . . They not only counted all his cash and securities, but went to his home and valued, with expert assistance, his paintings, his statuary, his furniture, also his household linen, his china and silverware. . . . The old gentleman looked over the long list carefully, and without a flicker of the eyelid, signed it all away.[1]

The 'old gentleman' was then in his fifty-sixth year, but he may well have looked twenty years older as he pledged, as security for his debts, the treasures of a lifetime. Not only his material wealth, but the edifice of his career, seemed ready to crumble away.

THE SECOND RIEL REBELLION

In the spring of 1885, the centre of interest in Canada moved westward. And just as in 1869–70 the need for direct communication

---

[1] Dalton C. Coleman, *Lord Mount Stephen*. Address to the Newcomen Society, New York, 11 July 1945. Princeton University Press.

with the newly-acquired Hudson's Bay lands had been brought into prominence, so the Second Riel Rebellion showed the wisdom of establishing such communication. In 1870 it had taken Colonel Wolseley's force three months to travel from Montreal to Fort Garry; in 1885 a force of between two and three thousand militia-men was transported to Qu'Appelle, near the new North West capital of Regina, in a matter of days. They had left the train only for a short distance north of Lake Superior; a few months later the journey would have been unbroken.

The Rebellion was not an unmixed blessing for the Canadian Pacific. Although the actual incidents took place several hundred miles north of the railway, exaggerated reports in the anti-C.P.R. Press caused a serious falling-off in that year's immigration. Even in the London *Times* there were alarming bulletins to the effect that 'almost all the Indian tribes in the North West Territory are on the warpath',[1] and that all the available forces in Eastern Canada had had to be sent to the seat of trouble.[2] At Stephen's instigation, the Governor-General protested to the Colonial Office, which in turn referred the matter to the High Commissioner. Tupper, who had already been doing all he could to allay public anxiety, addressed a private letter to the editor of *The Times*, but it took time to erase from the public mind such phrases as 'outrages upon frontier settlers' or 'long and bloody Indian war in prospect',[3] or the *Standard's* headline of 25 April 'Massacre in Canada'.

The *Toronto Globe*, of course, had not neglected the opportunity to attack both the Canadian Pacific and the Dominion Government. It declared on 16 May:

If the C.P.R. had not been built with such reckless haste, even Sir John Macdonald's misgovernment might not have caused a rebellion. . . . Either the whole white population must be withdrawn from these remote positions, or the number of troops employed for their protection must be greatly increased. Henceforward, every train of carts laden with supplies must be guarded by a force sufficient to repel any attack the Indians may make, and in the journeys across the prairies the teamsters, their convoy and their animals will consume the greater part of the supplies they are employed to transport. . . .

'If the Nor West succeeds', Stephen was wont to say, 'the C.P.R. cannot fail.' But life on the prairies, clouded by a menace such as the *Globe* visualized, would have been well-nigh impossible. Fortunately

[1] *The Times*, 1 April 1885. [2] *The Times*, 3 April 1885. [3] *The Times*, 9 May 1885.

these prophecies proved false; although a few Indians joined the half-breeds in their revolt they were a negligible minority.

GOVERNMENT REFUSES AID TO C.P.R.

The services rendered by the Canadian Pacific during the Second Riel Rebellion did not perceptibly accelerate the Government relief negotiations, but the Company's case was undoubtedly strengthened. The progress made can equally be attributed to the perseverance of George Stephen, backed by Sir Charles Tupper and Sir John Rose, in keeping the subject constantly before the Prime Minister. The High Commissioner was no longer a member of the Government, but he had offered to come back to Parliament as a private Member to support the cause of the railway.

It was no longer possible to conceal the fact that the railway was in financial straits, and delay—even politically—served no useful purpose, for the subject was brought up in the House as soon as the session began. Members of the Opposition moved for returns demanding the most minute information on all aspects of the Company's activities and policy, for all the world, as Stephen said, as if the railway was an enemy to be hunted down.[1] What was always at the back of the President's mind was the fear that by the time help came the Company would either be bankrupt or would have reached such a state of discredit that a Bond issue would be a complete failure.

On 18 March the Company made an official application to the Department of Railways and Canals, Stephen at the same time supplying Macdonald with memoranda giving answers to every conceivable objection that could be raised.[2] John Henry Pope, now Minister of Railways, and Collingwood Schreiber, the Government chief engineer, had been similarly briefed. Macdonald wrote in pessimistic vein to Tupper:

I don't know how Council or Parliament will take it. Stephen asks for a loan for a year of five millions—that Tilley can't face—that we should take 15 millions of Railway Bonds 5 per cents. at par and $7\frac{1}{2}$ millions of acres at $2 per acre. Council will not agree to give more than $1 an acre I think. . . . The Quebec M.P.s have the line to Quebec up again. The Maritimes are clamorous for the Short Line and we have blackmailing all round. How it will end God knows—but I wish I were well out of it. . . .[3]

[1] Macd.P. 'Stephen' 269, Stephen to Macdonald, 12 February 1885.
[2] Loc. cit. Stephen to Macdonald, 14 March 1885.
[3] Tupper Papers 319, Macdonald to Tupper, 17 March 1885.

Talking to Members at Ottawa in February, Stephen had found that some of them favoured the idea of the Government taking back land instead of securing the remainder of the 1884 loan with Land Grant Bonds, as earlier suggested. But Stephen had remonstrated against such a low price as $2 an acre; they had been selling land at an average of over $3 an acre. He had expected that the Government would jump at the chance of resuming the lands at the low figure of $1 or even $1¼, and even this would at least relieve the Company at once of part of its crushing burden of interest.[1]

The formal application was rejected. In answer to a question in the House by Blake, Macdonald stated that a second application might be made. But he succeeded in convincing Stephen that no further assistance would be forthcoming.

Stephen prepared to return to Montreal where, it seemed, his task would be merely to wind up the affairs of the Company. From the House of Commons he wrote a final note to Macdonald, asking him to let him have the Government's decision in writing, 'so as to relieve me personally from the possible charge of having acted with undue haste'. There was a faint chance that that day's Council meeting might alter the position; Stephen had little hope as he wrote:

The result of our conversation this morning has satisfied me that the Government will not be able to see its way to extend to the C.P.R. Company the aid it requires. . . .

I need not repeat how sorry I am that this should be the result of all our efforts to give Canada a railway to the Pacific Ocean. But I am supported by the conviction that I have done all that could be done to obtain it.[2]

FRIENDLY INTERVENTION; REVISED PROPOSALS ACCEPTED

It was at this point that certain members of the Cabinet, realizing what was happening, began to take a firm line. According to Beckles Willson, Donald Smith's biographer, it was Sir Frank Smith who persuaded Stephen to remain in Ottawa while another appeal was made to the Prime Minister. This is also the occasion on which, it is said, John Henry Pope bluntly told Macdonald that if the Canadian Pacific went down, the Government would fall the day after.

As a result of this friendly intervention Stephen took fresh heart, and the following day presented a revised draft proposal to

---

[1] Macd.P. 'Stephen' 269, Stephen to Macdonald, 6 February 1885.
[2] Loc. cit. Stephen to Macdonald, 26 March 1885.

Macdonald.[1] It was some time before agreement was reached as to terms, Stephen protesting to the last against the Government's determination to be repaid entirely in cash, accepting in the meantime the security of the proposed First Mortgage Bonds, and retaining a lien on the Company's unsold lands instead of receiving these back in part payment. Stephen realized that he was in no position to refuse aid on any terms that promised a measure of success; he did resolutely reiterate that he did not propose to attempt the impossible. Macdonald was adamant regarding the North Shore line; the Canadian Pacific had to take it over, even if it meant running it at a loss. The C.P.R. must reach Quebec city. To avoid further delay this was agreed to. It would take some weeks for the Bill to go through Parliament and there was no time to spare for trying to rid the affair of its political complexities.

It had seemed to Stephen in January that the Company could not possibly survive without early assistance. By putting off creditors with optimistic promises and, as has been seen, by further personal contributions, the life of the Canadian Pacific had somehow been prolonged from day to day. Nearly three weeks had passed since Stephen's fresh proposal had been submitted when he wrote to Macdonald:

It is impossible for me to continue this struggle for existence any longer. The delay in dealing with the C.P.R. matter, whatever may be the necessity for it, has finished me, and rendered me utterly unfit for further work, and if it is continued must eventuate in the destruction of the Company.

I must go home this evening and if anyone should be required here on behalf of the C.P.R. Company Mr. Van Horne will probably come up. . . .

I cannot refrain from saying here that I feel most keenly the position I am placed in. Every day now, obligations are maturing that three months ago were postponed till now on the faith that by this time we should be in a position to meet them, and our ability to pay these obligations, or to postpone them again, is gone. I do not wish to say anything here about the sacrifices I have made for the C.P.R., to make it a success, or to take up your time with complaints of any kind further than to say I have not met with the confidence and support from the Government which I felt I had a fair right to expect, and I will only add one more remark about the North Shore line. Before the outbreak in the Nor West and on the assumption that the coming season's crop would be a fair one, I estimated the net earnings of the Company for the present year (1885) at $2,400,000.

[1] Macd.P. 'Stephen' 269, Stephen to Macdonald, 27 March 1885.

The events that are taking place in the Nor West *may* reduce that amount by $300,000 or even $400,000. The fixed charges of the Company, now that the idea of taking lands as payment of $15,000,000 of the Government debt has been abandoned, will be $3,141,400 as per statement enclosed, or say $1,000,000 more than the estimated earnings. You can see what position the Company is in to undertake the additional liability involved in taking over the North Shore line at a rental far beyond its net earnings. . . . By your plan, as now proposed, the Company gets the benefit of a reduction of interest of $225,000 per annum and that is all. If the advantage of this reduction of interest for a few years is to be absorbed to a great extent by a forced assumption of the North Shore line on a basis involving an annual loss of over $100,000 the position of the Company will not be very much improved. . . . I now leave the matter in your hands and in the condition I am in must ask to be freed from all further responsibility in connection with the negociations with the Government.[1]

It really seemed now as if disaster were imminent. The following day Stephen, from Montreal, relayed to John Henry Pope a telegram he had just received from Van Horne:

Have no means paying wages. Pay car can't be sent out, and unless we get immediate relief we must stop. Please inform Premier and Finance Minister. Do not be surprised or blame me if an immediate and most serious catastrophe happens.[2]

Gangs of workmen on the Mountain Section who had received no pay for some time decided that they had waited long enough. They downed tools. Marching eastwards, they were joined by other groups until they had a force strong enough to compel even those who would willingly have stuck to their posts to stop work.

Macdonald, roused into action, asked the Bank of Montreal, at the request of the Company, to advance $500,000, to be repaid by the Government out of the sum to be voted in the coming Bill which the Prime Minister stated would be introduced 'at an early date this session'.[3] The Bank refused.[4] Eventually the advance was made, and the pay-car sent out. The mounted police had succeeded in reducing the strikers to order, but the latter refused to go back to work until the arrears were actually paid up.

On 30 April Stephen wrote to Sir Charles Tupper that the subject

[1] Macd.P. 'Stephen' 269, Stephen to Macdonald, 15 April 1885.
[2] Loc. cit. Stephen to Pope, 16 April 1885.
[3] Macd.P. 'Stephen' 268, Macdonald to C. F. Smithers, 24 April 1885.
[4] Loc. cit. Drinkwater to Macdonald, 27 April 1885.

of C.P.R. relief was to come up in caucus that day. He could not tell when it would be brought before Parliament:

Had you been here all our affairs would have been disposed of two months ago. . . . The delay has done us irreparable harm and so far as I can see nothing has been gained by it, even politically. . . . I have been almost living at Ottawa since 10th Decr. last trying but apparently in vain to impress Sir John with the extreme urgency of our case. I know and believe he has the best possible intentions but it seems as if it were impossible for him to act until the last moment arrives. . . . Sometimes it *looks* now as if the collapse of the Company were a matter of no consequence to the Government and I feel disappointed in consequence because I think I had a right to a more considerate treatment. Meantime I may tell you that my confidence in the success of the C.P.R. is greater today than it has ever been; every day seems to demonstrate its thorough soundness commercially. . . .[1]

John Henry Pope introduced the resolutions in the House on 16 June. Although Blake and several of his supporters took the opportunity to air their well-worn arguments the opposition seemed, by comparison with the debate of 1884, half-hearted. The Bill was passed in the Commons on 11 July, and on 20 July received the Royal Assent.

Three days later, Stephen cabled from London that the entire primary issue of $15 million of First Mortgage Bonds had been taken. The price was 95, and the business had been done by Baring Brothers and Company.[2]

BARINGS MAKE CRUCIAL BOND ISSUE

Once the C.P.R. Bill was fairly before the House, Sir Charles Tupper, ably assisted by Thomas Skinner and armed by Stephen with a wealth of documentary material which might enable the members of the firm to 'mature their views' regarding the soundness of the enterprise,[3] approached Baring Brothers. The market was in an unusually favourable state, and Stephen wrote to impress upon Macdonald the necessity of hastening the Bill on its way before the opportunity should be lost. If Barings were to handle the issue, it had to be made before 1 August.[4] On 6 July, Stephen told Macdonald that it was imperative he should sail for England on the 11th:

---

[1] Tupper Papers 323, Stephen to Tupper, 30 April 1885.
[2] Macd.P. 'Stephen' 269, Stephen to Macdonald, 23 July 1885.
[3] Tupper Papers 332, Skinner to Tupper, 3 July 1885.
[4] Macd.P. 'Stephen' 269, Stephen to Macdonald, 26 June 1885.

. . . Matters have gone so far with Barings that, unless some change comes over them, in the meantime, there is nothing to settle but the terms and that cannot be done without my presence there. . . . It is a terrible business for me to get away now, but I must let everything else go, and attend to this bond sale. . . .[1]

Stephen had so far recovered in spirits as to add a dry quip regarding the President of the Grand Trunk: 'Tyler goes over with me in the "Servia". I fancy he is a *wiser* man since he saw the N(or) W(est).'

On 20 July Stephen arrived at Liverpool. He was met by Thomas Skinner who came armed with the prospectus for the Bond issue. The President's approval was telegraphed to London, and by the time he arrived in that city the issue was out.[2] Stephen wrote to Macdonald:

Between ourselves, I doubt if much over half have been actually sold to *investors*. There was a dead set made against the bonds by G.T.R. folks, and there is not another House in London could have done what Barings have accomplished. . . .

This suspicion was shared by various enemies of the Canadian Pacific, and comments to that effect appeared in the *Financial News* of 30 July. Stephen, afraid that Barings might regret their action, was at great pains to nourish, as he put it, their confidence in the property. He and Donald Smith between them bought a substantial quantity of the Bonds.

By October it was clear that they had been fortunate in getting the issue out when they did; by that time the state of the market had so deteriorated that Stephen told Macdonald he had never seen things worse. Barings were, however, getting rid of the C.P.R. Bonds slowly but steadily, and Stephen was hopeful that by the following year he would find a ready market for the remaining $20 million worth, then in the hands of the Government, and thus be able to clear the debt which was not due until 1891.[3] By the end of October the Bonds were selling at 98 to 99, the ordinary shares had soared from $37\frac{1}{2}$ to $52\frac{1}{2}$, and Stephen cabled that he proposed paying off the $5 million temporary loan.[4] On 5 November he cabled in cypher: 'Railway now out of danger.'[5]

[1] Macd.P. 'Stephen' 269, Stephen to Macdonald, 6 July 1885.
[2] Loc. cit. Stephen to Macdonald, 23 July 1885.
[3] Loc. cit. Stephen to Macdonald, 1 August and 3 October 1885.
[4] Loc. cit. Stephen to Macdonald, 28 October 1885.
[5] Loc. cit. Stephen to Macdonald, 5 November 1885.

THE LAST SPIKE

Two days later, and five years ahead of schedule, Donald Smith drove the last spike of the main line at the point in British Columbia afterwards named Craigellachie. It had been planned that the Governor-General should perform this ceremony during a visit to the North West that autumn, but bad weather had delayed the joining of the tracks. But it was not inappropriate that the honour should fall to one who, in Stephen's words, had 'stood so courageously by the Company in its time of trouble'.[1]

Recognition of the Canadian Pacific as something more than just another new railway came two months later when Stephen received the following cable from the Colonial Office:

Much pleasure congratulate you Baronetcy conferred you by Queen in recognition great public services Canadian Pacific Railway.[2]

Writing to ask Sir John Macdonald whether there was a precedent for granting such an honour for services rendered in the 'colonies', the Governor-General, Lord Lansdowne, had said:

. . . Even, however, if this were not so, there is a disposition, and a natural one, to regard the C.P.R. as an Imperial work, and, if the matter be looked at in this light, the distinction given might without impropriety be different from that usually given for purely Colonial services.[3]

On the suggestion of Harry Northcote, Stephen was designated Baronet 'of Montreal, Canada'. Sir Robert Herbert wrote to Northcote:

. . . Although Mr. Stephen never asked for anything of the kind, and, I imagine, did not covet it, the honour has been conspicuously deserved and will give great pleasure to his many friends. . . .[4]

Shortly afterwards, Donald Smith's part in the creation of the national highway was marked by the award of K.C.M.G.

DEBT TO GOVERNMENT REPAID

For Stephen it was not a case of resting on his laurels. The completion of the contract did not end either his anxieties over the finances of the C.P.R. or the opposition of the railway's rivals. As

---

[1] Macd.P. 'Stephen' 267, Stephen to Macdonald, 10 February 1884.
[2] CO 448/2 (Honours/Canada 21889) 15 January 1886.
[3] Pope, *Correspondence of Sir John Macdonald*, p. 267.
[4] Macd.P. 'Stephen' 270, Herbert to Northcote, 14 January 1886, enclosed in Stephen to Macdonald, 28 January 1886.

Stephen observed in a cable to Macdonald after the ceremony at Craigellachie, the success of the enterprise commercially had still to be established. Thus, when the Company's enemies saw that the construction of the line was an accomplished fact, they renewed their assertions that it could not be profitably operated. The Grand Trunk, after thirty years, was only beginning to pay dividends. At the last meeting of the shareholders of that railway, in April 1885, Sir Henry Tyler had prophesied that sooner or later the C.P.R. would have to be taken over by the Government, and had added condescendingly that in that event the Grand Trunk would be glad to help the Government in any way to make as little loss as possible in working the road.[1]

Although the hopes of the Grand Trunk President were not fulfilled, the next two or three years were, in fact, critical ones for the Canadian Pacific, and unrewarding for the shareholders. The latter, it is true, drew their guaranteed annual dividend of 3 per cent, but that, as Stephen said, was merely receiving back their own money. There was no profit. Before the Company could begin to pay interest on its own capital the debt to the Government had to be discharged. There was no question of following the example of the Grand Trunk and allowing time to obliterate its obligations.

Repayment was due in 1891, but Stephen was determined that the $30 million due the Government should be paid as soon as possible. The credit of the Company demanded an early 'divorce' from all political connection. Moreover, payment of the loan would release the Company's lands, which the Government held as security.

Stephen's plan now was to let the Government retain 6 million acres of the land grant—equivalent to over $9 million—and to pay $20 million in cash, to be realized from the sale of the Mortgage Bonds deposited with the Government, and which he hoped Barings would be able to dispose of at par value. At that time the Dominion Government was itself in need of money, and it had the choice of issuing a new loan or settling with the C.P.R.

At first Stephen's plan was not popular; as the bulk of the lands had never actually been handed over to the Company, the theoretical resumption of 6 million acres in place of cash was not regarded with favour. The Government still owed the Company the residue of its subsidy and loan, but the railway would need all of this

[1] *Railway Times*, 2 May 1885.

money for equipment and extensions. In a letter to Macdonald, Stephen outlined the Company's immediate programme, which included construction in Quebec and the Maritimes, Ontario and Manitoba, but still took no account of possible expenditure on steamships on the Atlantic and Pacific, which Stephen foresaw that the Company would eventually be compelled to provide. In face of such commitments, Stephen was reluctantly obliged to suggest the modification of his agreement:

First let me say that nothing would give me greater pleasure than to make a full and final settlement with the Government in accordance with the literal terms of the original contract. It would be an inexpressible satisfaction and pleasure to me to pay back to the Government in cash every dollar of the money loaned to the Company, were such a thing within the range of possibility. I would do anything to accomplish it. It is anything but an agreeable task for me to be begging for the Government's assistance and for modifications of the terms of a contract, which I am bound to say was entered into with open eyes, though, as it has turned out, with a very inadequate knowledge of the difficulties moral and physical that had to be faced and overcome. Personally, there is almost no sacrifice I would not cheerfully make to shirk this disagreeable duty.

My main motive in urging a final settlement now, originates in the necessity in which the Company is placed, of having immediately to make arrangements by which the additional capital it requires may be provided as it is wanted. . . .[1]

Stephen felt justified in his demands. The Government had its long-projected national line ready for operation several years ahead of schedule, and, in addition, the much-desired branch lines could soon be provided, were the Company only able to use its resources freely. Even politically, Stephen's proposal had much to commend it, and eventually the Government agreed.

Barings were, at first, unwilling to issue more Canadian Pacific bonds,[2] but this did not dismay Stephen who, with recovered optimism, was confident that if necessary the C.P.R. could raise the $20 million in Canada. Then came an offer from another London firm to sell the Mortgage Bonds at 105, less commission. This quite unsolicited proposal worried Stephen much more than it pleased him, for he feared that Barings might think that it was a device for bringing them to terms, 'which is not my way of doing business',[3]

[1] Macd.P. 'Stephen' 270, Stephen to Macdonald, 22 February 1886.
[2] Tupper Papers 358, Tupper to Macdonald, 25 February 1886.
[3] Macd.P. 'Stephen' 270, Stephen to Macdonald, 6 March 1886.

It was Thomas Skinner who came to the rescue and, at Stephen's request, explained the whole position to Barings. As a result, Barings themselves made the new issue.[1]

The settlement with the Government was formally agreed to by an Order in Council and subsequently approved by Parliament, and the loan, which such confident prophets as the *Globe* had declared would never find its way back to the Dominion Treasury, was by 1 July 1886, completely cleared. It was, as McLelan, then Finance Minister, wrote to Sir Charles Tupper, 'a great triumph' for the Conservative Party.[2]

[1] Loc. cit. Stephen to Macdonald, 11 March 1886, and Macdonald to Tupper, 12 March 1886.

[2] Tupper Papers 369, McLelan to Tupper, 23 April 1886.

VII

Spanning the world

OLD FRIENDS AND FAMILIAR PLACES

ON 28 June 1886, the first through train from Montreal to the Pacific coast left Dalhousie Square station in a blaze of publicity. Stephen was not among the crowd on this occasion. At Causapscal he was entertaining for the first time his old schoolfellow, Donald Stewart.

Whereas George Stephen had gone westward to seek his fortune, the boy who used to sweep out the Mortlach schoolroom had turned to the east. Entering the Indian Army at the age of sixteen, after a brief sojourn at the University of Aberdeen where he had surprised everyone—himself included—by taking the class prize in Greek, he had become, by 1881, Commander-in-Chief, India, a General and a Baronet.[1] He it was who, during service in Afghanistan in 1879, despatched General Roberts on his afterwards celebrated march from Cabul to Candahar with the words: 'Off you go, Bobs, now is your chance so make the best of it.'[2] The fact is generally overlooked that Stewart himself had previously accomplished the march from Candahar to Cabul, under infinitely less favourable circumstances, and that Roberts had the benefit of all the intelligence his commander could give him regarding the state of the country and the nature of the road.

Stephen and Stewart had foregathered in London, after an interval in their acquaintance of some forty years. It is said that when Stewart called at the Stephens' substantial mansion, 25 St. James's Place, overlooking the Green Park (it was destroyed during the second World War) he could not help exclaiming: 'And is all this really yours, George?' On 29 May 1886, accompanied by Sir John McNeill,[3] nephew of the diplomat of the same name, the General

---

[1] G. R. Elsmie, *Field Marshal Sir Donald Stewart*, London, 1903.
[2] Robert Reford, Montreal, to J. G. Drummond, Aberdeen, 18 May 1950.
[3] See *Dictionary of National Biography*, 2nd Supplement, vol. 2, *Sir John Carstairs McNeill, 1831-1904*, Major-General, Indian Army.

sailed for Canada. Wrote the former, with more enthusiasm than regard for priorities:

Sir Donald had never killed a salmon or visited Canada, and he was like a boy in his delight at the idea of the trip.[1]

He added: 'I shall never forget seeing Sir Donald's excitement when fast to his first salmon.' When Stewart had gone fishing with John Macpherson, the schoolmaster, his activities were evidently limited to 'carrying the spoil'.

Nor was salmon-fishing the only excitement in store. Early in July Stephen despatched his guests in a private car by C.P.R. to the Pacific. On the way they were held up when a forest fire destroyed one of the wooden trestle bridges, but although officials offered to send them on by train from the other side Sir Donald was so much interested in the rapid repair operations that were going on that he insisted on remaining until the bridge was rebuilt. Three days later they were on their way again, over the new structure. The impression made on Stewart's mind by every aspect of the transcontinental enterprise was shortly to be turned to the service of the Company when, as a member of the India Council, and an authority on military matters, he was asked for his opinion of the value of Stephen's next project, the Pacific steamship service.[2] Stewart was no casual sight-seer; when being shown the new C.P.R. bridge a-building over the St. Lawrence at Lachine he was not satisfied until he had crossed it, climbing over the bare trestle-work.[3]

Stephen was to see quite a lot of his old friend in the years that followed. The summer of 1888 saw Stewart and McNeill back at the salmon-fishing, this time at Grande Metis, and Stephen had planned to spend the winter of 1890 with them in India. This trip had to be abandoned, however, as they found that Stewart's membership of the India Council precluded his spending more than sixty days out of England, and without him Stephen did not care to go.

Stephen and Stewart did make one journey together. September 1888 found them both on pilgrimage to the scene of their school-days. Dufftown was *en fête* for the occasion. The visitors were met by the local brass band playing 'Hielan' Laddie', and the whole town had turned out to welcome them, for the names of both had become legends in Mortlach. Barriers of time and rank vanished in the genuine pleasure both felt at being 'back home'. At a banquet given

---

[1] Elsmie, op. cit.   [2] CO 807/54, Confidential Print, North American 124.
[3] Oral evidence, Colonel George Stephen Cantlie, Montreal.

in their honour John Symon II, then Provost of Dufftown, proposed the health first of Sir George Stephen, who said in his reply:

. . . In all my varied career I have kept the memory of Dufftown and its people green in my mind. . . . It will cheer my father and mother in Montreal to know that you have honoured us so much. . . .

Sir Donald, in his turn, replied with equal simplicity:

. . . Whatever I may have done in the Service I attribute in a great degree to the training I received in the little school down in the village there, where I was educated by a gentleman whose memory I love and respect. Many of you will remember him. He was the most highly educated and cultivated gentleman I ever met—a charming companion, and manly in every respect. I refer to the late John Macpherson. . . .[1]

Stephen's parents, now aged eighty-seven and eighty-four, were then living in Dorchester Street West, Montreal. William Stephen still occupied himself in the making of violins, a craft learnt in his native district which was also the home of the famous Scottish violinist and composer, William Marshall. At their special wish, Stephen paid a visit to Glenrinnes, the new ecclesiastical parish formed in 1865 in which stood Croftglass, the family home. There an address of welcome was read by the minister, the Rev. Charles Bruce, whose son Randolph, then an engineer with the Canadian Pacific, was to become Lieutenant-Governor of British Columbia. On this occasion Stephen spoke more particularly to the children in his audience. While assuring them that the only road to success was within reach of everybody—all that was needed was an earnest purpose and determination to do well whatever they undertook—he added:

Of course it cannot fall to everyone to be President of the C.P.R., but enterprises of that kind have their drawbacks as well as their advantages. The sun does not always shine upon those who seem to be in a prominent position.

Although gratified by the public expressions of goodwill by which they were met, both Stephen and Stewart probably preferred to move about among old friends and familiar places in a more unobtrusive manner. And although Stephen's substantial benefactions to the districts of Mortlach and Glenrinnes, then and later, were only what might have been expected, it was by his less orthodox acts of generosity that he proved his true interest in his old home. A

[1] *Banffshire Journal*, 11 September 1888.

cottage by the Coulalt was badly in need of repair; a sum of money
was immediately forthcoming for the purpose. To Provost Symon he
said: 'Tell me the folks who remember my mother, and if they are
requiring anything. . . .' Stewart wanted to see his father's garden.
Leaning over the fence and pointing with a stick which had been a
present from an Indian rajah, he recalled: 'There's where the onions
were sown. I had to weed them on Saturday afternoons.' Stephen
had to call on his childhood sweetheart Jane Symon, then Mrs.
Thompson, to ask: 'Do you remember the Boys' Ball?'

The two visitors were staying with the Cowies at Dullan Brae, and
it was evidently Mrs. Cowie who first suggested to Stephen that he
might endow a cottage hospital in Dufftown. By his next visit, in
1891, the Stephen Cottage Hospital was an accomplished fact, and
at a ceremony there in June the then Lord Mount Stephen declared:
. . . The origin of the hospital belongs entirely to Mrs. Cowie. She it
was who put the thought into my head, and I am grateful to her for it. . . .[1]

WEAK LINKS IN THE CHAIN

Still Stephen's work for the Canadian Pacific was not over.
Several times, in the years 1885 to 1888, he spoke of withdrawing
from the scene of action and allowing men of more practical railroading experience to take his place. But before he did so there were
a number of 'loose ends' to be tied up.

For two particular problems Stephen felt himself directly responsible; first, he had allowed John Henry Pope and Charles
Hibbert Tupper, son of Sir Charles and a junior Minister, to persuade him, against his better judgment, into committing the C.P.R.
to the construction of the Short Line to take the Pacific to the
Maritime ports; secondly, by taking Pope's word for it that the
'Onderdonk Section' in British Columbia was a sound piece of work,
he had laid up a store of trouble for the Company.

Stephen's objection to the Short Line stemmed from the fact that
it had a purely political purpose—to satisfy the demands of the
Maritime Members of Parliament. It had been intended to run via
St. John, New Brunswick, through Maine to Halifax, Nova Scotia,
on the Atlantic seaboard But already these two Maritime Provinces
were served by the Government's Intercolonial Railway, which, as
has been mentioned, was originally built to honour a confederation

---

[1] *Banffshire Journal*, 9 June 1891.

pledge to link the Maritimes to the centre of the new Dominion. The fact that it was run at a loss showed that there was not yet sufficient traffic to sustain another railroad. The Short Line would be more direct than the I.C.R., but the shortest route to the Atlantic would still be that to Portland, Maine. Stephen had not, in the last instance, had any alternative but to agree to build the road; while the subject was under discussion—during one of the C.P.R.'s financial crises—a meeting of Maritime Members had threatened to oppose relief measures in Parliament unless the Short Line was promised. Even then, he had been given the assurance that the line would have all the through traffic, the I.C.R. becoming a purely local road.

In the matter of the Onderdonk Section, Stephen blamed himself more unreservedly. The work there, it will be remembered, was begun by Government contract before the Syndicate undertook the construction of the main portion of the C.P.R. The standard of the latter had, by the contract, been laid down as that of the Union Pacific when first built, but as finally completed the Canadian Pacific was a much superior proposition. When the Onderdonk Section was handed over to the C.P.R. Company, it was found that not only did it compare unfavourably with the rest of the work— that might have been defended on the grounds that the C.P.R. had set an unnecessarily high standard—but that without immediate improvements it was hardly fit to be used. It had been built as an isolated piece of work, not to be operated by the contractor himself but to be handed over by a certain date without reference to any other contract. From time to time it had, of course, been inspected by the Government's chief engineer, and therein lay the root of the trouble. To admit that the Section was not all that it might have been was to imply that Collingwood Schreiber had been at fault in passing inferior work. It reflected even more upon the then Minister of Railways, Sir Charles Tupper, and presented a highly disagreeable problem to his successor, John Henry Pope. The C.P.R. Company had experienced one financial crisis after another in its efforts to build a thoroughly good road; was it possible that the Department of Railways, rather than exceed its estimated expenditure, had sanctioned sundry economies and accepted work that was superficially satisfactory but would not bear closer inspection? Sir Charles Tupper, writing to Macdonald in 1889 of discussions which took place 'after we had decided to reduce the cost of the work' with the then Government engineer, Sandford Fleming, said:

. . . Mr. Fleming was so hostile to the construction of a cheap road that a quarrel took place between us on that point and he only yielded when I told him in so many words that I would get another Engineer to take his place. . . .[1]

It was only when Stephen himself went through to the Pacific in July 1886, that he realized that the assurances he had been content to accept from Pope were not justified. The matter was referred to arbitration, in order to determine who was to meet the cost of improving the line—Government or C.P.R. Company—and the course of the proceedings will presently be outlined.

These two problems, concerning the extremities of the transcontinental line, were by no means isolated from the main course of subsequent events, nor was another source of vexation, the recurrence of anti-C.P.R. agitation in Manitoba. Not content with linking the Atlantic and Pacific Oceans, the Canadian Pacific Company was looking ahead to the day when its system should 'span the world'. In the years following the completion of the main line, Stephen's energies were largely devoted to extending the eastern terminus to Liverpool and Cherbourg, and the western to Yokohama and Hong Kong. But in his negotiations, while he struggled to convince such authorities as the British Government of the merits of his railroad as a swift line of communication, he was constantly handicapped by the private knowledge of weak links in his globe-encircling chain. An Atlantic steamship service depended upon satisfactory rail connection at the Canadian seaboard, the Pacific service on the reliability of transcontinental train schedules. If the Canadian route were unsafe or liable to delay, both passengers and freight would travel instead through the United States. Stephen wrote to Macdonald in September 1888, saying that he had heard of passengers from Australia who had arrived at the Pacific coast with C.P.R. tickets in their pockets but, hearing rumours about the British Columbia section, had proceeded east over American lines.[2] Moreover, if American lines succeeded in penetrating into Manitoba, cutting the girdle in half, all idea of spanning the world might as well be given up at once.

Given time to establish itself, Stephen knew that the Canadian Pacific could hold its own against all rivals, but the infancy of the national line was an anxious time. In spite of all the financial and

[1] Tupper Papers 541, Tupper to Macdonald, 30 September 1889.
[2] Macd.P. 'Stephen' 271, Stephen to Macdonald, 9 September 1888.

other difficulties which the Company was known to have experienced the idea seemed to grow that the C.P.R. was a powerful, capitalist monster which must be watched at every turn lest it swallow everything in sight; an organization so well-equipped to defend itself that to take advantage of it was absolutely legitimate—akin to scoring over the Government. It was expected to continue to provide lines of communication from its reputedly limitless resources, regardless of whether or not these were profitable; it was a national institution with an altruistic mission in the land. It is possible that even the Manitoba agitators thought themselves perfectly justified in encouraging a 'foreign' railway system to provide what their national enterprise had disappointed them in not at once accomplishing.

All this might have daunted a less optimistic soul than Stephen's; as it was, his faith wavered more in the days after 1885 than ever before. The cumulative effect of years of anxiety were telling on even his courageous spirit. It was only the glimpses of a glorious future for the Canadian Pacific appearing at intervals through the gloom that enabled to him carry on with tasks that seemed thankless at the time, and perhaps only Macdonald was allowed to know that the C.P.R. President had his doubts.

PACIFIC STEAMSHIP SERVICE : TENDERS INVITED

In October 1885, the British Postmaster General, anticipating the termination of the Government's mail contract with the Peninsular and Oriental Steam Navigation Company, advertised for tenders not only for mail services on the eastern routes but also for one from Vancouver to Japan and China.

Stephen was still in England; it was just after Barings had made the First Mortgage Bond issue, and before the actual completion of the main line. Before long he received a letter from Macdonald, urging him to see either the Postmaster General or his deputy, and advising him also to try to enlist the co-operation of the Admiralty by offering to build the vessels to naval specifications so that in time of war they might be convertible to armed cruisers. Macdonald added:

You should tender so low that there might be no mistake about it, and I dare say we can persuade Parliament to give you a subsidy.[1]

---

[1] Macd.P. 'Stephen' 268, Macdonald to Stephen, 28 October 1885.

But it was not a case simply of tendering for the service called for by the Imperial Post Office. Macdonald told Stephen that he had had a note on the subject from Van Horne, and agreed with the latter that the average speed required—11 knots—was too slow if, besides carrying the mails, they hoped to compete successfully for the Pacific trade. What was wanted was a first class service run in conjunction with express trains on the C.P.R. It was useless to 'gallop' the mails over Canada if they were then to 'amble' on the Pacific.

Stephen foresaw that some diplomacy would be required to convince the British Government from the beginning that it must be prepared to move with the times. He suggested that as Macdonald was expected in London shortly it would be wiser to wait until he arrived and could personally vouch for the willingness of the Dominion Government to contribute a share of the subsidy.[1] Meantime he made a few enquiries as to the amount of the subsidy paid to the P. & O. Company for similar services, and finally drew up a memorandum for Macdonald's use, embodying his proposals for a subsidized Canadian Pacific steamship service.[2] For an annual subsidy for ten years of £100,000, he offered to provide a three-weekly mail service from one of Canada's Atlantic ports to Hong Kong by way of Yokohama, employing on the Pacific specially fitted vessels with a speed of from 14 to 15 knots. A comparative statement of the times estimated to be taken by the mails from London to Hong Kong and Yokohama by Gibraltar, by Brindisi and by the Canadian routes was appended, showing that the new service would probably save twelve days on the run to Hong Kong over the Gibraltar route, and three over the Brindisi. To Yokohama the saving would be twenty-five and sixteen days respectively. And Stephen estimated that if a fast Atlantic service, equal to that provided by the Cunarders, could be established between England and a Canadian port, a further reduction in time of three days could be achieved.

Even in the early days, when a Canadian Pacific Railway was still only a conception of visionaries, it was not thought of merely as a means of uniting eastern and western Canada. It was obvious that such a line of communication could not but be of international significance. In 1864, when by reason of its having been brought up in the British House of Commons the *Montreal Gazette* had the subject under review, it was stated as the opinion of that paper that the over-

---

[1] Macd.P. 'Stephen' 269, Stephen to Macdonald, 14 November 1885.
[2] CO 807/45, Confidential Print, North American 115.

land route to the Pacific was, for imperial purposes, essential; 'the monstrously circuitous route by Panama or Cape Horn should be abandoned as speedily as possible. . . .' It was also pointed out, from time to time, that the Pacific Railway might prove a useful substitute for the Suez or Cape of Good Hope routes, in conveying troops or supplies to British bases in the Far East. During the 'Russian scare' of 1885 there was actually some correspondence between the War Office and the C.P.R. Company on the subject of transporting war materials over the railway, although the 'scare' collapsed before the new route could be tested. It was these considerations that both Macdonald and the Company wished to stress in negotiating for a mail subsidy.

STEPHEN'S PROPOSALS BEFORE BRITISH GOVERNMENT

Macdonald's interview with Lord Salisbury, the British Premier, was all that could have been desired. The latter assured Macdonald that he recognized the Imperial value of the scheme; that it was of great importance for strategic and political reasons as well as on postal grounds.[1] It is not clear whether, at this point, the Canadian Prime Minister expressed his Government's willingness to contribute to a subsidy; at all events nothing to that effect was subsequently inserted in the C.P.R.'s official tender.

The next step was taken by the High Commissioner, Sir Charles Tupper, who, at the request of the Canadian Government, sent to Colonel Sir Frederick Stanley, the Colonial Secretary, Stephen's memorandum, which Stanley promptly had printed for the Cabinet with his personal recommendation appended.[2] He pointed out to his colleagues that the proposal was of more than financial importance, and that although the subsidy asked was large, he had reason to believe that Canada would contribute to the extent of £20,000 or £25,000. The matter was brought up in Cabinet on 13 January 1886, and was very well received. The proposal was agreed to in principle, provided that the details could be satisfactorily resolved by an Inter-departmental Committee representing the Colonial Office, Post Office, Admiralty, War Office and Treasury.[3] The White Paper containing the Committee's terms of reference stated that as the

---

[1] CO 42/786 (Canada 342) Minute by Sir Robert Herbert to High Commissioner's Despatch, 7 January 1886.   [2] CO 807/45.
[3] Tupper Papers 347, Northcote to Tupper, 13 January 1886. White Paper filed in CO 42/786 (Canada 342), 15 January 1886.

13

amount of the subsidy had been approved by the Cabinet, it was not necessary for them to consider this aspect of the scheme.

So far, events had moved with incredible swiftness. Within a fortnight, however, the Salisbury Government had resigned over the Irish Home Rule Bill, and everything came to a standstill. Stephen wrote to Macdonald from Montreal:

. . . It is clear that the Salisbury Government were pretty well 'enthused'. How we may get on with their successors is a riddle.[1]

In a subsequent letter he expressed the hope that Macdonald would from time to time remind the High Commissioner to keep pressing the matter in London.[2] Already, through Sir Robert Herbert who from first to last did his utmost to forward the scheme, Tupper had ensured that the retiring Colonial Secretary left for his successor a Minute to the effect that the Cabinet had accepted the principle of the C.P.R. proposal, subject to the Interdepartmental Committee's report on details, and had approved the amount of the subsidy.[3]

It cannot be said that the Gladstone Government adopted a markedly different attitude from that of Salisbury. Lord Granville, the new Colonial Secretary, was personally inclined to favour the grant, but the matter never actually reached the stage of discussion during the Liberal administration. The constitution of the Departmental Committee, when again it was instructed to continue its deliberations, was unaltered. Under the chairmanship of Mr. Bramston of the Colonial Office, the Committee was composed of permanent officials whose position was unaffected by the change of Government. It did not lack information, nor expression of opinion by interested parties, in coming to its decision. Stephen telegraphed the High Commissioner who passed on the information, that the Company was ready to guarantee an increased speed of 15 knots (average) instead of 14 as at first proposed, and that the service could be made fortnightly, instead of every three weeks, for the same subsidy.[4] Harry Moody, the London Agent of the C.P.R. (formerly Secretary to Lord Dufferin, an earlier Governor-General of Canada), furnished a more detailed memorandum on the proposed service, laying particular stress on the importance of a faster trade route than was contemplated by the Imperial Post Office.[5] This view was supported

---

[1] Macd.P. 'Stephen' 270, Stephen to Macdonald, 28 January 1886.
[2] Loc. cit. Stephen to Macdonald, 29 January 1886.
[3] CO 42/786 (Canada 342) Further Minute by Herbert, 30 January 1886.
[4] CO 807/46, Tupper to Herbert, 2 March 1886.
[5] CO 42/783, High Commissioner's Despatch, 4 March 1886.

by the Committee of the London Chamber of Commerce which, prompted by Sir John Rose, submitted to the Colonial Office its considered opinion that the commercial and imperial value of the proposals could not be overrated.[1] Mr. Bramston, in a Minute to the latter, commented: 'The new line of communication is attracting attention. . . .' The C.P.R. Company supplied the Committee with details regarding charges for the transport of troops, war materials and the like, and regarding the number of vessels intended to be put on the route.[2] So far only these and Stephen's memoranda were before the Committee, but Moody had meanwhile sent in a formal tender to the Post Office.[3]

The Departmental Committee issued its report in June. The matter had been considered from four angles: postal, commercial, strategic and imperial. The general conclusion was that although in time of war the presence of first class British vessels in the North Pacific, and the existence of an alternative route, through British territory, to the outposts of Empire in the Far East, should the Suez Canal be closed by enemy action, would be of inestimable value, from a postal point of view the grant of a subsidy would not be justified. It was considered that the commercial advantages would be reaped chiefly by Canada, although it was realized, too, that the opening of a new trade route would in time lead to a general increase in shipping activity. The imperial aspect had been stressed mainly by Sir Andrew Clarke, Inspector General of Fortifications, who observed that once a regular steamer service with the East by way of Canada and the Pacific was established, 'the whole Empire will be firmly knit together, and the chain of communication between British stations will literally girdle the world'.[4] This consummation was not, however, considered to be worth an annual expenditure of £100,000 for ten years.

Meanwhile the mercantile interest in the east, not waiting for Government officials to decide whether there was, or was not, a future for a Canadian Pacific trade route, were taking advantage of the opening of the railway to send cargoes—chiefly tea—by sailing ship to Vancouver, for transhipment to centres in Eastern Canada and the United States.[2] Said the Montreal *Trade Bulletin*:

---

[1] CO 42/789, London Chamber of Commerce to Colonial Secretary, 20 March 1886.
[2] Loc. cit. Moody to Colonial Secretary, 29 March 1886 and CO 807/46, Moody to Colonial Secretary, 26 March 1886.   [3] Loc. cit. Moody to Post Office, 31 March 1886.
[4] CO 42/789, Report of Departmental Committee.
[2] *Railway Times*, 17 July 1886.

This action has been taken by Japan merchants without even consulting parties here, which shows that they have, with their proverbial shrewdness, decided upon the best route. . . . Now that Japan has recognized the importance of the Canadian Pacific as regards tea, it is but natural to expect that it will attract the other leading products of the East, such as rice, coffee, spices, etc.[1]

George Stephen had not been a merchant and manufacturer for nothing. Imbued as he was with a desire to see Canada develop and prosper, he cannot have been blind to the great opportunities which lay open to her, given the initial impetus. He had not forgotten the exotic cargoes that had found their way to the establishment of James Morrison in Fore Street. He had no doubt heard what Bret Harte's engines said at the opening of America's Union Pacific Railroad.[2] Although in his letters at this time he was more concerned with the practical details of ways and means, it is reasonable to suppose that it was the vision of the system which eventually 'brought not just a continent, but the Orient to Montreal's backyard'[3] which inspired him to continue the fight for an Imperial subsidy.

In July 1886, Her Majesty sent once more for Lord Salisbury to form a Government, and the promoters of the Canadian Pacific steamship service took fresh courage. Nothing could of course be done during the Parliamentary recess, and there is no correspondence on the subject until some weeks later. But at the end of July Macdonald, in a speech at Victoria, British Columbia, referred to Lord Salisbury's determination to aid the establishment of a Pacific mail service, and added that the Dominion Government was equally anxious to secure a swift line on the Atlantic.[4]

By September, Stephen was back in London, and evidently setting in motion new machinery for the promotion of his plans in the Pacific. He had hoped that Macdonald would be able to join him, but the latter could not leave Canada.[5] Stephen cabled in November that there seemed good prospects of a decision by the Government that month.[6] As usual, the delay in settling the question of the moment was proving irksome to this man of action, and when a month later no progress had been made, he suggested that in order to

[1] Quoted in *Railway Times*, 17 July 1886.
[2] Western engine to Eastern: 'You brag of your East! You do? Why, I bring the East to you!'
[3] John Irwin Cooper, *Montreal : The Story of Three Hundred Years*, Montreal, 1942.
[4] *Railway Times*, 7 August 1886.
[5] Macd.P. 'Stephen' 270, Stephen to Macdonald, 22 October and 4 November 1886.
[6] Loc. cit. Stephen to Macdonald, 5 November 1886.

expedite matters Macdonald should cable Salisbury to the effect that the Dominion Government was on the eve of granting a subsidy for a fast mail and passenger service on the Atlantic, but could not commit itself until it was assured that the Imperial Government would do its share in establishing the proposed new route to the East.[1] The Canadian Premier, however, did not share Stephen's passion for prompt action. Stephen cabled Pope expressing his disappointment at Macdonald's reaction to his message and his opinion that nothing would be done in London without pressure from Ottawa.[2]

STEPHEN PRESSES FOR FAST ATLANTIC SERVICE

For some time Stephen had been urging on Macdonald the necessity of providing a better mail service between Britain and Canada. This route was still the preserve of the Allan and Dominion Lines, the Allans having the mail contract, and, probably mindful of the many disasters in the early history of the Line, the Allan ships made no attempt to compete with the speed of the Cunarders. So long as they continued to hold the mail subsidy they had no reason to change their practice. More than once, when a letter from England arrived long overdue, Stephen observed to Macdonald that it must have come by 'one of Allans' cattle-boats'. The Canadian Pacific did not want to undertake an Atlantic service itself if that could be avoided; it wanted to be free to use any or all of the existing lines, Canadian and American, fast and slow. The Pacific service, Stephen thought, would be 'quite enough "Navy" to begin with'.[3] But there was at least one member of the Canadian Cabinet who believed that when Stephen pressed the need for a new fast line on the Atlantic he was only seeking favours for the Company. The Postmaster General, Sir Alexander Campbell, plainly told the Prime Minister:

We should not take the chestnuts out of the fire for the C.P.R.—for other purpose than to spend money for them this line seems to me unnecessary and beyond our means.[4]

Stephen was quite aware of this feeling, which he thought was not confined to one Minister. But, as always, he was ready to disregard the mudslingers of either Party while concentrating on longer term

[1] 'Macd.P. Stephen' 270, Stephen to Macdonald, 11 December 1886.
[2] Loc. cit. Stephen to Pope, 13 December 1886.
[3] Loc. cit. Stephen to Macdonald, 4 June 1886 and 10 September 1886.
[4] Loc. cit. Van Horne to Macdonald, 1 January 1887, enclosing Campbell's note.

policies and wider aims. He concluded a diatribe on the fallacies of
the Liberals' 'anti-monopoly policy in railways' by appealing thus to
Macdonald's political sensibility:

In order to make good the claim of the party to be considered the Party of
Progress, I think it very important that the public should *always* have
something to look forward to. Finality and retrospection do not 'enthuse'.
The C.P.R. being now finished the Government or rather the Party is free
to turn its attention to the development of the resources of the country,
and of its Trade and Commerce. To that end, I should think it would be
good policy even if nothing ever came of it for the Government before the
House rises to take power to subsidize a line of steamers to run from
Vancouver to the Australian colonies by way of the Sandwich Islands.
Our people are quite ignorant as yet of the market for our products which
such a line of steamers would open up and the effect on their minds of
the Government taking steps to secure the trade and take it from the U.S.
would be very good. In the same way it would be a capital thing to take
power to grant a subsidy not exceeding say $50,000 a year for a term of
years to the Australian Cable Company should they take their cable to
Vancouver instead of San Francisco. It is quite possible nothing would
come of either at least for a time, but the effect in many ways would be
telling, affecting the public imagination most favourably. The dollar and
cent view would not be listened to. If I were to say one half of all this to
almost anyone in the Government but yourself I feel I would create an
impression that I was looking out merely for something for the C.P.R. I
feel I can trust to you to give me credit for more singleness of purpose.
Of course everything which helps the country benefits the C.P.R., but in
the present case C.P.R. interests are quite a subordinate consideration
with me.[1]

On arriving in London in the autumn of 1886 Stephen discussed
with Sir Charles Tupper the question of a fast Atlantic service and
wrote to Macdonald outlining the conditions required and advising
the latter to have an advertisement for tenders published.[2] He was
confident that he could persuade English shipping companies to
tender for the service. At the beginning of the year he had approached
Andrew Allan, describing to him what he considered necessary to
'perfect the Liverpool end of the C.P.R.' but the Canadian Pacific
President's ideas had apparently so startled Allan that it was obvious
there was no hope of co-operation in that direction.[3] Before the end
of the year Stephen had succeeded in interesting the Andersons of

---

[1] Macd.P. 'Stephen' 270, Stephen to Macdonald, 24 May 1886.
[2] Loc. cit. Stephen to Macdonald, 10 September 1886.
[3] Loc. cit. 270, Stephen to Macdonald, 29 January 1886.

the Orient Line in the project, and cabled Macdonald that a tender was forthcoming for a service superior to anything afloat.[1] It later transpired that Stephen and Sir Donald Smith had each undertaken to contribute £50,000 towards the Andersons' venture. A provisional syndicate had been formed largely dependent on the prestige which the C.P.R. men lent to the enterprise, but in no way directly connected with the railway company. Stephen had personally no desire to become involved in it, but to secure the end in view he was prepared to make any sacrifice required of him. The line was planned to run to Halifax, to connect with the proposed Short Line of the C.P.R.

Although no official communication regarding the Canadian Government's intentions on the Atlantic was made to the Colonial Office, it seems that the High Commissioner gave a hint of what was afoot to Mr. Stanhope, Lord Granville's successor.[2] As had been expected, the Colonial Secretary recognized that the fact that the Dominion Government was preparing to make a large expenditure in this direction had an important bearing on the question of the Pacific subsidy, then under discussion by a new Departmental Committee.

SUPPORT FOR STEPHEN'S PACIFIC SCHEME

On 23 December 1886, the second Departmental Committee submitted its report to the Colonial Office.[3] Whereas the first Committee had concentrated chiefly on the postal and commercial aspect of a Pacific mail service, mentioning its strategic and imperial advantages as being in the nature of expensive luxuries, the second Committee dwelt rather on the latter, recognizing that it was on those grounds that the matter had ultimately to be decided. It had become fairly plain that from a purely postal point of view the subsidy was unwarranted—the Japanese mails brought in annually only some £20,000 to the Exchequer—but that more important issues were at stake.

A different procedure had been adopted by the second Committee in acquiring information on which to base its decisions. Lord Dunraven, the Chairman, had begun by addressing a circular letter to various authorities, mostly naval or military, explaining the object

---

[1] Loc. cit. Stephen to Macdonald, 11 December 1886.
[2] Tupper Papers 403, Stanhope to Tupper, 11 December 1886.
[3] CO 42/789, 23 December 1886. Report contained in CO 807/54, Confidential Print North American 124.

of the enquiry and requesting the views of the addressees from the standpoint of their specialized knowledge. The naval witnesses were almost unanimous in their scepticism of the proposed service, a notable exception being Lord Charles Beresford, while the military experts were all in favour of it. In assessing the various viewpoints allowance must, of course, be made for the fact that at least two of the scheme's supporters were personal friends of George Stephen, even if they were also honest men and devoted public servants. It was at his suggestion that Sir Donald Stewart was consulted, although the late Commander-in-Chief, India, was an appropriate enough choice, especially as he had, in addition to his knowledge of the East, first-hand information respecting the Canadian route. Stephen wrote to Tupper in November 1886; 'Sir Donald told me last night that since he had seen the C.P.R. he now cared very little what happened to the Suez route.'[1] His friend rose admirably to the occasion, writing to Dunraven that in his opinion the importance of the proposal could not be exaggerated. 'No one who has seen the C.P.R. system can doubt that sooner or later it must be utilized in the manner advocated by the Dominion Government and the Railway Company', he declared, and went on to point out that besides giving the shortest route to Japan and China, the C.P.R. was the easiest to defend and traversed more temperate regions than any of the competing lines. The railway rolling stock, he added (no doubt prompted by Stephen) was peculiarly suited to troop transport, as it had been designed to accommodate all classes, including large numbers of emigrants.

Another staunch supporter was Viscount Wolseley, whose memories of Canada, and of moving an expeditionary force there before the advent of the Canadian Pacific, in addition to his personal regard for Stephen, made him particularly enthusiastic. After discoursing on all the possible contingencies in which the new steamers might play a valuable part, as well as dwelling on the need to stimulate British trade, Wolseley concluded:

There is something grand and imposing in the idea of our route to the East running for over three thousand miles through British territory. It appeals to even the coldest imagination.

The result was that once again the question came before the Cabinet for consideration. At the beginning of February 1887, when

[1] CO 42/789 (Canada 1714A)—Documents upon which the Report of the second Committee was founded.

no conclusion had yet been arrived at, Stephen wrote to Sir Robert Herbert asking for an interview with this ally of Canadian causes. The letter betrayed the customary impatience of the C.P.R. President:

. . . Though a firm believer 'that everything comes to him who can wait', I confess to be getting a little weary of waiting for the decision of the Government on Canada's proposal to establish a first class mail service in the Pacific Ocean and it would be a relief to me to have the matter disposed of one way or the other.[1]

Herbert replied that he would be glad to see Stephen, but had nothing definite to communicate. The Government, after repeated examinations of the proposals, had been unable to satisfy itself that the advantages of the trans-Pacific steam service, great as they were, would justify an application to Parliament for anything like so large a grant as £100,000 a year for ten years. Would it be possible, he asked, for the Company to modify the terms?[2] The following day Stephen called at the Colonial Office and told Herbert that while the Company could not build five first class steamers and maintain a fortnightly service for less than the sum named, it could give a monthly service, involving three vessels, for a subsidy of £60,000. He then said that the Canadian Government was unlikely to contribute because of its impending commitments on the Atlantic, but reminded Herbert that Lord Salisbury had thought that the case for granting the subsidy was fully made out.[3]

PACIFIC SUBSIDY HINGES ON BETTER ATLANTIC SERVICE

It was obviously the Treasury that was the stumbling block. The Colonial Office was all anxiety to forward the Canadian scheme, and in the hope of strengthening its hand with the Cabinet sent a carefully-worded cable to Lord Lansdowne, asking if there was any truth in the report that Canada was about to subsidize a fast Atlantic service, and, if so, what was the amount involved?[4] Lord Lansdowne's reply was disappointing; he merely stated that the Dominion Government was calling for tenders, but that no amount had been named.[5] Herbert's Minute to this was the exasperated comment:

[1] CO 42/789, Stephen to Herbert, 2 February 1887.
[2] Loc. cit. Herbert to Stephen, 4 February 1887.
[3] Loc. cit. Stephen to Herbert, 4 February, and Minute by Herbert, 5 February 1887.   [4] CO 42/792, 5 March 1887.   [5] CO 42/790, 8 March 1887.

The object of our telegram was to give the Dominion Government an opportunity of showing that they propose to incur heavy expenditure on the Atlantic portion of the steam service the Pacific portion of which they ask us to subsidize. This telegram however is of no use to them.

He was prepared, nevertheless, to give Canada another chance to wake up to his intention. Another cable was despatched, asking whether Canada was likely to contribute a share of the Pacific subsidy, but again the response was unsatisfactory. The Dominion Government was not prepared to propose a contribution.[1] Macdonald had introduced the matter in Council, but advised the Governor-General that his colleagues were of the opinion that Canada had done her share in building the C.P.R. and Intercolonial Railway, and in undertaking the Atlantic subsidy.[2] It has already been shown what Macdonald had to contend with in Council, but had he been in a position to make a more definite statement—or perhaps had he even made a provisional one—about the Atlantic service, the decision of the British Government might yet have been favourably influenced.

There would appear to have been a lack of liaison work at this point between the Colonial Office and the usually active official and unofficial Canadian agents in London, on the one hand, and the Dominion Government on the other.[3] Stephen must have been unaware of Herbert's ruses; in his communications to Macdonald he was invariably plain, so that his cable on 14 March: 'No decision yet about Pacific subsidy. Begin to fear friends here not in earnest. Can you suggest anything to hasten decision?' probably meant exactly what it implied.[4] Macdonald's reply conveyed the news that the Pacific subsidy had not been granted.[5]

COLONIAL CONFERENCE: PACIFIC PLANS AIRED

It is not clear whether the refusal of the Imperial Government to subsidize a C.P.R. Pacific steamship service was due to Canada's declining to contribute, or whether that was merely the excuse. In the opinion of Sir Robert Herbert, expressed in a Minute to a despatch from the Governor-General conveying his regret at the

[1] CO 42/790, 15 March 1887.
[2] Macdonald to Lansdowne, 15 March 1887, in Pope, *Correspondence of Sir John Macdonald*, pp. 395-6.
[3] Probably explained by Sir Charles Tupper's absence on a diplomatic mission to Washington.
[4] Macd.P. 'Stephen' 270, Stephen to Macdonald, 14 March 1887.
[5] Loc cit. 16 March 1887.

decision, the Dominion's failure to contribute was not a sufficient justification for denying the subsidy. His insight into Canadian affairs is manifest in the concluding sentence:

. . . Political exigencies of course require that the great expenditure in the West should not be further increased; that the Eastern maritime provinces should now have a pull at the Dominion purse.[1]

In a Minute to the same despatch Lord Onslow, the Permanent Under-Secretary, summed up the Colonial Office view thus:

We have not heard the last of this by a long way. I am afraid the 'great regret' expressed by the Canadian Government will be shared by Her Majesty's Government some day.

Far from blaming the Canadian Government for the miscarriage of his cherished scheme, Stephen supported the contention that Canada had made enough sacrifices in the cause of an all-British route to the East, and in his impatience with the Imperial Government told Macdonald that he proposed to open negotiations with the Norddeutscher Lloyd for the provision not only of a North Pacific service but also of a line from Canada to Australia.[2] Before resorting to such extreme measures, however, Stephen resolved to give the Imperial Government one more chance to reconsider its decision. The first Colonial Conference was due to meet the following month in London, and although Stephen regretted that one of the two Canadian delegates was to be the Postmaster General, Sir Alexander Campbell, whose unfriendliness to the C.P.R. had been amply proved, he saw in the Conference a last opportunity to have the Pacific mail service reconsidered on an imperial basis.[3] The other representative was to be the veteran engineer, Sandford Fleming, who, although deep in a plan of his own for a Pacific telegraph cable, could be relied upon to support the railway to which, in his term of office as Government engineer, he had devoted much skill and energy.

It was finally decided that the question would be reopened on the basis of the reduced subsidy of £60,000, Canada offering to contribute a quarter of this sum annually for ten years. Sir Robert Herbert welcomed this opportunity to reopen the question, especially as Canada was now willing to contribute, and the Colonial Office hastened to inform the Treasury of this development.[4]

[1] CO 42/790, 16 March 1887.
[2] Macd.P. 'Stephen' 270, Stephen to Macdonald, 20 March 1887.
[3] Loc. cit. Stephen to Macdonald, 12 March and 9 April 1887.
[4] CO 42/792, High Commissioner's despatch, 12 April 1887.

Campbell's speech to the Colonial Conference on 19 April realized Stephen's worst fears.[1] It was unconvincing and ill-informed. Although the Canadian delegate declared that his main task, and that of Mr. Fleming, was to discuss the new route to the East, he proceeded to discourse on the benefits of a fast service to Australia and New Zealand—on which the C.P.R. had admittedly prepared a memorandum for the Conference—entirely ignoring the North Pacific plan until reminded of it by the Imperial Postmaster General. Fortunately Sandford Fleming could speak with more authority on both routes, as well as on the contribution already made by Canada in subsidizing the Canadian Pacific Railway. Emphasizing the imperial significance of the latter, he declared:

Canada does not ask to be relieved of any of the burdens she has assumed; she brings all her costly works as a contribution to the common defence, and she desires that they may be made available in the most advantageous manner to the Empire.

—which in 1887 would have 'gone down' very well indeed.

LORDS DEBATE FAVOURS CANADIAN PACIFIC STEAMSHIP SERVICE

Meanwhile the question of the subsidy for the Hong Kong and Yokohama service was receiving considerable publicity. In an eloquent oration in the House of Lords the Earl of Harrowby, who had been a member of Lord Salisbury's previous Cabinet and had seen all the papers relating to the matter, appealed to the Government not to shirk the responsibilities of Empire. The Roman Empire, he pointed out, had been bound together by its great lines of communication on land; the British Empire now had the opportunity of making the sea its highway. Referring to the Canadian Pacific as 'the greatest revolution in the condition of the British Empire that had occurred in our time', he went on to show how modest had been even the subsidy of £100,000 originally demanded. The lowest tender for the Vancouver route received from any other party had been £108,000, and even that sum paled into insignificance before the fact that during the Russian war scare in 1885 Mr. Gladstone's Government had, at a cost of £33,000, for a period of six months, chartered nine vessels, only one of which could attain the minimum speed of the proposed C.P.R. ships. In addition, £1 million had been spent in chartering transports. He feared that procrastination on England's

[1] S.P. 76, 1889, CO 45/642, Report of Colonial Conference.

part would result in her being forestalled by Germany or Japan, both of whom had shown interest in opening up the route. 'Economise where you rightly can', he counselled, 'if necessary save the money devoted to the new Admiralty and War Offices; cease to buy works of art; cease decorating your parks; but do not postpone acquiring control over this great Pacific line'.[1]

Lord Onslow assured the noble Earl that the matter was still under consideration. Lords Carnarvon and Dunraven then added their support to the C.P.R. cause, the latter saying that he was somewhat suspicious of the word 'consideration'.

Stephen was equally suspicious of the term. Sir John Rose had cabled him the substance of the Lords' debate and added that an excellent article had also appeared in *The Times*, but Stephen feared that unless their advantage were followed up, success might yet elude them.[2] He appealed again to Macdonald to apply some pressure suggesting that he cable Rose to exert his influence in appropriate quarters. This Macdonald did. Rose approached several members of the Government, who were all favourable to the scheme, and were convinced that if Lord Salisbury insisted on the granting of the subsidy, the Chancellor of the Exchequer, Mr. Goschen, would give way. Rose hesitated, however, to see the British Premier while the Dominion's official representative, Sir Alexander Campbell, was still on the scene.[3] Stephen's solution to this impasse was to have Macdonald cable Campbell to ask Rose officially to attend to the matter of the Pacific subsidy after the Conference was over; this would afford an excuse for the latter to begin negotiations right away.[4]

This was done, and it was from Rose that Macdonald received news of subsequent developments. The Colonial Secretary, Rose wrote, had prepared a strong memorandum for submission to the Cabinet at a propitious time. Meanwhile the Council of the Colonial Institute had adopted a memorial on the subject which was to be sent to the Premier, and Rose was trying to get similar action taken by the London Chamber of Commerce.[5] Everyone, Rose thought,

---

[1] Hansard (Lords), 29 April 1887.
[2] Macd.P. 'Stephen' 270, Stephen to Macdonald, 30 April 1887.
[3] Loc. cit. Stephen to Macdonald, 4 May 1887, and Macd.P. 'Rose' 259.657, Rose to Macdonald, 6 May 1887.
[4] Macd.P. 'Stephen' 270, Stephen to Macdonald, 7 May 1887.
[5] Loc. cit. Stephen to Macdonald, 10 May 1887, enclosing Rose to Macdonald, 9 May 1887. See also CO 42/792, 15 July 1887, for Resolutions by London Chamber of Commerce.

favoured the better service entailing the subsidy of £100,000, and he cabled Macdonald to ask if the Dominion Government would, if absolutely necessary, contribute £20,000.[1] Macdonald replied that if the increased subsidy depended upon it, Canada would give the desired sum.

Stephen and Macdonald were agreed on letting their case rest on the Lords' debate. Harry Moody was anxious to have a question asked in the Commons, in order to bring matters to a head, but with negotiations in the hands of Rose it seemed that satisfactory progress was being made. The British Government was still preoccupied with Irish affairs, and, as Stephen with surprising acquiescence observed to Macdonald, might be expected to 'try their patience a little'.[2]

LINE STARTED WITH OLD CUNARDERS

The C.P.R. Company could afford to wait for a little until the Imperial Government incubated on the fresh opinions so forcefully expressed in the Upper House. With a minimum of fuss and publicity it had been putting on the Pacific the first three steamers of the Canadian Pacific Line. As one newspaper observed:

. . . almost the first notice the mercantile world receives is that the line is in operation and awaits the merchants' orders.[3]

The *Abyssinia*, *Parthia* and *Batavia* were old Cunarders, and were not actually owned by the railway company but ran under a working agreement with their second owners.[4] Although not adapted for luxury travel they were soon making the trip from Hong Kong via Yokohama to the Pacific terminus of the C.P.R. with a full complement of passengers and with substantial cargoes. Moreover, arrangements had been made with the Japanese Postal and Customs authorities for the carriage of mails by the Canadian Pacific route to Europe.[5]

C.P.R. agents were busy in the Far East mobilizing opinion in favour of the Canadian route. At first the Chamber of Commerce

---

[1] Macd.P. 'Stephen' 270, Rose to Macdonald, 11 May 1887.
[2] Loc. cit. Stephen to Macdonald, 10 May 1887.
[3] Loc. cit. Press cutting in Stephen to Macdonald, 20 May 1887.
[4] CO 42/792, High Commissioner's Despatch, 2 May 1887. See also W. Kaye Lamb, *The Pioneer Days of the Transpacific Service* (British Columbia Historical Quarterly, 1937), *Empress to the Orient* (same, 1940) and *Empress Odyssey* (same, 1948).
[5] CO 42/792, Foreign Office, 6 July 1887, and CO 42/794, Foreign Office, 15 July 1887.

of Hong Kong had been doubtful of the utility of the proposed service; then, after an interview with Harry Moody in London, the Governor of the Colony, Sir G. F. Bowen, wrote to the Colonial Office recommending the scheme from a strategic point of view,[1] and before long the commercial community had changed their minds and joined with their fellows on the mainland and in Japan in urging upon the British Treasury the importance of encouraging the efforts of the Canadian Pacific. There was appreciative laughter in the House of Commons when, in answer to a question, the Chancellor of the Exchequer described the 'somewhat remarkable simultaneous flow of telegrams from various parts of the world', all demanding action upon this subject.[2]

Earlier that year Lord Salisbury had sent a circular letter to various centres of commerce throughout the world, inquiring into the present state and future possibilities of trade with Canada.[3] The reply from Tokyo had been most enthusiastic; although there was not a great demand there for Canadian imports, the future for Japanese exports to the Dominion was extremely promising, and such merchants as Jardine, Matheson and Company, the tea merchants, were quoted as being convinced that a Pacific steamship service would rapidly expand trade.

Meanwhile the mails carried by the *Abyssinia*, the first of the C.P.R. steamers to reach Vancouver, had been delivered in London. Among them was a despatch from the British Minister at Tokyo to the Foreign Office, sent as an experiment so that Lord Salisbury might judge of the efficiency of the service.[4] The time taken was thirty-one days—the minimum time from Hong Kong quoted in Stephen's original memorandum as being possible for the first class vessels.

CANADA'S IRON DUTIES JEOPARDIZE SUBSIDY

There is no doubt that these events in the East compensated to a great extent for ground that had meantime been lost in the West. On 18 May 1887, Sir John Rose had cabled Macdonald:

Subsidy negotiations had nearly reached satisfactory conclusion, but Smith just sent for me say notice question given whether true Canadian

---

[1] CO 42/792, Individuals: Bowen, 26 April 1887.
[2] Hansard (Commons), 30 June 1887.
[3] CO 42/791, Foreign Office, 28 July 1887.
[4] CO 42/792, Foreign Office, 6 July 1887.

Government propose increase duty Pig Iron 100 per cent. Bar 150 Puddled Bars 350. Smith Goschen both fear unless satisfactorily explained must create great difficulty proposing vote House and make nearly impossible carry. Please cable me fully as soon as possible.[1]

Harry Moody also had communicated his distress at this news to Stephen, saying that he feared it would alienate sympathy for Canadian interests, and might be used by the Government as an excuse for further delay.[2] Macdonald's reply to Rose was: 'National Policy applied to iron as already to woollen and cotton,'[3] to which Rose responded; 'Holland, Smith think better suspend negotiations till adverse feeling subsides. . . .'[4]

The question on the subject of Canadian iron duties was duly asked in the House—by Lord Claud Hamilton, a director of the Grand Trunk Railway. Hamilton asked whether, in considering the C.P.R. request for a steamship subsidy, the Government had borne in mind the action of the Dominion Government in raising the duty on imported iron, and had estimated the consequent loss to the (British) iron trade.[5] In his reply, W. H. Smith stated that it had not been the practice to look upon the high tariffs which Canada found it necessary to impose as directly affecting general questions, but Her Majesty's Government could not but feel that the change in duties in this case must indirectly affect the consideration of the main question, which must ultimately be decided by Parliament.

Stephen's view was stated, in his usual forthright manner, in a letter to Macdonald:

Much as I would like to secure the Pacific subsidy, I would let it go, ten times over, rather than see the Canadian Government abandon *any line of policy* it saw fit to follow in the interests of the Dominion.[6]

It was a long road that the fervid Montreal free trader had travelled in only a decade—although a nationalist to the point of supporting, at one time, Canadian independence of all imperial ties, it was with a new assurance that Stephen felt that the Dominion was in a position where dignity as well as expediency demanded a resolute independence of action.

[1] Macd.P. 'Rose' 259.674, Rose to Macdonald, 18 May 1887. 'Smith' is W. H. Smith, First Lord of the Treasury.
[2] Macd.P. 'Stephen' 270, Stephen to Macdonald, 20 May 1887.
[3] Loc. cit. enclosed with Rose to Macdonald, 20 May 1887.
[4] Loc. cit. enclosed with Rose to Macdonald, 25 May 1887.
[5] Hansard (Commons) 20 May 1887.
[6] Macd.P. 'Stephen' 270, Stephen to Macdonald, 20 May 1887.

SIR JOHN A. MACDONALD
by G. Horne Russell
(In the possession of the author, it formerly belonged to
Colonel George Stephen Cantlie, D.S.O.)

In the same letter he enclosed newspaper cuttings about the C.P.R.'s new steamer service on the Pacific. He was confident that in spite of political setbacks the greater project of a first class Canadian Pacific Line could not ultimately fail. One aspect of the question was, however, giving him some anxiety: 'The worst feature of our case', he wrote, 'is the danger of the line being cut in two at Winnipeg.'

MANITOBA SOUTH-WESTERN BUILT BUT AGITATION CONTINUES

For some time now, the Manitoba Farmers' Union had been practically defunct, and although disappointed speculators continued to lead the agitation for 'free-for-all' railway building in the Province, the question had passed into the sphere of provincial politics. It was not a party issue, but it became clear that if Norquay's Conservative Government would not press for disallowance to be abolished, his opponent, Greenway, was ready to do so. Norquay, however, already disappointed in the negative results of applications to Ottawa, and being, it is thought, dependent upon his official salary, was prepared to bow to provincial demands.

There was no secret about the readiness of the Province to admit American roads. Knowing this, Stephen had been only too anxious to disarm opposition by pressing the construction of the Manitoba South-Western. Even during the last crisis of the Company in June 1885, he had, under the impression that the Dominion Government would agree to take back part of the C.P.R. land grant and thus relieve the financial situation, telegraphed Norquay to announce that the South-Western would be built that year.[1] The difficulty had finally been overcome by an arrangement with the Provincial Government whereby the land grant for the road, given by the Federal Government, was transferred to the Province, and in return the latter issued 5 per cent debentures on behalf of the railway.[2] The loan was placed in London, and was immediately successful.[3] The road was constructed that season from Manitou as far as Whitewater, but still the Province was not satisfied.

Knowing that there was no reasonable basis for the agitation, Stephen had all along urged Macdonald to take a firm stand on the disallowance question. He wrote in May 1886:

[1] Macd.P. 'Stephen' 269, Stephen to Macdonald, 26 June 1885.
[2] *Weekly Manitoban*, 15 July, 17 December 1885.
[3] *Railway Times*, 5 December 1885; also Macd.P. 'Stephen' 270, Stephen to Macdonald, 27 January 1886.

14

It is an illegitimate use of the word to call the restriction which prevents Yankee railways running into our Nor West and stealing the traffic simply for the purpose of striking at the C.P.R. and compelling it to work with them—a monopoly. It is not a monopoly and none of these agitators who have been ringing the changes on the cry has ventured to say that the C.P.R. rates are higher than their neighbours pay or than they ought to be. The fact is, no new country ever was so well served, and one can't help feeling how ungrateful these Manitoba people are considering all that has been done for them, however it won't do to say so [to] them just now, but they may, I feel sure, be easily won over to a national policy in railways as well as in commerce. They really do not wish to see the trade diverted into Yankee channels, though they often talk as if they did. . . .[1]

By the spring of 1887 Manitoba had become a veritable incubator for railroad plotting. A scheme in which a former Lieutenant-Governor, Alexander Morris, and a member of the Legislature, Gilbert McMicken, were involved and which had as its object the building of a rival railroad from Winnipeg to the boundary, was barely hatched when it died.[2] Like another similar venture in which the main promoter was one Duncan MacArthur, a prominent Winnipeg citizen, the project depended on a connection with the Grand Trunk.[3] Norquay had promised to put through charters for any company giving evidence of ability to carry out the terms. Stephen continued to impress upon Macdonald the necessity of standing fast by the policy of disallowance. When a further delegation from Manitoba to Ottawa was on its way he wrote:

. . . I hope you will not fail to ask the Winnipeg deputation to formulate their grievances if they have any. So far I have heard nothing but excited talk on Disallowance and Monopoly in the abstract. . . .

It is going to take some firmness to put an end to what I call Winnipeg's cry for practical annexation to the U.S.[4]

On 17 May Stephen received a telegram from J. J. Hill which demanded action. The Northern Pacific, said Hill, had agreed to build to the boundary if parties in Winnipeg would guarantee to meet them at Pembina or West Lynne. Those interested at the Winnipeg end were trying to get the Provincial Government to

---

[1] Macd.P. 'Stephen' 270, Stephen to Macdonald, 24 May 1886.
[2] Morris Papers, K5, K6, K7, K8, K9, McMicken to Morris, 9, 16, and 19 March and 2 and 11 April 1887.
[3] Macd.P. 'Stephen' 270, Stephen to Macdonald, 23 and 29 April 1887.
[4] Loc. cit. Stephen to Macdonald, 28 April 1887.

assume responsibility for building the connecting line.[1] Stephen first communicated this news to Macdonald, adding that if the demands of the Manitoba delegates could be disregarded for sixty more days the whole scheme would fall through; without authority to reach the 49th Parallel the road would end 'in the air'. He then sent the following telegram to Norquay:

I am informed that negotiations are in progress if not already completed between your Government and others, and the Northern Pacific Railway Company, with the view of giving that company an independent connection with Winnipeg. I cannot but regard this as an act of undeserved hostility towards the C.P.R., which in the end will do nothing but hurt to Manitoba and the North West, and further I consider it a breach of faith towards the holders of the $134,000,000 private capital invested in Canadian Pacific Railway securities. If the mischievous agitation in favour of diverting the business of the North West into American channels is continued and the Canadian Pacific Company is to be treated as a public enemy by the people of Winnipeg, the company will at once take steps to establish their principal workshops at Fort William, which, from an operating point of view has many advantages, leaving nothing at Winnipeg but the ordinary division shops. Pray do not be mistaken. This is not an idle threat, it is a fixed purpose, taken after full consideration. . . .[2]

Norquay, however, riding, as J. A. Jackson puts it, on a tidal wave of popular emotion, knowing that 'any attempt to stem it would have swept him under',[3] increased his popularity by returning a defiant answer in which was implied the determination of the Provincial Government to undertake the Manitoba portion of the Northern Pacific's proposed extension. The Bill to provide for the Red River Valley Railway was even then coming before the Legislature, and already a Philadelphia newspaper had predicted that should a clash occur between the Provincial and the Federal Government, Manitoba would defy Ottawa and secede from the confederation.

It was at this point that the negotiations for a Pacific steamship subsidy were threatened by Canada's proposed duties on imported iron. For Stephen, the last straw was a letter he received from Thomas White, now Minister of the Interior, deploring the continuance of the disallowance policy and declaring that it would be most desirable for the Grand Trunk, through a connection with the Northern Pacific, to become interested in the development of the

---

[1] Macd.P. 'Stephen' 270, Stephen to Macdonald, 17 May 1887.
[2] Winnipeg *Morning Call*, 21 May 1887.   [3] Jackson, op. cit. p. 84.

Canadian North West.[1] Regarding the messages he had received
from his agents in London, who were alarmed at the effect of the
proposed iron duties, Stephen wrote to Macdonald:

I have cabled Moody to keep cool and say nothing. If White's views are to
be carried out we do not want a steamship subsidy. The moment the
C.P.R. is placed under the control of the G.T.R. and its American con-
nections it ceases to be a true Canadian Pacific Railway line and the
Company will have to make the most of its property by working with the
American lines, leaving the through line to rot, and a monument of
Canadian folly. . . .[2]

[1] Macd.P. 'Stephen' 270, Stephen to Macdonald, 21 May 1887, enclosing White's
letter dated 18 May 1887.   [2] Ibid.

VIII

Stopping the cracks

MANITOBA AT THE CROSSROADS

BY the end of May 1887, Stephen was undoubtedly, as far as Winnipeg was concerned, the most unpopular man in Canada, with Van Horne a close second—only, as the latter said, when the Winnipeggers burnt Sir George in effigy one mattress sufficed, while to do justice to him required two. In Stephen's opinion, his wire to Norquay had had no appreciable effect; the Provincial Premier had already decided that the Red River road was to be built if at all possible. What Stephen had hoped was that his message would make Norquay pause before committing himself.[1]

What the agitators wanted was to gain popular support by making it seem that this move of the C.P.R. President forced them to extreme measures, and they were not disappointed. The Manitoba Legislature voted $1 million to be raised by the sale of Provincial Bonds, for the construction of the Red River Valley Railroad, and, in addition, offered a guarantee of 4 per cent for twenty-five years in aid of a Hudson's Bay Railway. According to Stephen, what they wanted was money to be spent in their midst, no matter on what, to give real estate speculators a 'boom'.[2] There was no one left in Manitoba who had money to burn; McMicken's railway scheme had presumably failed for want of capital, and it was obvious that the Canadian Pacific did not contemplate throwing any more millions into the Province just yet.

The Province of Manitoba stands, as it were, at the crossroads of the Dominion. It has been seen how, in the early days, the Red River settlers lived in a world that ran from north to south; they had been glad to be united by rail with the commercial centres of Minnesota, and although at that time they had also looked forward to the building of the Canadian Pacific, they had perhaps expected that the expansion of trade would operate freely in both directions,

[1] Macd.P. 'Stephen' 270, Stephen to Macdonald, 25 September 1887.
[2] Loc. cit. Stephen to Macdonald, 4 and 6 June 1887.

so that they would be twice blessed. The national line conferred the greater benefit, but it had meant a partial eclipse of the older route, and the 'monopoly clause' had imposed a check on the immediate further development of the north-south traffic. Had the new road compensated for this by lavish expenditure there might have been no trouble, although the attractions of potential competition as a lever with which to force even better terms out of the railway company might in any event have proved irresistible. The fact remains that the Manitobans' first loyalty had been to the Minnesota route, and despite ancient complaints that the Hill-Kittson company had 'ground down the people of Manitoba', they were ready, when the Canadian Pacific did not come up to expectations, to seek American alliances.

The immediate result of the introduction of the Red River Valley Railroad Bill in the Manitoba Legislature was a slump in Canadian Pacifics on the London market.[1] With the credit of the Company 'utterly shaken', Stephen saw that after all there was nothing for it but to surrender at once the C.P.R.'s exclusive privileges in Manitoba. He suggested to Macdonald that when the Bill came up to Ottawa for 'disallowance' it should be intimated that the Dominion Government intended to negotiate with the C.P.R. Company for the cancellation of clause 15.[2] Stephen's solution was, however, somewhat naïve. Manitoba was not to be so easily pacified.

Disallowance of the Bill only served to increase the Province's determination to proceed with the railway project, but thanks to the allies of the Canadian Pacific it did not prove so easy to dispose of the Provincial Bonds which were to finance the scheme as had been expected. Just in time, Morton, Rose and Company were prevented from making the issue by the intervention of Sir Donald Smith and Sir John Rose.[3] The Province's agents had been unaware of the full circumstances when they agreed to make the issue. Stephen still feared that money could be found elsewhere. Macdonald, on the other hand, took a more optimistic—or complacent—view. He was not in favour of the Canadian Pacific's giving

[1] Macd.P. 'Stephen' 270, Stephen to Macdonald, 9 and 26 June 1887.   [2] Ibid.
[3] Macd.P. 'Donald A. Smith' 265, Smith to Macdonald, 24 June 1887. Macd.P. 'Rose' 259.691, Morton, Rose & Co. to Macdonald, 24 June 1887. Macd.P. 'Rose. 259.693, Macdonald to Rose, 24 June 1887. Macd.L.B. 24.197, Macdonald to Rose, 25 June 1887. Macd.P. 'Rose' 259.694, Rose to Macdonald, 27 June 1887. *Railway Times*, 9 July, 1887.

up its rights just then, and suggested that a reduction in rates might achieve all that was desired. To this Stephen replied:

. . . I cannot take any comfort in your view that the Winnipeggers will soon regain their senses. I see no indication of anything of that sort and when you reflect that the whole agitation has no real basis of any grievance to act upon, that it is simply the work of a half dozen desperadoes who have got control of the Government, and who care for nothing so long as they can accomplish their own selfish ends, you will at once see that nothing in the way of a reduction of rates, were that possible without loss, would do any good. . . .

Stephen realized that while the farmers might benefit indirectly from such a reduction—and it was only indirectly that freight rates affected them, for they sold their grain at the stations to millers such as Ogilvie—it would not appease the real-estate speculator. He concluded his letter with a *cri de coeur* comparing the two areas, one on either side of the 49th Parallel, which were the scenes of his two great railway enterprises:

On one side it is all turmoil and agitation and politics, on the other every man is working and saying nothing.[1]

The C.P.R. was still paying no supplementary dividend, and Stephen feared that many investors would prefer to risk a loss for the sake of getting clear of the concern.

Soon rumours were afloat that Norquay was after all succeeding in his quest for funds. First it was said that the Catholic Seminary had agreed to make a loan[2]; then it appeared that the Provincial Government intended to appropriate certain trust funds which were in its keeping.[3] At all events the work of construction was progressing, and Canadian Pacifics, which a year before had stood at 75, were quoted at 49½. On 12 September Stephen addressed a letter to the shareholders (Appendix V) explaining the position in Manitoba.

In October it was reported that the building of the Red River Valley Railroad had stopped for lack of money, but almost immediately it became known that the Winnipeg City Council had offered to come to the rescue with an issue of municipal bonds.[4] This was to be secured by the City's sinking fund, and Stephen at once

---

[1] Macd.P. 'Stephen' 270, Stephen to Macdonald, 12 July 1887.
[2] Thompson Papers, 6590, Stephen to Macdonald, 8 September 1887.
[3] Macd.P. 'Stephen' 270, Stephen to Macdonald, 14 September 1887.
[4] Macd.P. 'Van Horne' 288, Van Horne to Macdonald, 9 October 1887.

communicated with Morton, Rose and Company with the object of getting some bondholders to restrain the City from such action. It was found impossible to persuade any bondholder to act.[1] In the end, Norquay failed to come to terms with the City Fathers, who would only advance the money if the Premier would guarantee the completion of the road.[2] As the contractor would not guarantee completion if the military intervened, this was impossible.[3]

Even although it seemed that the Red River Valley road might never reach the boundary, Stephen was now more than ever convinced that in the interests of the Company, and for the sake of peace in the North West, the Canadian Pacific must surrender clause 15. He had a double motive. If competing railways were to be admitted into its preserves, the Company had to be able to hold its own, and this could only be brought about by further large expenditure on rolling stock and other equipment. If, in exchange for the surrender of clause 15, the Dominion Government would agree to guarantee an issue of Land Grant Bonds, this—together with the news that trouble in Manitoba was at an end—would, Stephen felt sure, result in a ready sale.[4] This scheme would benefit both Company and Government, for moderate politicians in Manitoba agreed that although not everyone approved of the Red River Valley Railroad, the people of the Province were practically unanimous against the policy of disallowance on principle, and until it was discontinued Manitoba would remain a source of unrest.[5]

Stephen was about to leave for England when he made this suggestion to Macdonald, urging the latter to let him have the Government's decision in time for him to discuss it with Baring Brothers at his first interview. In addition to making an issue of Land Grant Bonds, he was hoping to launch securities in connection with the projected Algoma Branch which was to take the C.P.R. to Sault Ste. Marie.[6] At first Macdonald wanted to postpone consideration of the question until 1891 (the original date for completion of the contract) but Sir Donald Smith, in Stephen's absence, persuaded him that the situation demanded early action.[7] A provisional agreement was made, and Stephen was able to make

---

[1] Macd.P. 'Stephen' 270, Stephen to Macdonald, 10 and 14 October 1887.
[2] *Railway Times*, 22 October 1887.   [3] *Railway Times*, 5 November 1887.
[4] Macd.P. 'Stephen' 270, Stephen to Macdonald, 19 October 1887.
[5] Loc. cit. Stephen to Macdonald, 14 October 1887.
[6] Loc. cit. Stephen to Macdonald, 11 November 1887.
[7] Macd. P.'Donald A. Smith' 265, Smith to Macdonald, 23 January 1888.

his arrangements with Barings.[1] On his return to Canada in January 1888, however, he was still having to argue with Macdonald about the advisability of abolishing disallowance. He had to point out that not only was the C.P.R. suffering, but the Dominion Government was being represented as hindering the development of the North West.[2]

Work on the Red River Valley road was still held up, and the Provincial Legislature, seeing that as a means of impressing Ottawa this project was something of a failure, resorted to other methods. A memorial was prepared embodying Manitoba's version of the case for ending disallowance, and was sent, after routine perusal by the Privy Council at Ottawa, by the Governor-General to the Colonial Office for presentation to the Queen.[3] Obviously the Privy Council expected that it would be summarily dismissed by the Imperial authorities as unworthy of serious consideration. On the contrary, the Colonial Office staff studied it industriously, and, observing that the Canadian Government based its case not on policy but on law, proposed to refer the matter to the Judicial Committee of the Imperial Privy Council.[4] This the Dominion Government did not want, but had the Governor-General not shortly informed the Colonial Office that an early settlement with Manitoba was in sight, it is probable that the Imperial authorities would have pressed their point.[5] As it was, the latter decided to await developments, hoping for an amicable solution. A Despatch of 13 March conveyed the news that such had been achieved. After considerable discussion over terms it had been agreed to propose to Parliament that the Dominion Government should guarantee $15 million worth of C.P.R. Land Grant Bonds in exchange for the Company's surrender of clause 15.[6]

THE BATTLE OF FORT WHYTE

In January 1888, Norquay's Administration had been replaced by Greenway's Liberals. Perhaps the best illustration of how a

[1] Macd.P. 'Stephen' 270, Stephen to Macdonald, 26 November 1887 (two letters); also Macd.P. 'Stephen' 271, Stephen to Macdonald, 18 January and 19 February 1888.
[2] Macd.P. 'Stephen' 271, Stephen to Macdonald, 25 February 1888.
[3] CO 42/795, Governor-General's Despatches 4 and 5 January 1888; also CO 42/791, his Despatches 30 August and 21 September 1887.
[4] See Thompson Papers 7454.   [5] CO 42/795, Despatches 17 and 18 February 1888.
[6] CO 42/795, Despatch 13 March 1888. Also Macd.P. 'Stephen' 271, Stephen to Macdonald, 15, 16, 17 and 20 March 1888, and CO 42/796, Governor-General's Despatch 25 April 1888.

farmer could support the speculator's view of the situation is given
in a letter addressed to the new Premier by a Waskado farmer who
wanted an extension of time in which to pay for his pre-emption
land:

> . . . I have had very hard luck since I have been here. I have lost too
> [*sic*] crops by hail and one by frost and it has thrown me pretty well
> back . . . but still I am bound to stay when we have got a better Govern-
> ment in power and the railway Monopoly is done away with know [*sic*]
> it will give us farmers a chance. . . .[1]

It appeared that Greenway still intended to proceed with the
construction of the Red River Valley Railroad whenever money
for the purpose could be secured. Stephen had offered to lease to
the Province the C.P.R.'s Emerson Branch, running from Winnipeg to the boundary on the opposite side of the river from the
Pembina Branch. A third line was obviously not required and
Stephen considered that if the Province was determined on an
independently worked road the C.P.R. might as well make good a
little of their loss through competition by drawing rental from the
rival concern. His conviction that only fresh expenditure would
satisfy Manitoba seemed borne out by Greenway's refusal of his
offer, after much prevarication, on the pretext that the rental
demanded was too high.[2]

By August of that year Greenway had evidently discovered some
possible source of finance and had agreed with the Northern Pacific
to build the road with what amounted to a subsidy of $6,000 a mile
from the Provincial exchequer.[3] Again Stephen was filled with
apprehension. In vain did Macdonald protest that the entry into
the North West of the Northern Pacific was only to be expected
when the C.P.R. surrendered its exclusive rights, and that
Greenway could not be blamed for trying to get as much
railway accommodation for his Province as he could.[4] Stephen had
been prepared to compete with the Northern Pacific on equal terms,

---

[1] Greenway Papers (G300-349), Wellington W. Tamblyn to Greenway, 9 April 1888.
[2] Macd.P. 'Stephen' 271, Macdonald to Stephen, 28 February 1888; Stephen to
Macdonald, 17 March, 30 April, 4, 5, 7 and 15 July 1888; Piers to Stephen, 16 July and
Stephen to Piers, 17 July 1888 (Arthur Piers, assistant general manager, C.P.R., later in
charge of steamship operations), also *Winnipeg Free Press*, 18 May 1888; correspondence
between Lieutenant-Governor Aikins, Van Horne, Superintendent Whyte (C.P.R.) and
Greenway.
[3] Macd.P. 'Stephen' 271, Stephen to Macdonald, 2 August 1888; *Railway Times*, 8
September, *Winnipeg Sun*, 28 and 30 August, and *Winnipeg Free Press*, 30 August 1888.
[4] Macd.L.B. 25.111, Macdonald to Stephen, 4 August 1888.

but not with the subsidized ally of a hostile Government.[1] Nor could he take comfort from Macdonald's assurance that Manitoba had neither the means nor the credit to carry out her intentions; he no doubt knew that earlier that year an envoy of the Province had with winning words almost persuaded Baring Brothers and Company to bring out a loan for it.[2] It was still possible to challenge the legality of the Provincial Government's proceedings. The question was even then before the Supreme Court, and Macdonald was confident that when the Province was proved to be in the wrong the American company would 'drop the thing like a hot potato'.[3]

Stephen went over to England in the autumn of 1888 unable to shake off the deep depression that had settled upon him. In August he had retired from the Presidency of the Canadian Pacific, deeming it right that someone more experienced in railway administration should take his place, but without having solved the various problems which had confronted the Company on the completion of the main line three years before. There was still, at the back of his mind, the nagging doubt that the whole enterprise was one big mistake. The attitude of Manitoba, and the apparently inevitable invasion from the south, made him wonder once more whether the line north of Lake Superior ought ever to have been built. Yet once more he told himself that without that line there would have been no *Canadian* Pacific Railway. When Macdonald, who took a more cheerful view of the future, rebuked him for his pessimism, Stephen admitted that as his nerve and courage were no longer what they once were he was disqualified from making an accurate forecast.[4]

He was hurt to the core by the apparent apathy and even hostility of the people of Canada towards the C.P.R.,[5] and was worried beyond bearing at the prospect of some great catastrophe befalling the shareholders. As always, he unburdened himself to Macdonald:

It is not, need I say to you, anxiety lest I should suffer pecuniarily myself that bothers me. It is the apprehension that I may turn out to be the cause of loss and disaster to others, who trusted and believed in the C.P.R. because of my connection with it, that depresses me and makes 'life hardly worth living'.[6]

[1] Macd.P. 'Stephen' 271, Stephen to Macdonald, 8 August 1888.
[2] Greenway Papers (G251-299), C. S. Drummond to Greenway, 27 March 1888.
[3] Macd.L.B. 25.181, Macdonald to Stephen, 11 October 1888.
[4] Macd.P. 'Stephen' 271, Stephen to Macdonald, 19 November 1888.
[5] Loc. cit. Stephen to Macdonald, 2 August 1888.
[6] Loc. cit. Stephen to Macdonald, 19 November 1888.

So far as Manitoba was concerned, Macdonald proved the truer prophet. The rest of the story of the Red River Valley Railroad, culminating in the melodramatic 'Battle of Fort Whyte', when the Provincial railway-builders found their crossing of the C.P.R. line challenged by a body of men under the Western Superintendent, William Whyte, does not require retelling.[1] Although the newspapers made the most of the incident, even *The Times* publishing a leader which it afterwards regretted,[2] the *Railway Times* more exactly described the event: 'Nobody was injured, but the Manitobans are greatly exasperated.'[3] In December it was reported that work on the Red River Valley road had been suspended 'because of bad weather',[4] but by this time the law had decided in favour of the Dominion Government's right to restrain the Province, and the Northern Pacific was consequently discouraged.

HUNGARIAN SETTLERS FOR THE NORTH WEST

Before continuing to deal with the other main topics of this phase of Stephen's career, progress must be reported on one aspect of his work for the C.P.R. which tended to be overshadowed during the later stages of construction, but not entirely neglected, namely, the task of filling up the North West with settlers. Stephen's experience with the Gladstone Government over this question had not daunted him, but he saw that the one great difficulty in the way of systematic colonization was lack of capital. Voluntary bodies continued to send out occasional batches of emigrants, and independent farmers settled on isolated locations, but these sporadic efforts were not enough.[5] Stephen had himself settled one of his Scottish cousins, William Stephen, on a farm at Virden, Manitoba, in 1883, and the latter, by his industry and that of his sons, proved what could be done on a large scale, if only the initial capital were forthcoming.[6]

Such was his belief in the potentialities of the North West that Stephen was not slow to risk his own capital gratuitously in promoting settlement. At the end of 1883 he contemplated financing

---

[1] See J. A. Jackson, *The Background of the Battle of Fort Whyte*, Historical and Scientific Society of Manitoba, Winnipeg, 1946.

[2] *The Times*, 23 October 1888; Macd.P. 'Stephen' 271, Stephen to Macdonald, 26 October 1888.   [3] *Railway Times*, 3 November 1888.

[4] *Railway Times*, 1 December 1888.

[5] Macd.P. 'Stephen' 270, Stephen to Macdonald, 25 February 1886.

[6] *Western World*, April 1892 (Winnipeg): *A Virden Farmer*, with illustrations of 'Mr. William Stephen's Gopher Creek Farm, Virden, Manitoba.'

the establishment of French communities in Alberta, proposing to enlist the aid of Father Lacombe, the veteran Catholic missionary in these parts, in the process of transplantation. Archbishop Taché of St. Boniface, whom he had approached on the subject, had admitted that the French could make a better living in the North West than down on the Gulf of the St. Lawrence, but was evidently not too anxious to have the faithful scattered. Father Lacombe, on the other hand, was very favourable to the idea.[1] But it would seem that the Archbishop won the day, and Stephen was obliged to look elsewhere for his settlers. Archbishop Taché found himself, instead, trying to meet the needs of some Scottish Catholics in Lady Gordon Cathcart's crofter settlement in the North West Territories; the *Weekly Manitoban* of 22 July 1885 reported that he had written to W. B. Scarth of the parochial visit of one Father McCarthy to this settlement where it was found that what was needed was someone 'to teach the catechism in the Gaelic language'.

Stephen had in 1883 persuaded some of his Dutch friends to interest themselves in colonization schemes,[2] and he also used his influence in Germany to the same end. A letter from Prince Hohenlohe,[3] whom Stephen had met while travelling, explains to some extent the lack of success in attracting Germany's surplus population to the Canadian North West:

. . . I advise people, who ask me where to go, if I can't prevent them leaving the country, I direct their steps to Canada. . . . Nevertheless my wish is . . . that we may soon find a land where our surplus population may settle without giving up its nationality. We are far more than ever forced to look out for such a land, as England tries in every way to prevent us from acquiring territories abroad, whilst England itself never hesitates to swallow as much land as it can get. The way in which English papers and also some of the different colonial governments show their jealousy towards the smallest German annexation and try to prevent them, has raised a very bitter feeling in Germany against England, and prevents a great many Germans to settle where British sovereignty exists. . . . They will therefore be forced to settle in the United States. . . .

In the summer of 1885, however, Stephen met someone who was looking for the very thing the C.P.R. President wanted to provide.

[1] Macd.P. 'Stephen' 267, Stephen to Macdonald, 30 December 1883.
[2] Loc. cit. Stephen to Macdonald, 14 May 1883.
[3] Macd.P. 'Stephen' 269, Stephen to Macdonald, 28 January 1885, enclosing Hohenlohe to Stephen, 10 January 1885. (Chlodwig Karl Victor, Prince of Hohenlohe-Schillingsfürst, German Chancellor.)

Count Paul O. Esterházy was a Hungarian exile who had been banished from his native land after the revolution of 1848. Wandering in the United States, his attention had been drawn to the plight of some of his fellow-countrymen in the mines of Pennsylvania.[1] These exiles had been acustomed to working on the land, and the hardships of their uncongenial toil had of late been accentuated by conflicts with miners of other nationalities during recent coal and iron workers' strikes.[2] Esterházy had made one attempt to settle some of these Hungarians in the Western States, but the scheme had not succeeded, and in it the Count had lost his own capital. Then, through the C.P.R.'s agents in America, he got in touch with the Canadian Government. It was the time of the 'Russian scare', and Esterházy's proposal for 'military settlements' in the Canadian West—of farmers trained in warfare who would act as emergency militia—roused a good deal of interest. The scare passed, however, and Government interest waned. The land was still there, nevertheless, and on a promise of financial aid from Stephen himself, Esterházy went ahead with his plans. In July 1885 the first Hungarian settlement was established west of Minnedosa, Manitoba, and the following month another group settled alongside. They called the place Hun Valley.[3] Had unlimited capital been available, the problem of populating the North West would by such means have been to a great extent solved. The news of the new Canaan spread through old Hungary like wildfire, even being disseminated from pulpits along with spiritual food to the land-hungry. Sir George Stephen's purse was not, however, bottomless. After assisting Esterházy to obtain a loan of $25,000 on behalf of prospective colonists[4] with which the latter founded another colony in Saskatchewan, named Esterhazy,[5] Stephen could do no more.[6] The Hungarians deserved more official encouragement, as they proved

[1] Andrew A. Marchbin: (i) 'Early Emigration from Hungary to Canada', in *Slavonic Review*, xiii, 1943-5. (ii) *The Origin of Migration from South-eastern Europe to Canada*, in Canadian Historical Association Report, 1934.
   [2] *Montreal Gazette*, 14 July 1885.
   [3] Marchbin, op. cit. (i) p. 132.
   [4] Marchbin, op. cit. (i) p. 135. See also SP 12, 1887, CO 45/612, Appendix 49, for Report on Hungarian Immigration and Colonization, by Count Paul O. Esterházy, 31 December 1886.
   [5] Esterhazy, now a 'town' of four elevators, is about 150 miles east of Regina, and is served by a branch line of the C.P.R. from that city to Brandon. (Oral evidence from resident.)
   [6] See also Robert England, *The Colonization of Western Canada*, London, 1936, Chapter 14 on Hungarian and other communities. Also J. of C.H.C. CO 45/584, Appendix 6 on Immigration.

to be model settlers.[1] Some years later, Clifford Sifton, Minister of the Interior, who with Lord Strathcona, then Canadian High Commissioner, had worked to promote Central European immigration to Canada, endorsed the opinion which had led Stephen to give his support to Hungarian colonization:

I think a stalwart peasant in a sheepskin coat, born on the soil, whose forefathers have been farmers for ten generations, with a stout wife and half-a-dozen children, is good quality.[2]

Stephen also helped to finance a Scandinavian settlement in the North West which had equally good results,[3] so that the settlers were able to induce a number of their fellow-countrymen to join them.

BRITAIN CAUTIOUS ABOUT STATE-AIDED EMIGRATION

From time to time the question of state-aided emigration from the United Kingdom recurred in the Imperial Parliament, a nucleus of interested parties in the House of Lords especially helping to keep the subject open.[4] In May 1886, Stephen perceived what he thought was a 'little gleam of sunshine for us' in a speech of Lord Salisbury's in which he had recommended that a portion of the money which was being devoted to 'buying out' the Irish landlords should be spent in helping the Irish to emigrate.[5] Stephen erred, however, in thinking that the British Premier was an earnest advocate of state-aided colonization.

In 1887, Stephen happened to be in London when a deputation waited on Lord Salisbury at the Foreign Office with a scheme for state-aided colonization.[6] Lord Brabazon, the spokesman, after pointing out the urgent need of some measure to relieve the distress arising from unemployment, proposed the appointment of an Imperial Commission, on which representative colonists should be *ex officio* members, empowered to raise funds in the open market for the purpose of sending out suitable emigrants to the free lands

---

[1] Marchoin, op. cit. (i), p. 138, quoting Report of Department of the Interior, SP 7, 1892.
[2] John W. Dafoe, *Clifford Sifton in relation to his Times*, Toronto, 1931, p. 318. Note: Unrestricted emigration propaganda was prohibited in most European countries.
[3] James B. Hedges, *Building the Canadian West*, New York, 1939, p. 122.
[4] Hansard (Lords): 2 April 1886, p. 587; 7 June 1886, p. 1139; 1 February 1887, p. 383; and (Commons): 18 June 1886, p. 1847; 7 February 1887, p. 767; 8 August 1887, p. 1555. Also Accounts and Papers, 1886, vol. xlv.
[5] Macd.P. 'Stephen' 270, Stephen to Macdonald, 17 May 1886.
[6] *The Times*, 5 February 1887.

of the colonies. Lord Salisbury's reply was hardly constructive. While professing to agree personally with the sentiments of the deputation, he proceeded to enlarge upon the difficulties of such a scheme:

You have not only to achieve a victory in the lists of pure logic or pure political philosophy, but you have to provide the arguments which would carry the measures through the House of Commons, and that is not exactly the same thing. . . . You say you do not want money—you want State-directed colonization. Well, you want direction, then. But you know direction is the one thing than an English Government cannot give you. It has no power to give it to you the moment you go into a colony. . . . Then there is beyond that the great difficulty of finance. . . .

Although it was not suggested that the Government should do more than appoint the Commission, Lord Salisbury went on to stress the impossibility of raising the required sum—he put it at £100 to £150 per man. It would be far too much for private enterprise, and how could Parliament be persuaded to guarantee such an outlay? 'I fear that you are asking Parliament to undertake a great speculation.' He considered that the deputation had not gone sufficiently deeply into the details of their scheme, but concluded by assuring them it would give him the greatest satisfaction if they succeeded in resolving their great idea into a practical shape in which Parliament could give it effect.

This was, of course, too much for Stephen. After all his efforts with the Gladstone Government he now had to begin all over again to try to convince Lord Salisbury and the general public that investment in the North West was no 'leap in the dark'. On 9 February his letter was printed in *The Times*:

Referring to Lord Salisbury's answer to the deputation on the subject of state-aided colonization which waited upon him a few days ago, will you grant me space to briefly point out that the financial obstacles in the way of a well devised and effective scheme of colonization from the congested districts of Ireland and Scotland are not nearly so serious as Lord Salisbury seemed to fear?

For example, a capital allowance of £120 is sufficient to take a crofter family of man, wife and four children from their home in Scotland or Ireland, and, in 14 days, place them in any of the new North-West Provinces of Canada, upon 160 acres of good agricultural land ready for the plough, without obstacle of either stick or stone, with a comfortable house to live in, with the cattle and implements necessary to enable the crofter to begin his work of cultivation and with sufficient means to maintain his family for the first year.

Upon this basis, an expenditure of £360,000 would emigrate, and settle comfortably in the Canadian North-West, 3,000 crofter families—18,000 souls in all; and, if this expenditure were continued for 5 years, the result would be the emigration and settlement of 90,000 souls, or about one-third of the distressed Scotch crofter population.

The capital required to carry out this scheme would have to be provided by the State, but such arrangements could—I am satisfied and I am prepared to show—be made by which its repayment within ten years would be rendered perfectly secure; though it is the basis of this plan that the State should, for that period, forego interest. So that the actual cost to the nation of transplanting a Scotch or Irish crofter family to their new home, and thoroughly establishing them in it, would simply be 3 per cent. interest per family, or £6 per head. It will thus be seen that the emigration of a million persons would only cost £6,000,000, and not the £100,000,000 or £120,000,000 which was mentioned by Lord Salisbury and not corrected by the deputation.

Surely this scheme, which I am satisfied is quite practicable, is not beyond the power of a great nation like this, especially when all sides admit that emigration, or colonization, is the one remedy for a growing and already nearly unbearable difficulty.

What more could Lord Salisbury want? Here was a scheme, all cut-and-dried, proposed by one who had at his command the facilities for carrying it into operation, and at extremely modest cost. The crofter problem in Scotland had, although in a quieter way, been causing almost as much anxiety as the Irish land question, and the opportunity to solve both with such seeming simplicity ought to have stirred the Government into immediate action. A more cautious approach was, however, decided upon. A committee consisting of 32 Peers and 135 Members of Parliament met to consider the best means of bringing the subject before Parliament,[1] and in November of that year they issued a Report on State Colonization, recommending that a Board be officially formed with power to raise a public loan for colonization purposes, interest to be guaranteed by the Imperial Government.[2] They had ascertained that the Canadian Government were ready to help with advice and assistance and free grants of land, provided that they were not made immediately responsible for the immigrants.[3]

[1] *The Times*, 12 February 1887.   [2] *The Times*, 14 November 1887.
[3] *The Times*, 29 November 1887.

15

Stephen had meanwhile enlisted the sympathy of Lord Lothian, Secretary of State for Scotland, in his proposal to deal with the crofters. Lord Lothian had found the Treasury unwilling to agree to the terms of Stephen's scheme as it stood, and was anxious to have these modified in order to make them more acceptable to 'the guardians of the public purse'.[1] Sir John Rose had revived the old suggestion of having the Canadian Government guarantee the security of the three land companies to be involved (C.P.R., Hudson's Bay and Canada North West Land Companies) but this was no more acceptable in 1887 than it had been in 1883.[2] Stephen maintained that he was offering the Imperial Government 'a very cheap remedy for the crofter question'.[3] He had hoped to have Lord Lothian visit the North West in person that summer so that he might 'judge how well it and the poor crofters would agree', but at the last moment Lord Salisbury had prevented the Scottish Secretary from leaving before the House rose.[4]

The following year the Government sanctioned the advance of £10,000 to start a colonization scheme for the crofters of the Western Highlands and Islands of Scotland, on condition that £2,000 was raised by private subscription. The fund was to be administered by four trustees, representing respectively the Imperial Government, the Canadian Government, the private subscribers and the Land Companies.[5] The individuals chosen were the Secretary of State for Scotland, the High Commissioner for Canada, the Lord Provost of Glasgow and Mr. Thomas Skinner.[6]

Stephen communicated his reaction to Macdonald:

It is hard to keep one's temper with these people on the other side. . . .
The absurdity of creating a big commission to watch over an expenditure of £10,000!!![7]

To Rose he cabled in a similar sense, referring to the Government's scheme as 'absurdly homeopathic and useless'. The suitability of the North West for the settlement of crofter families had been proved by experience, and there was no need for such tentative

---

[1] Macd.P. 'Stephen' 270, Stephen to Macdonald, 26 May 1887. The phrase in quotation is Lord Salisbury's.

[2] Loc. cit. Enclosures in Stephen to Macdonald, 26 May 1887; Cables, Rose to Stephen, 25 May 1887; Stephen to Rose, 25 May 1887; Rose to Stephen, 26 May 1887.

[3] Loc. cit. Stephen to Macdonald, 26 May 1887.

[4] Loc. cit. Stephen to Macdonald, 19 September 1887.

[5] Accounts and Papers, House of Commons, C.5403, 1888.

[6] Hansard (Commons): 4 April 1889, p. 1680; answer to question by Mr. Rankin.

[7] Macd.P. 'Stephen' 271, Stephen to Macdonald, 30 April 1888.

measures.[1] In answer to a question in the British House of Commons in March 1889, it was stated that 193 crofters had been sent out to date[2]; a Scottish and an Irish settlement, at Saltcoats and Killarney, were established in Saskatchewan and Manitoba respectively, but nothing further was done, as a new Committee had been appointed to look into the whole question.[3] After sitting for three parliamentary sessions, this Committee reported that the success of the Canadian experiment was sufficiently established to justify a further despatch of 'a moderately numerous party'.[4] By the time that more money was made available, even the crofters had lost interest, and in 1893 none applied to emigrate.[5]

Although his own scheme for systematic colonization proved comparatively fruitless, Stephen may nevertheless be said to have played a not inconsiderable part in the settlement of the Canadian North West. Apart from the small colonies which he personally helped to finance, the very fact that he was instrumental in the building of the railway through the fertile districts secures him a substantial share of the credit. It may be added that the time was peculiarly ripe for the development of prairie farming. In the harvest of 1883 a new phenomenon had appeared on the western scene—the Massey Harris binder. Today in every prairie town the agricultural machinery store is as essential and inevitable as the row of grain elevators, and although the binder is now a museum piece, the author of *Harvest Triumphant* may justly claim that 'nothing can ever rob the binder of its historical significance. With the Canadian Pacific and David Fife's hard red wheat, it made possible the settlement of the Canadian northwest'.[6]

MORE OBSTACLES TO PACIFIC STEAMSHIP SUBSIDY

By June 1887, it had become obvious to the British Government that whatever might be thought of Canada's fiscal policy as applied to pig iron—bar or puddled bar—the proposed Pacific steamship service had aroused so much interest that the question demanded

---

[1] Macd.F. 'Stephen' 271, Stephen to Macdonald, 30 April 1888. Copy of cable to Rose enclosed.
[2] Hansard (Commons): 21 March 1889, p. 400; answer to question by Mr. Watt.
[3] Loc. cit. 20 February 1890, p. 753, answer to question by Mr. Seton-Kerr.
[4] Hansard (Lords): 24 April 1891, p. 1302, speech by Earl of Meath.
[5] Hansard (Commons): 10 February 1893, p. 1043, answer to question by Mr. Seton-Kerr.
[6] Merrill Denison, *Harvest Triumphant : The Story of Massey-Harris*, Toronto, 1948, p. 84.

consideration on its own merits. British prestige seemed likely to be endangered by rumours that negotiations were in progress with Germany for supplying the service should the Imperial Government fail to give its support. How serious Stephen was when he first suggested such an expedient is conjectural; when Macdonald, prompted by Sir Henry Holland, the Colonial Secretary, asked him what foundation there was for the rumours Stephen telegraphed the laconic reply:

Would like you to answer that Pacific are not and will not negotiate with any foreign Company unless compelled by failure to induce England to aid in the establishment of the service.[1]

A month later, Rose reported that Goschen was 'still procrastinating', and that although the Cabinet as a whole was favourable it seemed that it would be impossible to obtain legislation that session.[2] Stephen thereupon cabled both Rose and Tupper, the High Commissioner, that if the Imperial Government would but make the contract that autumn, he would accept it, subject to its ratification by Parliament the following session.[3] Stephen had heard that unless action could be taken in the near future, the Canadian Pacific was likely to be forestalled by a San Francisco line operating in connection with American railways.[4] Moreover, following a depression in the shipyards in 1885, conditions there were steadily improving and every year increased the cost of shipbuilding.

After a further meeting with Mr. Goschen and Sir Henry Holland, both Rose and Tupper were confident that the Imperial Government would agree to Stephen's suggestion.[5] Then came a further and most unexpected setback. In response to a request by the Chancellor, Tupper wrote to Mr. Goschen the following day enclosing a memorandum by Harry Moody embodying the C.P.R.'s alternative proposals for the fortnightly and monthly services. He also enclosed a copy of Stephen's cable respecting the danger of competition from San Francisco and, on the advice of Rose, Holland and Sir Robert Herbert, added, as a spur to action by the Treasury, his opinion that lack of support from the Imperial Government would be exploited for propaganda purposes by the

---

[1] Macd.P. 'Stephen' 270, Macdonald to Stephen, 21 June 1887, and answer.
[2] Macd.P. 'Rose' 259.699, Rose to Macdonald, 15 July and 259.704, Rose to Macdonald, 21 July 1887.
[3] Macd.P. 'Stephen' 270, Stephen to Macdonald, 23 July 1887.
[4] Tupper Papers 428, Stephen to Tupper, 23 July 1887.
[5] Macd.P. 'Rose' 259,709, Rose to Macdonald, 28 July 1887.

advocates of commercial union between Canada and the United States.[1]

Goschen's reaction was exactly the opposite of what had been intended. He replied:

. . . I cannot help feeling that if there is really a strong movement in Canada in favour of such a Commercial Union, the proposed subsidy to the C.P.R. could go but a very little way to counteract it. And on the other hand your remark fills me with some alarm as to the position in which this country might be placed if, after it had committed itself to a considerable subsidy to the Canadian Pacific, and that not so much for postal as for general political objects, the Commercial Union between Canada and the United States should nevertheless, in a short time, become an accomplished fact. . . .[2]

While assuring the High Commissioner that he appreciated the exertions of Canada in creating the Pacific route, he declared the whole question was complicated by so many delicate political and financial considerations that he did not believe the Government 'as at present advised' would be able to make an announcement regarding the subsidy that session. The Chancellor also averred that Moody's memorandum on the monthly service was the first he had heard of the modified offer, which statement Tupper, in his reply, firmly denied, reminding Goschen that he had himself referred to it in the House on 23 June.

This correspondence was forwarded to Stephen with Tupper's comment that the Imperial Government were 'afraid of their shaddows [sic]'. The House of Commons, he said, would be no trouble.[3] Some days previously, in fact, the Premier had received a letter signed by nearly 300 Members declaring their approval of the scheme.[4] In face of this document it seemed strange that when, shortly afterwards, Lord Lorne and Sir Donald Smith discussed the matter with the Chancellor, the Postmaster General and the Colonial Secretary, Lorne got the impression that the members of the Cabinet were favourable to the subsidy, but were afraid that the case they had to submit to Parliament was not sufficiently strong.[5] Their professedly main anxiety was lest the railway could not be kept open in winter. Tupper had already explained to them the measures

---

[1] Tupper Papers 435, Tupper to Macdonald, 11 August and 430, Tupper to Goschen, 28 July 1887.
[2] Loc. cit. 432, Goschen to Tupper, 8 August 1887, and Tupper's reply, 11 August.
[3] Tupper Papers 434, Tupper to Goschen, 11 August 1887 and 535 (1889 in error), Tupper to Macdonald, 4 August 1887.   [4] *Railway Times*, 6 August 1887.
[5] Tupper Papers 438, Lorne to Tupper, 22 August 1887.

that were being taken to ensure this—the building of snowsheds at the points marked out by surveyors as likely to be threatened by avalanches.

It is not clear what finally swayed the Imperial Government in favour of granting the subsidy. It may have been the collective persuasions of the C.P.R. Company's friends and allies in London and the representations of the commercial community; it may have been, in the last instance, the result of Harry Northcote's spending a Sunday in August with Mr. Goschen.[1] At all events, it was announced in September that a subsidy of £45,000 for the monthly service was to be proposed to Parliament, conditional on the Dominion Government's supplying the balance of £15,000.[2]

The news was received with enthusiasm by the Press, although *The Times* regretted that the Government had not taken the bolder course and subsidized the fortnightly service. For this it blamed the Post Office: 'Possibly the habit of selling pennyworths of stamps and engaging in banking transactions of a few pence insures the predominance of the niggling spirit of retail trade. . . '.[3] *The Times* had no doubt that Mr. Cook would come forward to add his persuasions as to the advisability of the more frequent service.

Mr. Thomas Cook did not fail it. From Algeria he wrote to testify that he personally had seen English travellers who had had to go by the American route because the C.P.R. vessel was full, and they could not wait a month for the next. He already had pamphlets prepared giving through fares from Europe to Japan by the new route, and added that far from eclipsing the old, the Canadian steamship line would act as a feeder, as many travellers would wish to go one way and return by the other.[4]

Stephen himself was for the moment quite content, having come to the conclusion that at first there would not be sufficient steady trade for the larger fleet.[5]

ATLANTIC SERVICE STILL DELAYING FACTOR

It now seemed that the Canadian Pacific Company had only to hasten through the formalities of the contract and order its ships,

[1] Tupper Papers 434, Tupper to Stephen, 11 August 1887.
[2] Macd.L.B. 24.226, Macdonald to Tupper, 12 September 1887; Macd.P. 'Stephen' 270, Tupper to Macdonald, 15 September 1887; Tupper Papers 454, Goschen to Tupper, 19 September 1887; CO 42/792, Governor-General's Despatch, 21 September 1887.   [3] *The Times*, 26 September 1887.   [4] *The Times*, 10 October 1887.
[5] Macd.L.B. 24.226, Macdonald to Tupper, 12 September 1887.

but it soon became clear that its difficulties were not yet at an end. Mr. Goschen had directed the High Commissioner to have the Company begin negotiations with the Post Office, the Department responsible for the drafting of the contract, saying that he would communicate with the latter regarding the Treasury's views on the essential points.[1] Two months later the High Commissioner's secretary informed the Colonial Office that the Post Office was still awaiting notice of the Government's decision on the subsidy.[2] It appeared that Goschen had indeed written a memorandum for the Post Office in September, but possibly owing to its informality—it was not a Treasury Instruction—it had not been acted upon.[3]

This obstacle was cleared away before the arrival of Stephen who had come over to sign the contract, but its clearance only made way for another, and greater, stumbling-block. Writing to Macdonald on his return to Canada, Stephen broke the news:

. . . I have had a most tedious time with Goschen over the Pacific Ocean subsidy, and after I thought everything settled Moody cables that they will not sign the contract until the Government are notified that the tender for a satisfactory Atlantic service has been accepted. . . .[4]

Although the Canadian Government had informed the Colonial Office in March 1887 that it proposed calling for tenders for an improved Atlantic service, the actual advertisement did not appear until August. What caused the delay is obscure; as Stephen pointed out, there was no risk attached to publishing the advertisement; the Government would still be free, if it saw fit, to throw all the tenders into the waste-paper basket.[5] Both he and Tupper had at intervals continued to impress upon Macdonald the need for a really first class service, but when the advertisement did finally appear the conditions hardly met with either Stephen's or Van Horne's approval. The former lost no time in expressing himself upon the subject to the Prime Minister:

. . . Van Horne says that if they had been drawn for the purpose of preventing anyone tendering but the Allans and their allies they are perfect. I give up bothering about the matter; it seems to me clear that the Government are resolved on accepting an inferior and useless service

[1] Tupper Papers 454, Goschen to Tupper, 19 September 1887.
[2] CO 42/792, High Commissioner's Despatch, 17 November 1887.
[3] Loc. cit. Milner to Holland, 16 November 1887.
[4] Macd.P. 'Stephen' 270, Stephen to Macdonald, 18 January 1888.
[5] Loc. cit. Stephen to Macdonald, 9 August 1887.

to the country from the Allans and giving them an increased subsidy therefor. . . .[1]

He concluded by saying that if the country could not afford a first class line they should at least refrain from subsidizing freight boats, to the detriment of other vessels of the same class. Macdonald did not take this rebuke too seriously; Stephen, he wrote to Tupper, was looking at everything just then 'with a jaundiced eye'.[2]

Stephen had by no means given up bothering about it. On arriving in London in December 1887, he had once more got in touch with the Andersons. The latter were still anxious to tender for the Atlantic service, and had been in communication with the High Commissioner on the subject.[3]

Another appeal to Macdonald from Stephen to insist upon a 20-knot service elicited the response that although the former agreed that speed was very desirable, the Privy Council feared that the subsidy required for it would be beyond their means.[4] To this Stephen replied by cable:

Message received. Canada 30 years ago comparatively poor country with its money costing 6 per cent. gave Allan hundred and four thousand pounds subsidy practically equal to £200,000. Will be throwing money away or worse to subsidize service that must fail to compete with New York. Folly swallow cow and stick on tail. Present mail service positive injury to Canada. Am indifferent who gets contract provided best service secured.[5]

In January 1888, Mr. W. R. Anderson visited Canada and arranged with J. J. C. Abbott to engage an agent for his firm to carry on negotiations with the Government,[6] but there seemed to be no immediate possibility of the matter's being settled. Arrangements for the Pacific service were at a complete standstill owing to the indecision which clouded the future of the Atlantic portion of the Canadian route.

It was April 1888 before any definite information on the subject reached the Colonial Office. It came in the form of a cable from

---

[1] Loc. cit. Stephen to Macdonald, 12 August 1887.
[2] Tupper Papers 439, Macdonald to Tupper, 24 August 1887.
[3] Loc. cit. 441, Tupper to Stephen, 25 August 1887 and 444, Tupper to Stephen, 30 August 1887.
[4] Macd.P. 'Stephen' 270, Stephen to Macdonald, 22 December 1887 and answer.
[5] Loc. cit. Stephen to Macdonald, 23 December 1887. Note: The Andersons' tender involved a subsidy of $500,000—about £100,000.
[6] Macd.P. 'Abbott' 186, Abbott to Macdonald, 18 January 1888.

Tupper—then in Canada—announcing that the Dominion Government had given notice to the present contractors for the Atlantic mails to terminate their contract in one year's time in order that a much more rapid and efficient service might be provided.[1] On the same day Harry Moody wrote to Sir Robert Herbert expressing the hope that Mr. Goschen would be satisfied with this indication of the Canadian Government's intentions, and would allow the Pacific contract to be completed.[2] The Treasury would not at first accept Tupper's cable as an official communication, and refused to proceed unless some more definite guarantee were given.[3]

Eventually, after some further correspondence between Tupper and Goschen, the Chancellor appeared satisfied as to the future speed of the Atlantic steamships, and by September 1888, it seemed that the formalities of the Pacific contract were at last about to be concluded.

No actual figures for the speed of the proposed Atlantic service, or of the subsidy to be paid, had yet been disclosed. Tupper was afraid lest in his letters to Goschen he had committed the Canadian Government too far merely by saying that the Chancellor might confidently rely on a very much improved service being provided,[4] but Macdonald calmed his fears. In his opinion the High Commissioner had only expressed 'or rather conveyed' their desire for an accelerated service; the degree of acceleration had not been pledged. Although he agreed that more speed was desirable, Macdonald was still convinced that Canada could not afford to compete with the New York lines. Nothing, he thought, would so greatly injure the financial credit and status of the Dominion as to have it said that its Government was reckless and extravagant. He concluded:

Remember, that the day or two we may lose on the Atlantic is more than regained by the speed of the C.P.R. across the continent. Let us then get as great an acceleration of speed under the new Contract as we can afford and be satisfied with it.[5]

So much for the conception of the Conservative Party as the Party of Progress! This was hardly Stephen's idea of the new Canadian route to the East.

[1] CO 42/797, High Commissioner, 18 April 1888.
[2] Loc. cit. Moody to Herbert, 18 April 1888.
[3] Loc. cit. Treasury to Herbert, 19 April 1888. See also Minute by Lord Knutsford to Treasury Despatch of 11 May 1888, in same volume.
[4] CO 42/797, High Commissioner, Tupper to Goschen, 6 July 1888.
[5] Macd L.B. 25.94, Macdonald to Tupper, 30 July 1888.

The British Treasury was so content with the High Commissioner's assurances that when, at the last moment, the Post Office suggested that before signing the Pacific contract it should have a written understanding as to the speed of the Atlantic service, the reply was that this could be waived; the Dominion Government did not wish to name a definite speed lest it prejudice prospective tenders.[1] On a further point submitted by the Post Office the Treasury did consent to ask for definite information. This was the question of the connection between the Atlantic steamships and the C.P.R.; the Post Office wished to ensure the smooth transference of the mails. This new consideration delayed the signing of the contract for a further eight months. It was finally provided in a Privy Council Minute that the points of connection should be Halifax in winter and Quebec in summer.[2] The Canadian Prime Minister confirmed this in a cable to the High Commissioner, adding that his Government would stipulate for such landings in the Atlantic contract, and would be responsible for the mails at these points.[3]

SUBSIDY GRANTED DEPENDENT ON HALIFAX CONNECTION

Although this assurance satisfied the Imperial authorities, Stephen was not so happy about it. It was as yet by no means certain that the C.P.R. would ever get to Halifax, except by giving in to the Government's demand that a new line be built, and Stephen could not help thinking that to build a second line, when already the Intercolonial was being run at a loss, was sheer folly. At least the Government, by leasing its line to the Canadian Pacific, might recoup itself for past losses.[4] For some reason the Government did not think it desirable for the Pacific to get control of the Intercolonial; this much Macdonald later confirmed to Hickson, the Grand Trunk manager,[5] and it may well be that it was the recurrent fear of favouring the C.P.R. at the expense of the Grand Trunk that dictated the Prime Minister's attitude.

The Short Line to St. John, New Brunswick, was due to open on 2 June 1889, and an extension was planned to run via Harvey,

[1] CO 42/797, G.P.O./Treasury correspondence, 3 October 1888.
[2] CO 42/800, Governor-General's Despatch, 12 June 1889.
[3] Macd.L.B. 25.476, Macdonald to Tupper, 25 June 1889.
[4] Macd.P. 'Stephen' 271, Stephen to Macdonald, 20 May 1889; and 270, Stephen to Macdonald, 20 February 1886.
[5] Macd.L.B. 26.325, Macdonald to Hickson, 30 November 1889.

Fredericton and Moncton to Halifax, the terminus of the Intercolonial Railway. On 18 May 1889, the *Halifax Morning Chronicle*
declared:

Halifax has been sold. . . . St. John, New Brunswick, has got a short
line railway to Montreal, and Halifax can connect with it by the good old-
fashioned Intercolonial route. . . .

Provincial plaints weighed with Macdonald even if it meant holding
up a project of more than national importance. Halifax should have
its Short Line. As always, he was confident of wearing down a
resistance born of impatience with the trivia of politics.

There was a limit, however, to the lengths Stephen or Donald
Smith would go with their altruism.[1] They had offered to contribute
£50,000 each to a fast Atlantic Service which would set Canada in
the forefront of ocean commerce, but they were not, at their time of
life, looking for precarious investments. Of such they had had their
fill. A service that just missed its mark was of no interest to them,
and if, in addition to losing time on the Atlantic, the new service was
further impeded by the lack of a satisfactory connection at the
Atlantic seaboard, the whole new route would fail to justify its
existence.[2]

In spite of Stephen's misgivings the Pacific contract was duly
signed and presented to the Imperial Parliament in August 1889,
where it met with little opposition. An order was placed with the
Naval Construction and Armaments Company at Barrow for three
first class passenger steamers, and less than a year later the first
White Empress, the *Empress of India*, was launched. In 1891 the
Canadian Pacific's first class steamship service on the Pacific became
a reality, but meanwhile the plans for a fast Atlantic service had
completely miscarried.

ATLANTIC PLANS: CONFLICTING MARITIME DEMANDS

In August 1887, the Canadian Government had called for tenders
for an Atlantic mail service. Both the Allans and the Andersons had
made offers; it is not known what the Allans proposed, but it seems
that the Andersons, backed by a syndicate of which Stephen and

[1] The previous year Sir Henry Tyler was writing to his wife: 'He (Sir Donald Smith)
says he and Sir George Stephen have each lost £300,000 by the Canadian Pacific.' (M.G.
A22, 26 August 1888, in Public Archives of Canada.)
[2] Macd.P. 'Stephen' 271, Stephen to Macdonald, 20 May and 5 July 1889.

Smith were prominent members, offered a speed of 18 to 20 knots
for an annual subsidy of $500,000. It also appears that neither
tender was accepted, although there is no evidence that either was
refused. It is possible that the question was left open to permit the
contestants to improve their offers, the one as regards speed, the
other as regards reduction of subsidy. In December 1888, Macdonald
told Tupper that the Cabinet was considering the matter and would
probably decide on an increased subsidy, but that it could not rise
to the Andersons' figure.[1]

Early in 1889, Stephen saw the Andersons in London. They had
just received a cable from the Canadian Minister of Finance
inviting them to go out to Canada to negotiate about the Atlantic
service.[2] The Andersons were, however, unwilling to go through all
the process of getting up another syndicate, without which they
would be unable to act, unless they were assured that this time the
Dominion Government really meant business, and really meant to
have a fast service.

A week later the Andersons again approached Stephen. They had
decided to take up the business if they could get it on reasonable
terms, and wished to know whether Stephen's and Smith's former
offers still held good.[3] Neither was so enthusiastic as he had been,
but it seems that they undertook to make good their offers to the
Andersons provided that the difficulty of getting the C.P.R. to
Halifax could be overcome.

In response to Stephen's inquiries as to the intentions of the
Canadian Government, Macdonald said that Council was inclined to
give a maximum subsidy of $350,000; when to this was added a
grant from the Admiralty and the Imperial postal subvention, it was
hoped to be able to secure a fast service. The subsidy, however, was
likely to be opposed in Parliament by the Maritime Members unless
the Canadian Pacific carried out its contract to complete the second
line via Harvey to Halifax.[4]

To this Stephen replied that, owing to increased costs, he
doubted if the Andersons, or anyone else, could provide for the sum
named such a service as Canada ought to have, and he hoped that
the Maritime people would soon recover their senses.[5]

[1] Tupper Papers 523, Macdonald to Tupper, 11 December 1888.
[2] Macd.P. 'Stephen' 271, Stephen to Macdonald, 4 January 1889.
[3] Loc. cit. Stephen to Macdonald, 11 January 1889.
[4] Macd.L.B. 25.320, Macdonald to Stephen, 12 January 1889.
[5] Macd.P. 'Stephen' 271, Stephen to Macdonald, 30 January 1889.

Three weeks later he cabled Macdonald that he should lose no time in closing the Atlantic contract; with the increase in ship-building costs resulting from the placing of large Government orders, it would soon be impossible to get capital even on the Andersons' terms sufficient to establish the required service.[1]

The Dominion Government acted with commendable decision. It had promised the Allans to wait until 1 March for their tender, but at the last moment the latter withdrew altogether.[2] On 6 March Macdonald cabled the Andersons to the effect that the Government proposed a subsidy of £104,000 (rather more than $400,000) exclusive of outside mail earnings, for a 20-knot service to be performed by first class vessels sailing from Southampton or Plymouth to Quebec or Halifax, calling at a French port either way. If a fully authorized agent were sent over, the details would be settled at once.[3]

At last Stephen seemed to be getting what he wanted. He immediately set about helping the Andersons to raise the capital required, not only for the Atlantic service but for the Pacific service and for one to Australia. For, as an extra inducement to the Andersons to undertake the fast Atlantic service it had been agreed to offer to them the C.P.R. Company's Pacific steamship contract, while there was some prospect of the Canadian Government also subsidizing a service to New Zealand and Australia. Stephen impressed upon Macdonald, however, that if he himself was obliged to take a substantial interest in this venture it would be for the sake of encouraging others, and not from any motive of self-interest; he wished to be under no obligation to the Government as a result of its subsidizing these steamship lines.[4]

Meanwhile the Minister of Justice was being besieged by petitions from the Maritime Provinces. The Board of Trade of St. John enumerated the advantages of that city as an Atlantic port,[5] while its fellow in Halifax desired that it should be made a condition of the Atlantic service that all Canadian cargo and mails should be landed at Halifax.[6]

[1] Loc. cit. Stephen to Macdonald, 21 February 1889 and answer.
[2] Loc. cit. Stephen to Macdonald, 23 February 1889, and answer, and 9 March 1889.
[3] Macd.L.B. 25.374, Macdonald to Andersons, 6 March 1889.
[4] Macd.P. 'Stephen' 271, Stephen to Macdonald ,9 March 1889.
[5] Thompson Papers 9024, February 1889.
[6] Loc. cit. 9520, 16 April 1889.

THE SHORT LINE DIFFICULTY

Negotiations with Mr. W. R. Anderson at Ottawa were not proceeding too smoothly. Besides demanding a large commission from the C.P.R. Company, Anderson was insisting on various minor conditions and, more important, was refusing to guarantee a minimum speed of 18 knots.[1] Stephen advised Macdonald to concede everything but the reduction in speed.[2] If the Andersons failed them he was confident that on the terms now offered an independent company might be organized to undertake the service. At the same time he thought that if the Government stood its ground the Andersons would give in.

When next Stephen saw him, Anderson protested that he was ready to guarantee an average speed of 18½ knots,[3] and on 17 June the Minister of Justice, J. S. D. Thompson, was informed by G. E. Foster, the Finance Minister, that the terms of the contract had been satisfactorily settled.[4] The Pacific contract had just received the signature of the Imperial Postmaster General, but arrangements for amalgamating the management hung fire until it was certain that the Andersons could raise the necessary capital. Stephen's contribution remained conditional on the solution of the Short Line difficulty. There was still no prospect of building the Harvey-Moncton line to Halifax, and the direct line was still in Government hands.[5]

Three months passed. Early in October Stephen met the Andersons in London and appealed to them to use their persuasions with Macdonald with a view to inducing the Canadian Government to grant the Canadian Pacific running powers over the Intercolonial Railway to Halifax.[6] The Andersons, he thought, would be so alarmed at the prospect of his and Smith's withdrawal from their syndicate that they could not fail, as he had failed, to impress the Prime Minister with the urgency of their case. At the same time Stephen cabled in this sense to Van Horne, who was trying to negotiate a settlement of the Short Line question,[7] receiving the reply that a favourable result was expected when the Minister of Justice returned

---

[1] Macd.L.B. 25.450, Macdonald to Stephen, 5 June 1889.
[2] Macd.P. 'Stephen' 271, Stephen to Macdonald, 4 and 5 June 1889.
[3] Loc. cit. Stephen to Macdonald, 6 June 1889.
[4] Thompson Papers 9959, Foster to Thompson, 17 June 1889.
[5] Macd.P. 'Stephen' 271, Stephen to Macdonald, 5 July 1889.
[6] See Macd.P. 'Van Horne' 288, Andersons to Stephen, 9 October 1889.
[7] Loc. cit. Stephen to Van Horne, 8 October 1889, and answer.

from Halifax, where he was looking into the matter. Before communicating with Macdonald, however, the Andersons wrote to Stephen asking if there was any other difficulty in the way of his co-operation.[1] They did not mention that some days before they had written to their agent in Canada saying that after discussion with an eminent naval architect they had evolved plans for an even better service, conditional on the Government's agreeing to the omission of the call at a French port, and at Quebec in summer. They gave the impression that they thought the political difficulties involved in such a change could be overcome,[2] although it subsequently appeared that they had been deliberately proposing the impossible. Then, instead of making an attempt to persuade the Canadian Government to end the impasse over the Short Line, they informed Stephen that on account of his and Sir Donald Smith's prospective withdrawal, they proposed to surrender their contract to the Dominion Government.[3]

To this Stephen replied that as he fully expected to hear in a day or two that the difficulty over the Short Line had been overcome, he would still be ready and willing to implement his promises to the full. He assured them:

I am much more concerned about the success of the proposed scheme in its entirety than I am about the fate of my promised subscription of £50,000, and must confess myself puzzled and not a little disappointed at the apparent alacrity with which you appear to have seized the first opportunity to surrender your contract with the Government upon grounds which I think have no real foundation. . . .[4]

There was some further correspondence between Stephen and the Andersons, Stephen reiterating his willingness to resume negotiations whenever the C.P.R. was assured of access to Halifax, and the Andersons at first proclaiming their readiness to take the matter up again if the cordial co-operation of the C.P.R. were guaranteed, then, in their final letter, stating that they desired now to withdraw their previously expressed suggestion about a possible renewal of negotiations.[5] They denied that Mr. W. R. Anderson

---

[1] Macd.P. 'Van Horne' 288, Andersons to Stephen, 9 October 1889.
[2] Loc. cit. Andersons to C. H. Mackintosh, 28 September 1889.
[3] Loc. cit. Andersons to Stephen, 11 October 1889, and to Macdonald, 12 October 1889.
[4] Loc. cit. Stephen to Andersons, 14 October 1889.
[5] Loc. cit. Andersons to Stephen, 16, 21 and 24 October, and Stephen to Andersons, 19 and 22 October 1889.

had been told, while in Canada, of the Short Line difficulty, but there is evidence that this was not so.[1]

Colonial Office correspondence on the subject of the Australian service gives a clue to the reason for the Andersons' decision. On 12 August 1889, the Andersons wrote to the Colonial Secretary asking whether the Imperial Government was prepared, on the expiry of its contract with the San Francisco line, to contribute to the Canadian service to Australia instead. Mr. W. R. Anderson had evidently had an interview with Sir Robert Herbert on the subject, and had pointed out to him that the Post Office paid some £16,000 a year for the conveyance of mails by the San Francisco route, and had expressed a hope that a similar sum might be awarded the Canadian line.[2] On 20 September, writing to acknowledge a communication from Herbert to the effect that Lord Knutsford had passed on their enquiry to the Treasury, Andersons stated that their negotiations with the Australian colonies over the latter's contribution were proceeding favourably; all that was wanted was an assurance of the co-operation of the Imperial Government.[3] The Treasury's reply to the Colonial Office, dated 28 September, was presumably communicated at once to the Andersons. The question of replacing the present service from San Francisco by one from Vancouver had been under consideration for some time, both by the Treasury and by the various Colonies concerned. In order to give them more time to come to a decision, the San Francisco contract had been extended on a temporary basis for one year. The Lords of the Treasury could not, therefore, give a definite reply to the Andersons, except that they were 'certainly not prepared to pledge themselves to pay to a company carrying mails between British ports the extravagant sum now paid on the San Francisco service'.[4]

According to Van Horne, the Andersons had hoped to claim commission upon the ships for the Pacific Line, but as the time remaining before the commencement of the service was so short, the C.P.R. Company had had to place the order without reference to the Atlantic contract.[5] The Andersons' cable to Macdonald surrendering the contract had been sent on the same day that the Canadian Pacific signed the contract with Barrow.

[1] Loc. cit. Stephen to Andersons, 22 October, and Van Horne to Macdonald, 30 October 1889.

[2] CO 42/802 Individuals, 'Anderson, Anderson and Company,' 12 August 1889, and Minute by Herbert. [3] Loc. cit. 20 September 1889.

[4] CO 42/801 Treasury, 28 September 1889.

[5] Macd.P. 'Van Horne' 288, Van Horne to Macdonald, 30 October 1889.

POLITICAL RAILROADING

Evidence of public feeling in Canada against the Canadian Pacific as a ruthless giant, bent only on its own all-devouring progress through the land, found its way at this time into the columns of the *Railway Times*:

. . . It is evident that the withdrawal of the Andersons, who were in league, or at least acting with the Canadian Pacific, is due to a failure to extort from the Government concessions which would have been highly injurious to the interests of the Government in the Intercolonial Railway, concessions which, had they been granted, would have resulted in diverting the ordinary business of the Intercolonial Railway and other roads having traffic arrangements with it to the Canadian Pacific, which aims at owning the whole earth and would aspire to owning the planets as well, if the road could be extended to them. . . .[1]

A different point of view was expressed to Macdonald by Van Horne, the new Pacific President, concerning the plight of the Company whose new Short Line, lacking Government permission to send its Halifax traffic via the Intercolonial, had to see the latter carry through freight not only from Halifax west to St. John but past it, poaching on the preserves promised to the new line. The Government line appeared to have no intention of becoming a purely local road. Van Horne wrote:

Our loss growing out of the Short Line is equal to one half per cent on the entire capital stock of the C.P.R. Company, and if you will consider the effect on the credit of the Company of the payment of even this half per cent to its shareholders, in addition to what can otherwise be paid, together with the fact that Sir George has all along and almost alone had to supplement the credit of the Company by carrying heavy financial burdens for it, keeping him in a state of constant and consuming anxiety, you can better understand his present feelings. There has not been a year in the history of the Company that the assistance of his money and credit was not of vital consequence to it, and I fear that it would be in a sorry plight even now were it withdrawn. . . .[2]

Stephen himself had by then given up trying to make Macdonald see reason on this subject. His last word was written in a letter dated 3 September, 1889, but not sent until August 1890. At first he had thought better of it, for the letter was full of the kind of complaint to which the Premier had learnt to turn an insensitive ear; but finding

[1] *Railway Times*, 21 December 1889, quoting an earlier issue.
[2] Macd.P. 'Van Horne' 288, Van Horne to Macdonald, 17 October 1889.

16

that there seemed no end to the injustices suffered by the Company at the hands of the Government, Stephen had subsequently resolved to let the Prime Minister have the full blast of his accumulated woe:

. . . As to the 'Short Line,' you know what the influences were that induced me to touch it. Tupper had a political object to serve; Pope had, in addition to that, a personal advantage to gain; that, I am free to say, weighed with me quite as much as the former. Further, at a meeting of the Maritime members—which I have since learned originated with Pope—under the threat that they would not support one of our life-and-death measures then before the House unless I agreed to build the Short Line, I was forced to commit the Company to build the line. Tupper and Pope repeatedly said, by way of inducement to undertake the work, that, on the opening of the Short Line, the ICR would be run as a local road, that the through business would all come over the Short Line, that the ICR, worked as a local road, would be just as useful to the people of the country traversed by it and the annual loss to the Government would be much less than by operating it as an expensive fast through line;—and much more to the same purpose. . . . In this, as in many other things, I have been the victim of my own credulity and of my criminal confidence in the Government—especially in the then Minister of Railways—and the C.P.R. is today suffering the consequences. . . .
. . . If the Government . . . has decided that the C.P.R. Short Line is not to be permitted to do business in Halifax and on the line between that and St. John, it is only fair to the Company to say so, and to let the Company abandon its efforts to do so, and stop its trains at St. John, and make the best it can of the Short Line with which it has been saddled by my failure to protect the interests of the Company. . . . The absurdity of giving a large subsidy in aid of the construction of the Short Line, and, the moment the road is built, and ready to do its work, telling the Company in effect that the line shall not be permitted to do the very thing for which it was ostensibly created, is astounding.

I am thoroughly sick and tired of these wretched squabbles with the Government, when I confidently looked for harmony and pleasantness, and shall not be happy until I get away from them all.[1]

It was, in fact, nearly a year before the Short Line question was settled, although Macdonald was confident, in November 1889, that he was on the point of engineering a satisfactory compromise. He reckoned without Van Horne when he wrote, first to Tupper, that as the terms on which the C.P.R. could use the I.C.R. between St. John and Halifax had been 'pretty well settled', there would be

[1] Macd.P. 'Stephen' 272.

nothing to prevent Smith and Stephen interesting themselves in the fast Atlantic service,[1] and then to Hickson, the Grand Trunk manager, as follows:

Wainwright [general manager of the North Shore Railway] wrote me that he had mentioned to you the Government proposition as to the arrangement with the C.P.R. for rates (both freight and passenger) from Halifax via St. John New Brunswick to Montreal and back. Schreiber goes to Montreal to arrange the tariffs &c with the C.P.R. and will communicate with you. Our desire is to secure to the G.T.R. a fair share of the business via the Chaudière and it is important you should agree to the arrangements even if all the details may not suit you. Otherwise we may be obliged to yield to the pressure of the C.P.R. They come into the arrangement very unwillingly, as they expected to get in effect the control of the I.C.R. line between Halifax and St. John, which in my opinion is not desirable.[2]

A week later Macdonald was writing to sympathize with Hickson over Van Horne's refusal to compromise with the Grand Trunk over the Short Line. Van Horne, he said, was 'in rather a bitter humour just now, as he cannot (*entre nous*) get concessions which the Government does not think it in the public interest to grant. However,' concluded Macdonald, 'the world will continue to go round notwithstanding these little tempers'.[3]

The world went round for seven months before Stephen wrote to Macdonald saying that he had heard from Van Horne that a satisfactory settlement had at last been reached.[4] He had himself been unaware of the most recent developments; it was such a sore subject with him that he thought Van Horne purposely refrained from mentioning it unnecessarily. Even now, although C.P.R. trains might be running through to Halifax, Stephen could only reflect that they were doing so with little profit to the Company. Another sacrifice to political exigency had been made, another superfluous provincial trimming tacked up.

[1] Macd.L.B. 26.316, Macdonald to Tupper, 25 November 1889.
[2] Macd.L.B. 26.325, Macdonald to Hickson, 30 November 1889.
[3] Macd.L.B. 26.332, Macdonald to Hickson, 7 December 1889.
[4] Macd.P. 'Stephen' 272, Stephen to Macdonald, 6 July 1890.

IX

Lord Mount Stephen

THE ONDERDONK SECTION

Of what might be termed the aftermath of the building of the Canadian Pacific, there remains only the British Columbia arbitration to be dealt with. The broad facts of the case have already been outlined; it serves as a last illustration of the difficulties confronting the business man who becomes involved in an enterprise in which political considerations exist alongside commercial.

From time to time during the construction of the Onderdonk Section, from Kamloops to Port Moody, reports had percolated to Montreal that the work being done there was of inferior quality, but Stephen had accepted John Henry Pope's word that these rumours were groundless.[1] When he himself inspected the Section in the summer of 1886 he had a rude awakening. The particular defects of which he complained are listed in a letter to Macdonald in which he begged the latter, who was then in the Pacific Province, to satisfy himself that these were no idle statements.[2] It was obvious that only a large expenditure of money would make the Section fit to form part of the through line. At that time the Company was incurring considerable expense over the provision of snow-sheds in the mountains, but even if it had been in a position to do so it seemed too much to expect it to spend a further sum in virtually finishing the Government's work. The ultimate question, therefore, was who was liable for this outlay?

It was clear that the Government dreaded being forced to come to Parliament with an enormous bill to be paid. In 1891, when the smoke of battle had cleared a little, Macdonald recapitulated the position thus:

It is a simple matter. The C.P.R. had a claim against the Railway Department which the latter disputed as excessive, though willing to pay a considerable sum. This therefore could only be settled by arbitration, or a

---

[1] Macd.P. 'Stephen' 271, Stephen to Macdonald, 25 June 1889.
[2] Macd.P. 'Stephen' 270, Stephen to Macdonald, 6 August 1886.

suit in the courts. Both sides preferred arbitration, and a very able trio of referees were appointed. Both sides selected very competent counsel, and both have very properly left the case to be managed by them.[1]

It is implicit in this statement that the Government did not deny its liability to meet the cost of repairs on the Section. If the bill was going to mount up too high, however, then it was desirable for the Government to deny responsibility. Early in 1885, in the House of Commons, Blake had raised the question of the Onderdonk Section. He too had heard that the work was not up to standard, and was afraid that reclamations would later be made by the C.P.R. Company upon the Government. John Henry Pope had replied that the engineers had always expressed themselves very well satisfied with the work done; the chief engineer had passed over the Section every year, and would do so again.[2] Clearly, the Grits must not be proved to have been correct.

There was another factor in the case which was more or less political. Stephen feared that the Canadian Pacific might suffer at Pope's hands, not because the latter wished to be unjust, but because some of his colleagues felt that in the past he had been too favourable to the Company. It was possible that in order to disabuse them of this idea Pope might go to the opposite extreme.[3] Even when the tribunal was sitting, Pope still hoped by his own efforts to be able to affect the course of proceedings. This is indicated in a letter to Macdonald in which he says:

. . . I have instructed (Schreiber) and our three Solicitors to leave nothing undone however long it may take to see that we are not placed in a false position in Parliament. . . . I am running up a big bill out there but it must be done. . . .[4]

Although even in 1891 Macdonald did not appear to be unduly perturbed by the delay in settling the case, Stephen had by 1887 begun to grow restive. He wrote to Macdonald in August:

. . . If the line is not put in order this fall, and it is now August, so as to show it can be kept open next winter the chances of our ocean subsidy will be greatly diminished. . . .[5]

The arbitrators had not then commenced their sittings—they did not do so until February 1888—and as the arbitration agreement was

[1] Macd.L.B. 27.14, Macdonald to Stephen, 31 March 1891. See also Macd.P. 'Pope' 256.410, Pope to Macdonald, 23 July 1888.
[2] D. of C.H.C. 1885, vol. i, p. 204, 23 February 1885.
[3] Macd.P. 'Stephen' 269, Stephen to Macdonald, 14 November 1885.
[4] Macd.P. 'Pope' 256.416, Pope to Macdonald, 31 July 1888.
[5] Macd.P. 'Stephen' 270, Stephen to Macdonald, 2 August 1887.

drawn up no provision was made for expenditure incurred prior to the final decision.[1] This was later provided for.

In July 1888 an alarming situation threatened to develop, after Van Horne had given evidence before the tribunal. The prospective President made no attempt to conceal his opinion regarding the state of the Section, and one of the arbitrators was heard to say, out of court, that if one half were true the Government ought to stop the operation of the line at once.[2] Collingwood Schreiber, the Government engineer, wrote to Pope that by decrying the Government work and asserting that the road was not safe to run, Van Horne would, in the event of an accident, 'find it difficult to keep outside the walls of the Penitentiary'.[3] Pope described it as 'all in all a curious specimen of volunteer evidence',[4] but Stephen could only applaud his successor's stand.[5]

Already the Minister of Railways had been considering the expediency of acting under the provisions af a recent law which decreed that on being informed that a railway was unsafe it was the Minister's duty to order its closing. He had consulted Macdonald on this point, begging him to impress on Stephen that by declaring the Onderdonk Section to be dangerous he was putting him (Pope) in a false position.[6] Pope's anxiety lest he should be liable to an action for failing in his duty did not appear to be in the least assuaged by his professed conviction that the Government Section was perfectly sound. It was Macdonald who pointed out to him the incongruity of carrying out the provisions of the Act:

. . . as the Government contention is that the road is safe, and the Government portion better built than that constructed by the Company, I don't see how you can stop the road as dangerous under the Act. To do so you must satisfy yourself that Schreiber and . . . your Engineers are wrong and the testimony of the American Engineers [witnesses for the C.P.R.] to be relied on.

This is a responsibility that you should not take unless you disbelieve your own Engineers and trust implicitly to the Company's witnesses. . . .[7]

Pope, however, was determined to proceed, and instructed

---

[1] Macd.P. 'Van Horne' 288, Van Horne to Stephen, 24 July 1888.
[2] Loc. cit. Van Horne to Stephen, 24 July 1888.
[3] Macd.P. 'Pope' 256.406, Schreiber to Pope, 22 July 1888.
[4] Loc. cit. 256.410, Pope to Macdonald, 23 July 1888.
[5] Macd.P. 'Stephen' 271, Stephen to Macdonald, 28 July 1888.
[6] Macd.P. 'Pope' 256.400, Pope to Macdonald, 19 July 1888.
[7] Macd.L.B. 25.96, Macdonald to Pope, 30 July 1888.

Schreiber to carry out an inspection, not only of the Onderdonk Section, but of the whole line, as a letter had reached the Department from some aggrieved person alleging that the Lake Superior Section was defective.[1] Alarmed at the prospect of the unfavourable publicity which would doubtless attend such a procedure, even although the Company were completely exonerated, Stephen appealed to the Prime Minister to restrain Pope.[2] Although in his reply Macdonald said that he had already advised Pope against holding an inspection of the road, he took the opportunity also to try to persuade Stephen to have the Company retreat from its stand on the Onderdonk Section. He pointed out that if Van Horne's testimony were published, the reputation of the Canadian Pacific would be greatly injured, and, taking his cue from Collingwood Schreiber, whose letter to Pope he had seen,[3] that should an accident happen, Van Horne would be liable to indictment for manslaughter. If the latter's statements were accurate, said Macdonald, then he ought to have stopped the operation of the road. 'The truth seems to be', he concluded, 'that both sides have got their blood up and have become reckless. We must try to assuage this *furore*.'[4]

But if Stephen was powerless to restrain Van Horne, he was also unwilling to do so. The Government had based its case upon the contention that it had a right to build any sort of road it pleased, and this was so contrary to all Stephen's conceptions of the essential partnership between Government and Company that he could not allow such ideas to go unchallenged. He could not bring himself to believe that it had ever been intended to hand over an inferior road to the C.P.R., and flatly told Macdonald that he would not do either Pope or Tupper the injustice of accepting this as the truth.[5]

That Stephen's references to John Henry Pope were made 'more in sorrow than in anger' is constantly illustrated. Pope was, at this time, in an exceedingly precarious state of health, and many of Stephen's letters to Macdonald contain appeals to the latter to use his influence with the Minister of Railways to have him conserve his energy.[6] It was difficult for Stephen to approach Pope himself, for

[1] Macd.P. 'Van Horne' 288, Abbott to Van Horne, 1 August 1888 and Van Horne to Stephen, 4 August 1888.
[2] Macd.P. 'Stephen' 271, Stephen to Macdonald, 4 August 1888.
[3] Macd.P. 'Pope' 256.400, Pope to Macdonald, 19 July 1888.
[4] Macd.L.B. 25.117, Macdonald to Stephen, 7 August 1888.
[5] Macd.P. 'Stephen' 271, Stephen to Macdonald, 25 June 1889.
[6] Macd.P. 'Stephen' 270, Stephen to Macdonald, 21 May 1886 and 271, 12 January 1888, for example.

Pope had become so infuriated over the arbitration that calm conversation between them was impossible. On one of their last meetings, however, before Stephen went over to England in the autumn of 1888, Pope appeared very much better and an amicable discussion took place. Stephen urged Pope to have Macdonald relieve him of his post, but Pope confessed that he was afraid to do so lest it be said that he was running away from the British Columbia matter. Although Stephen pointed out that the case was now taken out of his hands by the arbitrators, Pope remained adamant; he did not tell Stephen that he was still fighting to be proved right. In writing of this conversation to Macdonald, Stephen expressed his conviction that if Pope did not get relief he would not live.[1] The prophecy was only too correct, and the news of his old friend's death the following spring was made doubly bitter by the evidence, revealed by the arbitration proceedings, of Pope's seeming betrayal of the C.P.R. and its President.[2]

It was a deep disappointment to Stephen that after all the years of close, if not always happy, association the relations of Government and Company should have reached such a parlous state. It was to him a truly personal grief. Stephen's almost naïve confidence in those whom he had once decided he could trust is hardly compatible with the popular conception of the railway baron. It worried him more to have his faith proved unjustified than to sustain any material loss. His friend George Laidlaw wrote to him in those days of disillusionment:

It is of no use to worry about the mean and truculent spirits that cannot understand your nature for 'God has made them so' as the old hymn has it. . . . Within and without your circle you may have experienced ingratitude, jealousy, cowardice or worse, but who can deal much with human nature and not encounter that which recalls its great variety and frailty. The sound heart of all Canada is with you as it has never been with a man before, bar the Premier. . . .[3]

Although Laidlaw had in mind chiefly the Manitoba trouble-makers, his words had a more general application than he knew. It was unfortunate that in his state of mind Stephen was inclined to magnify his difficulties, for he could never change his nature. When

---

[1] Macd.P. 'Stephen' 271, Stephen to Macdonald, 15 August 1888.
[2] Loc. cit. Stephen to Macdonald, 24 April and 25 June 1889.
[3] Loc. cit. Laidlaw to Stephen, 15 August 1888, enclosed in Stephen to Macdonald, 4 September 1889, written shortly after Laidlaw's death.

Macdonald rebuked him for worrying over Pope's evidence in the arbitration, Stephen replied with some resignation:

. . . It has perhaps been a fault of mine all through life to believe too firmly in the constancy of friendship, though I suppose I shall go on confiding and trusting to the end, and being laughed at for my simplicity. . . .[1]

In the absence of comprehensive data on the subject of the British Columbia arbitration, it would be futile to attempt to form, from the occasional references in the Macdonald correspondence, a true picture of the proceedings. To the end Stephen blamed himself for bringing what he termed 'this injury' upon the C.P.R. Company. He had given up trying to convince Macdonald, who had obviously lost interest, that the Company had received less than justice at the hands of the Department of Railways.[2] Macdonald was fond of telling Stephen that he ought to read Charles Reade's book *Put Yourself in His Place*, his way of reminding him that the Prime Minister of Canada could not always see things in the same light as could the President of the Canadian Pacific. In 1891, when the arbitration was still going on, Stephen wrote to Macdonald from Scotland:

. . . I note what you say about my harping on the British Columbia arbitration matter. If you could only put yourself in my place you would harp on it too though with your gift of forgetting an injury done to yourself which I have not been born with, you would probably ere this have accepted the situation on the theory that it is useless expecting too much of poor human nature. . . .[3]

In his next letter Stephen promised never again to allude to the subject, and in fact he wrote only two more letters to Macdonald, for in June 1891, the latter died, having overtaxed his already waning strength in his last election campaign. This must have been a sad and, in spite of Macdonald's precarious state of health, an unexpected blow to Stephen, who had written on 21 April (from Faskally House, Pitlochry, where he was fishing):

We are all coming out in August hoping to spend the Fall at Metis and to see you before you leave Rivière du Loup . . . .

The arbitration finally resulted in an award to the railway company of $579,225. The estimated expenditure on improving the Section had been cited variously as between $6 million and $10 million, but

---

[1] Loc. cit. Stephen to Macdonald, 25 June 1889.
[2] Macd.P. 'Stephen' 272, Stephen to Macdonald, 23 April 1891.
[3] Loc. cit. Stephen to Macdonald, 21 April 1891.

rather than prolong the controversy the Company accepted the verdict without further appeal.

CONTROL OF THE SOO LINE

In a letter addressed to the Canadian Pacific shareholders in August 1888, on the occasion of his retirement from the Presidency (Appendix VI), Stephen referred to a transaction which he had earlier described to Macdonald as his 'greatest service to the maintenance of the power and independence of the national highway'.[1] It concerned two American railroads, and ensured C.P.R. control in perpetuity of—again in Stephen's words—'the Soo gateway to the North West'. The 'Soo Line'—otherwise the Minneapolis, St. Paul and Sault Ste. Marie Railway—had been opened at the end of 1887, destined to connect with the Canadian Pacific's Algoma Branch, linking Sudbury, Ontario, with Sault Ste. Marie. The second line, the Duluth, South Shore and Atlantic Railway, connected Sault Ste. Marie with Duluth.

While these two lines might well have brought traffic to the Canadian Pacific, they might equally well, in hostile hands, have diverted it into other channels. The Grand Trunk, by a process of absorption, was spreading its influence in the direction of the Sault, while the westward progress of the Northern Pacific, and the reports at the time of that Company's activities relating to Manitoba, were calculated to force the C.P.R. to look to its own defences. There was also the Vanderbilt system to be reckoned with.

At the beginning of 1888 the Canadian Pacific was in no state, financially, to undertake expensive commitments in any direction. Baring Brothers had agreed to launch the Land Grant and Algoma Bond issues, but the proceeds of these were already earmarked for improvements in the main line and for the building of the Algoma Branch. Once more Stephen and Donald Smith stepped into the breach; by coming to the rescue of the 'Soo Line', which was in financial difficulties, and by negotiating a pact with the South Shore road, they gave the Canadian Pacific, on the same platter, perpetual traffic agreements with these American lines and control over a vital sphere of railway influence.[2] At the time Stephen expected that J. J. Hill would take over the 'Soo Line',[3] but Hill had ceased to be inter-

[1] Macd.P. 'Stephen' 271, Stephen to Macdonald, 22 April 1888.
[2] Loc. cit. Stephen to Macdonald, 29 January, 22 April, 4 July and 14 December 1888.
[3] Loc. cit. Stephen to Macdonald, 25 July 1888.

ested in anything east of St. Paul, and in 1890 the Canadian Pacific, then in safer financial waters, assumed the responsibility which Stephen and Smith had shouldered on its behalf.

'SHALL A NATION BE BORN AT ONCE?'

The fact that by their action both Stephen and Smith came in for a good deal of criticism is evidence of the current lack of appreciation which was more and more bringing home to Stephen the realization that, so far as his contemporaries were concerned, his far-sighted efforts for the country of his adoption were virtually in vain. People could not believe that they were not acting on behalf of their own American railroad, and it must indeed have seemed incomprehensible that the long-expected connection between St. Paul and the Sault was to be used for the benefit of the Canadian Pacific, for the protection of the much abused North of Lake Superior route, and not to forward the selfish interests of the old 'St. Paul Syndicate'. Stephen complained bitterly to Macdonald of the suspicious attitude of his incredulous countrymen. He knew that time would prove that such criticism had been misplaced, yet in the meantime it was hard to bear. 'I cannot help asking myself', he wrote, 'why should I bother myself and work for a people so blind and prejudiced as so many of your people seem to be to their own interests. . . .'[1] He realized, however, that the general public had not quite grasped the great idea behind the Canadian Pacific. It was still, to most people, something new to think in terms of nationhood, to see beyond mere provincial and parochial interests. It is easy now to criticize their attitude from a vantage point nearly eighty years on, and after witnessing on many occasions concerted action by a country from which, even yet, neither provincialism nor parochialism have by any means vanished. The really remarkable fact is that so soon after Confederation there should have been found at all in Canada a man like Stephen whose natural impatience expressed itself thus:

The real trouble rises from the fact that not one man in a thousand in Canada appreciates the magnitude and importance of the C.P.R. as the instrument by which the Nor West is to be developed and Canada *made* and kept for ever a nation. In other words, the C.P.R. is ahead of its time, though I do not like to think the people will not expand and grow up to it, but it is discouraging waiting for that which I fear will not come in my railway days. . . .[2]

---

[1] Macd.P. 'Stephen' 271, Stephen to Macdonald, 22 April 1888.   [2] Ibid.

Thus it was that when Stephen retired from the Presidency of the Canadian Pacific he could almost have been described as a disappointed man. On 4 June 1889, the eve of his sixtieth birthday, he took up his pen and wrote to Macdonald:

. . . Tomorrow I begin my sixty-first year, and looking back ten years I am far from being the free man I then was. (It was on 23 May 1879 that the St.P.M.&M. was born.) When I think of the misery I have suffered in these ten years I cannot help thinking what a fool I was not to end my work and enjoy the leisure which I had earned by forty years' hard work. I began to earn my own living at the age of ten. 'But what maun be maun be.' It was not so ordained. . . .[1]

Surprising words to come from the pen of one whose activities during those ten years had gained for him an international reputation as a financier and railway-builder, and a baronetcy of the United Kingdom? Even allowing for the familiar exaggeration and self-pity, what was uppermost in Stephen's mind in June 1889, was not his success but what appeared to him to be his failures. Many things troubled him in connection with the national highway which was so much his creation. He had done what he set out to do, and the potentialities of the Canadian Pacific, both from a national and a commercial point of view, were as great as he had ever imagined they might be. But had this wonderful and expensive toy been placed in the hands of too young a child? For lack of knowledge or appreciation of its true value, would the infant Dominion prejudice the future of its new acquisition by thoughtless destruction of its carefully planned system? Would short-term, narrow views triumph over vision and foresight? In 1889, with the British Columbia arbitration still unsettled, with the Short Line still short of Halifax, and the fast Atlantic service which was to complete the new Canadian route to the East not by any means certain of establishment, the man to whom a task well done meant more than a brilliant façade of achievement might conceivably wonder whether, after all, he had been wasting both his substance and his energy.

STEPHEN WITHDRAWS FROM CANADIAN PACIFIC

Exhausted as he was after the years of strain, Stephen had no reason to expect that he had still over thirty years ahead of him. While both Macdonald and John Henry Pope were deaf to his

[1] Macd.P. 'Stephen' 271, Stephen to Macdonald, 4 June 1889.

entreaties that they should seek relief from the toils of office, Stephen, holding firmly to the belief that no man is indispensable, gradually withdrew from active participation in the affairs of the Canadian Pacific. In the same letter from which the above extract is quoted he told Macdonald:

. . . I am trying hard to accustom the C.P.R. people to manage the affairs of the Company without always looking to me for help; not that I am, or ever can be, unwilling to aid them in every possible way, but it is better that they should not count on me. . . .

After his retirement from the Presidency, Stephen had remained on the Executive of the Company, but towards the end of 1889 he privately announced his intention of resigning altogether from the Directorate. In alarm, Van Horne appealed to Macdonald to use his influence to prevent this:

. . . He has half promised to remain as a director until our annual meeting in May, but he is determined to go out then, and we have to shift for ourselves financially even now. . . . Sir George has in the past, as you to some extent know, made many things possible for the Company by undertaking obligations and carrying burdens which it could not itself undertake to carry, and many of them have now to be provided for because he will carry them no longer. His withdrawal is full of danger to the Company, and it is just as full of danger to the country, for it can hardly be disputed that the Canadian Pacific has for the past five or six years been the active commercial nerve of the country, and paralysis of that nerve would mean widespread disaster. Sir George is in an unreasoning mood— has made himself believe that he has in some way sacrificed or betrayed the interests of the Company, and I don't know what all . . . if there is anything you can do without injury to the country that will help us to hold him, I hope and pray that you will do it. . . .[1]

Eventually, Stephen was persuaded to remain on the Directorate a little longer. In 1892 he again made an attempt to withdraw from active connection with the Canadian Pacific, and again Van Horne raised objections, writing to him:

You have been, as nearly as possible, President and Board of Directors combined right up to the present time, for we have been substantially governed by your views in all cases, however much everyone here may have opposed them. Your withdrawal would not be the withdrawal of a director, but of the soul of the enterprise. . . .[2]

[1] Macd.P. 'Van Horne' 288, Van Horne to Macdonald, 13 January 1890.
[2] Walter Vaughan, *Life of Sir William Van Horne*, Makers of Canada Series, vol. x, p. 230.

To this the reply was that Van Horne enormously exaggerated the importance of Stephen's name remaining on the Directorate; since 1888 he had been careful to keep his name out of sight in all matters coming before the public, so that now his connection with the Company was almost forgotten. The C.P.R. was now, moreover, independent of his personal support, and the interests of the Company were so completely identified with the name of Van Horne that no one would care who were his co-directors.[1]

At the annual meeting on 11 May, however, Stephen—he was then Lord Mount Stephen—was re-elected a Director, although his place on the Executive was taken by Thomas G. Shaughnessy. The following year he had his way and retired completely. He was then resident in England, and the Directors' Report stated with regret that the Right Honourable Lord Mount Stephen, owing to his absence from Canada, found himself unable to discharge the duties pertaining to the position of a Director to his own satisfaction, and therefore declined re-election. The shareholders were assured that the severance of his official connection with the Company would not in any way lessen the deep interest which he had always taken in the Company, and in everything connected with it calculated to promote its prosperity, nor would he be less willing than he had been in the past to assist the Directors in their efforts to advance the Company's interests.

THE BARINGS CRASH

At the end of 1890 an incident occurred which was to show Stephen that his old reputation as a financial wizard was as strong as ever. At the same time it gave him an opportunity to repay an old debt. It was not like Stephen to make a song about a personal service, but when the great firm of Baring Brothers and Company crashed in November 1890, in the midst of a general collapse of western security markets, and sent for him to help them to reorganize their affairs, he permitted himself to write an account of the matter to Macdonald, so great was his pleasure at having been of service, in their hour of need, to the men who had had the courage, five years earlier, to take the step which had saved the Canadian Pacific.

It was through a very similar transaction that the firm had come to grief. In July 1885, they had made the issue of C.P.R. First Mortgage Bonds, but it was widely believed, and it seems with some

---

[1] Loc. cit. p. 231.

reason, that at the time very few of the Bonds were taken by the public. Similarly, it appears, Barings had bought out and out certain South American securities which, in Stephen's words, 'given time to turn round . . . were sure to come right',[1] and in the natural course of things, Barings would no doubt have disposed of their holdings at a favourable time and in a favourable manner. But it had been decided, perhaps by some rival in the field, that not only could these investments be prevented from 'coming right', but that in the process this old-established house might be robbed for ever of its power to attract much of the most important business in the financial world. In December 1888, the *Montreal Gazette*, quoting the *Statist* of 1 December, was already reporting attacks on Barings which criticized the firm's South American dealings with the apparent object of discouraging public investment in the securities in question.

When the crash came, it looked at first as though Barings had indeed fallen never to rise again. In the initial panic which followed in the wake of what he described as a financial cyclone,[2] Stephen had cabled Macdonald suggesting that the latter should himself come over to England at once to arrange about the Dominion's financial agency, until then held jointly by Barings and Glyn, Mills and Company.[3] What Stephen feared was that overtures might be made by firms of doubtful capacity who desired to have the management of the Canadian Government's affairs, but who would seek their own advantage before that of the Dominion.[4] Macdonald was inclined, as usual, to think Stephen over-precipitate, but he despatched Courtney, his Deputy Minister of Finance, to guard the interests of the Government.

Almost immediately, however, reassuring cables came from Stephen to the effect that Barings were forming a new company among the family, with the help of a few outside friends, to take over the Commission Department of the old business, and that the new organization promised to be strong beyond question. There was therefore no necessity for any change in the existing relations with the Canadian Government, Glyn, Mills having agreed to work with the new firm as with the old.

As soon as Lord Revelstoke and his partners had arranged for the liquidation of Baring Brothers and Company, and had begun to

---

[1] Macd.P. 'Stephen' 272, Stephen to Macdonald, 3 January 1891.
[2] Loc. cit. Stephen to Macdonald, 22 November 1890.
[3] Loc. cit. Stephen to Macdonald, 17 and 18 November 1890.
[4] Loc. cit. Stephen to Macdonald, 3 January 1891.

think of the future, they had sent for Sir George Stephen, and with scant optimism had outlined to him a plan of reconstruction, asking his advice on it, and on its feasibility. At once Stephen told them that he himself would find £50,000 of capital for it, that he was sure his cousin Donald Smith would subscribe another £50,000, and that furthermore he would undertake to get another £150,000 in New York. Stephen wrote to Macdonald:

. . . You never in your life saw anything like the effect of this prompt response upon their spirits. It seemed to lift a cloud off their minds and since then all has gone on most swimmingly.[1]

So great was the name of Baring that as soon as it was known that a new company was being formed they were, in Stephen's words, 'so flooded with offers of fresh capital as to be embarrassing to know how to refuse them without seeming ingratitude'. Stephen concluded his letter:

One thing is beyond question, that is their honor and honesty. These have been as conspicuous during their troubles as ever they were in their most prosperous operations. Their character stands as high today as it ever did and this of itself will prove as good to them as an extra million of capital.

STEPHEN AND 'THE INDEPENDENCE HERESY'

The death of Sir John Rose in September 1888, had deprived Canada of a true friend and Sir John Macdonald of a trusted adviser. Just as in 1869 Rose's place in Canada had been in some measure filled by George Stephen, so after Rose's death Stephen became unofficial commentator on Canadian affairs from England, where he finally took up permanent residence in the autumn of 1890, until the death of the Prime Minister cut short the correspondence which has revealed so much of contemporary history.

One of the most prominent questions of the day was that of the future political and commercial relations of Great Britain, Canada and the United States. In the late 1860's Stephen had adhered to what he afterwards referred to as 'the independence heresy', in whimsical deference to the more orthodox views of such as Macdonald. He believed that political separation from Great Britain was Canada's 'manifest destiny', but at no time did he imagine that this necessarily involved annexation to the United States. He deplored

---

[1] Macd.P. 'Stephen' 272, Stephen to Macdonald, 22 November 1890.

SOME PROMINENT DUFFTOWN MEN
The central figure is John Symon, Provost

1 Provost John Symon: 2 Baillie McKay, carpenter: 3 Baillie Spence, tailor: 4 The Tower Bellringer: 5 Tom Dow, molecatcher: 6 Alex Grant, blacksmith: 7 Brady, exciseman: 8 Halkney, tailor: 9 Robertson, druggist: 10 Proprietor of Fife Arms Hotel: 11 McLennan, bookseller: 12 13 dairymen: 14 George Jessiman, Town Crier: 15 John McDonald, son of the Minister's Man: 16 David Cruickshank, son of the stationmaster: 17 Tom Guild, Band Leader, foreman tailor

The Band made up of tailors and their apprentices, and painters

the tendency on the part of some Canadians to depend on the neighbouring country for their own prosperity.[1] Prior to 1866 he had hoped for the continuance of the Reciprocity Treaty, but when this was cancelled, and Canada had responded by establishing and developing her own manufactures, Stephen considered that, having shown what she could do, the new Dominion should continue to assert her right and her ability to remain independent. If ever some form of reciprocity should be re-established he would be only too happy, but he wished the two nations to negotiate on equal terms, not as though one were obliged to seek favours of the other.

Macdonald, for his part, could not believe that independence and annexation were not inseparable, and was therefore less eager for the event. Even Stephen admitted, in 1872, that the time was not yet ripe for Canada to stand alone. Writing to Macdonald in that year advising against the imposition of a protective tariff affecting British goods on the grounds that the imperial tie would not stand the strain, he declared that if Britain found that she was not being accorded preferential treatment she would be only too glad to get rid of this part of her 'Colonial' burden:

I want to see the separation take place in the 'fullness of time'—not before—and with the most perfect good feeling between the two countries. . . .[2]

Nineteen years later, referring to the views of a former Governor-General, he wrote to Macdonald:

I have never forgotten what Lord Lisgar said about Canada as an independent nation in *alliance* with England. . . .[3]

But by then he apparently thought the time for independence was ripening fast, for he ended the letter with the words 'It would surely be a pleasure to you to see Canada "come of age" under your Government'. But within four months Macdonald had died, as he had wished, 'a British subject'.

Stephen's views were destined to remain on a somewhat idealistic plane. He continued to support a National Policy for Canada, advocating its extension until all anomalies were eradicated, while at the same time looking forward to a Free Trade millenium. He longingly contemplated the prospective market of 65 million people that lay to the south of the 49th Parallel, comparing it with Canada's

---

[1] Macd.P. 'Stephen' 272, Stephen to Macdonald, 5 September 1890.
[2] Macd.P. 'Stephen' 267, Stephen to Macdonald, 22 February 1872.
[3] Macd.P. 'Stephen' 272, Stephen to Macdonald, 28 February 1891.

own mere 5 millions.[1] Yet he did not fail to remind Macdonald that with adequate communications—a fast steamship service on the Atlantic, a fortnightly instead of a monthly service on the Pacific and steam and cable connection with Australia and New Zealand— Canada could afford to regard with equanimity the tariff barrier to the south, and could negotiate on her own terms when the question of reciprocity did recur.[2] His confidence in the Dominion's ability to hold her own even against the manufacturers of the United States was hardly reflected in England where, as he regretfully told Macdonald, 'the prevailing opinion is that Canada ought to devote her energies to the production of what they call "corn" and raw materials and import their manufactured goods from England'.[3]

In 1891 the farmers of Canada, in contrast to their ancient adherence to the policy of protection, became obsessed with a desire for unrestricted reciprocity, so that Macdonald, still holding that such a step spelt annexation, won the Election of that year largely by raising 'the loyalty cry'.[4] It was now Stephen's turn to charge his friend with undue pessimism about the future, which Macdonald was facing with a diminished majority, while the new McKinley tariff hung like a dark cloud over Conservative and Liberal alike. Stephen's bracing response to this threat had in it some of the forceful optimism of the young Montreal merchant of the 'sixties'— the youthful idealist whom artists portrayed with held head high, short, straight nose poised in hopeful attitude, not, as in later days, head sunk on chest and the cares of the world causing the tall figure to droop as though its very height was a burden too:

. . . Don't you think you exaggerate the damaging effect of the McKinley tariff? Has not your mind been affected by the pretensions of the Grits that it was certain to ruin Canada? I believe Canada can not only live but prosper if the Yankees built an impassable barrier along the whole frontier. In saying this I do not mean that a treaty of commerce as wide and comprehensive as it can be made consistent with our political and commercial independence would not be a very good thing for both countries. But we shall never get such a treaty so long as our people howl about it as essential to our very existence as an independent community. The moment the Yankees make up their mind that annexation or even

---

[1] Macd.P. 'Stephen' 272, Stephen to Macdonald, 5 and 12 September and 5 October 1890.
[2] Loc. cit. Stephen to Macdonald, 11 October 1890.
[3] Loc. cit. Stephen to Macdonald, 25 November 1890.
[4] Macd.L.B. 28.14, Macdonald to Stephen, 31 March 1891. See also Creighton, op. cit. (*The Old Chieftain*) Chapter Fifteen, VI.

commercial subserviency are things not to be discussed or thought of they will be ready to trade on a business basis. . . .[1]

KIND HEARTS AND CORONETS

Tho' yon be the land that ye're grand and
ye're great in,
Come hame. . .

Mary Symon

In May 1891, Lord Salisbury wrote to Stephen saying that he had Her Majesty's permission to ask whether he would be disposed to accept a Peerage of the United Kingdom. It was the first time that such an honour had been accorded a 'colonist', and Stephen himself probably quite genuinely regarded it more as recognition of the growing importance of the Dominion than as a personal compliment. He was to get a good deal of quiet amusement in his later years from Press references to himself as the 'herd-boy millionaire', and was inclined also to smile at the manner in which his cousin Donald Smith wore *his* coronet. But he accepted the honour, and chose as his title the name of the mountain at the summit of the Rockies which had first been named for him. Nor was the place of his boyhood forgotten, for his full title was Baron Mount Stephen of Mount Stephen, British Columbia, and Dufftown, Banffshire.

While the inspiration for the Mount Stephen arms and crest was Canadian, the arms featuring fleurs-de-lis and maple leaves and the crest consisting of 'a dexter arm embowed proper, vested azure, charged with two fleurs-de-lis or, and holding in the hand a pickaxe proper', the motto was Scottish, and typical. It consisted of one word 'Lippen', meaning 'Trust'.

It was a happy coincidence that soon after the news of the peerage was announced Lord and Lady Mount Stephen paid their first joint visit to Dufftown. Encouraged by their discovery in 1888 that their eminent contemporary still retained a keen appreciation of local efforts to entertain, the people of Mortlach had prepared an even more elaborate reception and programme of events than had confronted Stephen and Stewart.[2] Besides the recent honour bestowed upon their guests, the opening of the Stephen Cottage Hospital had to be celebrated; moreover, Dufftown had not lagged in the march of progress, and it had been arranged that Lady Mount Stephen should perform the ceremony of turning on a new water supply from

[1] Macd.P. 'Stephen' 272, Stephen to Macdonald, 21 April 1891.
[2] *Banffshire Journal*, 9 June 1891.

the Conval Burn which was to put an end to the old pilgrimage of householders to the well in the Square. (The 'Maister's Well' was subsequently removed and re-erected with ceremony on a new s te in 1901.)

Practically all the local dignitaries took part in the pageant of welcome, to the delight of the general public.

At the head of the procession there were on horseback Provost Symon, Quartermaster Grant and Mr. Peter Innes. Mr. Innes rode a sturdy black pony, and his appearance evoked hearty cheers. . . .

The three gentlemen on horseback, with Sergeant Instructor Swingler, along with members of [the reception] committee, were marshals of the procession, which in its progress through the town attracted much attention. The tradesmen made an excellent appearance. The butchers were represented by a cart, on one end of which was the head of a black-faced sheep, and at the other the horns of a Highland ox. In the cart was the carcass of a sheep, and riding on the cart, with the blue apron of the butcher, were Mr. Alex. Mackenzie and Mr. Myron. A cart in which there was a plough, and in which rode Mr. Stewart and Mr. Kemp, represented the agricultural interest. Mr. Watt, Mr. Gordon and assistants rode in a cart which represented the grocery trade, and distributed to the crowd as they passed through the streets large quantities of sweets. The fourth and last cart represented the druggists, and in it were three or four young lads busily at work in making the mysterious compounds of the druggists' shops.

At nine o'clock in the evening came the ceremony in which Lady Mount Stephen, dressed in brown plush trimmed with gold, her bonnet fashioned of brown feathers, was the central figure. As she turned on the new water supply, water rose 'in pretty jets' from the fountain specially erected. Speaking on her behalf of this 'interesting ceremony', Lord Mount Stephen remarked on the great change from the days when most of the townspeople had to carry water from the Square, adding, amid laughter and cheers, 'My wife is not in a position to know what that means'. Then, amid further cheers, 'I hope . . . that the inhabitants who hear me will long live in the enjoyment of the benefits of a bountiful water supply, and if you will not mind'—looking slyly around the landscape even then fragrant with a mixture of peat reek and malt from the pioneers among Dufftown's seven distilleries—Pettyvaich, Mortlach, Glendullan, Parkmore, Glenfiddich, Balvenie, Convalmore—'sometimes we all find even the best of water a little "wersh"; when you do dilute it, don't make the mixture too strong'.

At the public banquet which preceded a display of fireworks and other illuminations the Provost, a noted orator and never at a loss for an apt phrase, voiced the general sentiment thus:

Forgive me if I air a hackneyed quotation and say, 'Kind hearts are more than coronets.' Pleased as we were when we heard of the coronet, it was a mild feeling compared with what we felt when we learned with what princely generosity Lord Mount Stephen had remembered his native parish. . . . The children amongst us, I suppose, verily know the life of George Stephen as they know the fairy tales of history [*sic*]; the elders amongst us are accustomed to speak of it as one grand example of the possibilities in our Highland character . . . today he comes back to us in the summit of his prosperity, neither forgetting nor forgot by those whom he has left so far behind in the race of life. . . .

And so the bonfires were lit, and when darkness fell at last on that June night the people gathered on the Market Green to watch the fireworks from the town, while George Stephen, seeing through the eyes of his friends not the imagined failures of his great adventure, but the positive achievements, reflected with amused content that the journey from Halifax to the Pacific seemed now no longer than had once appeared the road from Dufftown to Aberdeen.

APPENDIX I

The C.P.R. Contract

(From Journals of the House of Commons of Canada, 1880-81. CO 45/51€.)

December 10, 1880. THIS CONTRACT and agreement made between Her Majesty the Queen, acting in respect of the Dominion of Canada, ard herein represented and acting by the Hon. Sir Charles Tupper, K.C.M.C., Minister of Railways and Canals, and George Stephen and Duncan McIntyre of Montreal, in Canada; John S. Kennedy, of New York in the State of New York; Richard B. Angus and James J. Hill, of St. Paul, in the State of Minnesota; Morton, Rose & Co., of London, England; and Kohn, Reinach & Co., of Paris, France.

Witnesses: That the parties hereto have contracted and agreed with each other as follows, namely:

(1) For the better interpretation of this contract, it is hereby declared that the portion of Railway hereinafter called the Eastern Section, shall comprise that part of the Canadian Pacific Railway to be constructed, extending from the Western terminus of the Canada Central Railway, near the East end of Lake Nipissing, known as Callander Station, to a point of junction with that portion of the said Canadian Pacific Railway now in course of construction extending from Lake Superior to Selkirk on the East side of Red River, which latter portion is hereinafter called the Lake Superior Section. That the portion of the said Railway, now in course of construction, extending from Selkirk to Kamloops, is here n-after called the Central Section, and the portion of said Railway now in course of construction, extending from Kamloops to Port Moody is hereinafter called the Western Section. And that the words 'the Canadian Pacific Railway', are intended to mean the entire Railway, as described in the Act 37th Victoria, cap. 14. The individual parties hereto, are hereinafter described as the Company, and the Government of Canada is hereinafter called the Government.

(2) The contractors, immediately after the organization of the said Company, shall deposit with the Government $1,000,000 in cash or approved securities, as a security for the construction of the Railway hereby contracted for. The Government shall pay the Company interest on the cash deposited at the rate of 4 per cent. per annum half-yearly, and shall pay over to the Company the interest received upon securities deposited, the whole until default in the performance of the conditions

hereof, or until the repayment of the deposit to the Company on the completion of the Railway, according to the terms hereof, with any interest accrued thereon.

(3) The Company shall lay out, construct and equip the said Eastern Section, and the said Central Section, of a uniform gauge of four feet, eight and a half inches and in order to establish an approximate standard whereby the quality and the character of the Railway and of the materials used in the construction thereof, and of the equipment thereof may be regulated, the Union Pacific Railway of the United States as the same was when first constructed, is hereby selected and fixed as such standard. And if the Government and the Company should be unable to agree as to whether or not any work done or materials furnished under this contract are in fair conformity with such standard, or as to any other question of fact, excluding questions of law, the subject of such disagreement shall be from time to time referred to the determination of three referees, one of whom shall be chosen by the Government, one by the Company, and one by the two referees so chosen, and such referees shall decide as to the party by whom the expense of such reference should be defrayed. And if such two referees should be unable to agree upon a third referee, he shall be appointed at the instance of either party hereto, after notice to the other, by the Chief Justice of the Supreme Court of Canada. And the decision of such referees, or of the majority of them, shall be final.

(4) The work of construction shall be commenced at the eastern extremity of the Eastern Section not later than the first day of July next, and the work upon the Central Section shall be commenced by the Company at such point towards the eastern end thereof on the portion of the line now under construction as shall be found convenient and as shall be approved by the Government, at a date not later than the first May next. And the work upon the Eastern and Central Sections, shall be vigorously and continuously carried on at such rate of annual progress on each section as shall enable the Company to complete and equip the said sections in conformity with this contract, unless prevented by the act of God, the Queen's enemies, intestine disturbances, epidemics, floods and other causes beyond the control of the Company. And in case of the interruption or obstruction of the work of construction from any of the said causes, the time fixed for the completion of the Railway shall be extended for a corresponding period.

(5) The Company shall pay the Government the cost, according to the contract of the portion of Railway, 100 miles in length, extending from the city of Winnipeg westward up to the time at which the work was taken out of the hands of the contractor, and the expenses since incurred by the Government in the work of construction, but shall have the right to assume the said work at any time and complete the same, paying the cost

of construction as aforesaid so far as the same shall then have been incurred by the Government.

(6) Unless prevented by the act of God, the Queen's enemies, intestine disturbances, epidemics, floods or other causes beyond the control of the Government, the Government shall cause to be completed the said Lake Superior Section, by the date fixed by the existing contracts for the construction thereof, and shall also cause to be completed the portion of the said Western Section now under contract, namely from Kamloops to Yale, within the period fixed by the contracts therefor, namely, by the thirtieth day of June, 1885; and shall also cause to be completed, on or before the first day of May, 1891, the remaining portion of the said Western Section, lying between Yale and Port Moody, which shall be constructed of equally good quality in every respect with the standard hereby created for the portion hereby contracted for. And the said Lake Superior Section, and the portions of the said Western Section now under contract, shall be completed as nearly as practicable according to the specifications and conditions of the contracts therefor except in so far as the same have been modified by the Government prior to this contract.

(7) The Railway constructed under the terms hereof shall be the property of the Company; and pending the completion of the Eastern and Central Sections, the Government shall transfer to the Company the possession and right to work and run the several portions of the Canadian Pacific Railway already constructed or as the same shall be completed. And upon the completion of the Eastern and Central Sections, the Government shall convey to the Company, with a suitable number of station buildings and with water service (but without equipment), those portions of the Canadian Pacific Railway constructed or to be constructed by the Government, which shall then be completed; and upon completion of the remainder of the portion of Railway to be constructed by the Government, that portion shall also be conveyed to the Company, and the Canadian Pacific Railway shall become, and be thereafter, the absolute property of the Company. And the Company shall thereafter and forever efficiently maintain, work and run the Canadian Pacific Railway.

(8) Upon the reception from the Government of the possession of each of the respective portions of the Canadian Pacific Railway, the Company shall equip the same in conformity with the standard herein established for the equipment of the sections hereby contracted for, and shall thereafter maintain and efficiently operate the same.

(9) In consideration of the premises, the Government agrees to grant to the Company a subsidy in money of $25,000,000 and in land of 25,000,000 acres, for which subsidies the construction of the Canadian Pacific Railway shall be completed, and the same shall be equipped,

maintained and operated, the said subsidies respectively to be paid and granted as the work of construction shall proceed, in manner and upon the conditions following—that is to say

(*a*) The said subsidy in money is hereby divided and appropriated as follows, namely:

Central Section
  Assumed at 1,350 miles—
    1st—900 miles at $10,000 per mile   .. $9,000,000
    2nd—450 miles at $13,333 per mile   .. $6,000,000
                                              —————————— $15,000,000

Eastern Section
  Assumed at 650 miles, subsidy equal to
    $15,384.61 per mile $10,000,000
                                         —————————— $25,000,000

And the said subsidy in land is hereby divided and appropriated as follows, subject to the reserve hereafter provided for.

Central Section
  1st 900 miles at 12,500 acres per mile   11,250,000
  2nd 450 miles at 16,666.66 acres per mile   ..   7,500,000
                                                    ——————————
                                                    18,750,000

Eastern Section
  Assumed at 650 miles, subsidy equal to 9,615.35
    acres per mile   6,250,000
                                              ——————————
                                              25,000,000

(*b*) Upon the construction of any portion of the Railway hereby contracted for, not less than 20 miles in length, and the completion thereof so as to admit of the running of regular trains thereon, together with such equipment thereof as shall be required for the traffic thereon, the Government shall pay and grant to the Company the money and land subsidies applicable thereto, according to the division and appropriation thereof made, as hereinbefore provided; the Company having the option of receiving in lieu of cash, terminable bonds of the Government, bearing such rate of interest for such period and nominal amount as may be arranged, and which may be equivalent according to actuarial calculation to the corresponding cash payment, the Government allowing 4 per cent. interest on monies deposited with them.

(*c*) If at any time the Company shall cause to be delivered on or near the line of the said Railway, at a place satisfactory to the Government, steel rails and fastenings to be used in the construction of the Railway, but in advance of the requirements for such construction the Government, on the requisition of the Company, shall upon such terms and conditions as shall be determined by the Government, advance thereon three-fourths of the value thereof at the place of delivery. And a proportion of the amount so advanced shall be deducted according to such terms and conditions from the subsidy to be thereafter paid, upon the settlement for each section of 20 miles of railway, which proportion shall correspond with the proportion of such rails and fastenings which have been used in the construction of such sections.

(*d*) Until the first day of January 1882, the Company shall have the option instead of issuing land grant bonds as hereinafter provided, of substituting the payment by the Government of the interest (or part of the interest) on bonds of the Company, mortgaging the Railway and the lands to be granted by the Government running over such term of years as may be approved by the Governor in Council in lieu of the cash subsidy hereby agreed to be granted to the Company or any part thereof; such payments of interest to be equivalent, according to actuarial calculation, to the corresponding cash payment, the Government allowing 4 per cent. interest on monies deposited with them; and the coupons representing the interest on such bonds shall be guaranteed by the Government to the extent of such equivalent. And the proceeds of the sale of such bonds to the extent of not more than $25,000,000 shall be deposited with the Government, and the balance of such proceeds shall be placed elsewhere by the Company, to the satisfaction and under the exclusive control of the Government; failing which last condition the bonds in excess of those sold shall remain in the hands of the Government. And from time to time as the work proceeds, the Government shall pay over to the Company: firstly, out of the amount so to be placed by the Company—and, after the expenditure of that amount, out of the amount deposited with the Government,—sums of money bearing the same proportion to the mileage cash subsidy hereby agreed upon, which the net proceeds of such sale (if the whole of such bonds are sold upon the issue thereof) or, if such bonds be not all then sold, the net proceeds of the issue, calculated at the rate at which the sale of part of them shall have been made, shall bear to the sum of $25,000,000. But if only a portion of the bond issue be sold, the amount earned by the Company according to the proportion aforesaid, shall be paid to the Company, partly out of the bonds in the hands of the Government, and partly out of the cash deposited with the Government, in similar proportions to the amount of such bonds sold and remaining unsold respectively; and the Company shall receive the bonds so paid as cash at the rate at which the said partial sale thereof shall have been made. And the Government shall receive and hold such sum of money towards the creation of a sinking fund for the redemption of such bonds and upon such terms and conditions as shall be agreed upon between the Government and the Company.

(e) If the Company avail themselves of the option granted by clause (d), the sum of $2,000 per mile for the first 800 miles of the Central Section shall be deducted *pro rata* from the amount payable to the Company in respect of the said 800 miles, and shall be appropriated to increase the mileage cash subsidy appropriated to the remainder of the said Central Section.

(10) In further consideration of the premises the Government shall also grant to the Company the lands required for the road-bed of the railway, and for its stations, station-grounds, workshops, dock ground and water frontage at the termini on navigable waters, buildings, yards, and other appurtenances required for the convenient and effectual construction and working of the Railway, in so far as such land shall be vested in the Government. And the Government shall also permit the admission free of duty, of all steel rails, fish-plates and other fastenings, spikes, bolts and nuts, wire, timber and all material for bridges, to be used in the original construction of the Railway, and of a telegraph line in connection therewith, and all telegraphic apparatus required for the first equipment of such telegraph line. And will convey to the Company, at cost price, with interest, all rails and fastenings bought in or since the year 1879, and other materials for construction in the possession of or purchased by the Government at a valuation; such rails, fastenings and materials not being required by it for the construction of the said Lake Superior and Western Sections.

(11) The grant of land hereby agreed to be made to the Company, shall be so made in alternate sections of 640 acres each, extending back 24 miles deep, on each side of the railway, from Winnipeg to Jasper House in so far as such lands shall be vested in the Government, the Company receiving the sections bearing uneven numbers. But should any of such sections consist in a material degree of land not fairly fit for settlement, the Company shall not be obliged to receive them as part of such grant, and the deficiency thereby caused and any further deficiency which may arise from the insufficient quantity of land along the said portion of Railway, to complete the said 25,000,000 acres, or from the prevalence of lakes and water stretches in the sections granted (which lakes and water stretches shall not be computed in the acreage of such sections) shall be made up from other portions to be selected by the Company in the tract known as the fertile belt, that is to say, the land lying between parallels 49 and 57

degrees of north latitude, or elsewhere, at the option of the Company, by the grant therein of similar alternate sections extending back 24 miles deep on each side of any branch line or lines of railway, to be located by the Company, and to be shown on a map or plan thereof deposited with the Minister of Railways; or of any common frontline or lines agreed upon between the Government and the Company, the conditions hereinbefore stated as to lands not fairly fit for settlement to be applicable to such additional grants. And the Company may, with the consent of the Government, select in the North West Territories any tract or tracts of land not taken up as a means of supplying or partially supplying such deficiency. But such grants shall be made only from lands remaining vested in the Government.

(12) The Government shall extinguish the Indian title affecting the lands herein appropriated, and to be hereinafter granted in aid of the Railway.

(13) The Company shall have the right, subject to the approval of the Governor in Council, to lay out and locate the line of the Railway hereby contracted for, as they may see fit, preserving the following terminal points, namely, from Callander Station to the point of junction with the Lake Superior Section; and from Selkirk to the junction with the Western Section at Kamloops by way of the Yellow Head Pass.

(14) The Company shall have the right, from time to time, to lay out, construct, equip, maintain and work branch lines of railway from any point or points along the main line of the railway, to any point or points within the territory of the Dominion, provided always that before commencing any branch they shall first deposit a map and plan of such branch in the Department of Railways. And the Government shall grant to the Company the lands required for the roadbed of such branches, and for the stations, station grounds, buildings, workshops, yards and other appurtenances requisite for the efficient construction and working of such branches in so far as such lands are vested in the Government.

(15) For twenty years from the date hereof, no line of railway shall be authorized by the Dominion Parliament to be constructed south of the Canadian Pacific Railway, from any point at or near the Canadian Pacific Railway except such line as shall run south-west, or to the west-ward of south-west nor to within 15 miles of Latitude 49. And in the establishment of any new Province in the North West Territories, provision shall be made for continuing such prohibition after such establishment until the expiration of the said period.

(16) The Canadian Pacific Railway, and all stations and station grounds, workshops, buildings, yards and other property, rolling stock

and appurtenances required and used for the construction and working thereof, and the capital stock of the Company, shall be forever free from taxation by the Dominion, or by any Province hereafter to be established or by any Municipal Corporation therein, and the lands of the Company, in the North West Territories, until they are either sold or occupied, shall also be free from such taxation for twenty years after the grant thereof from the Crown.

(17) The Company shall be authorised by their Act of incorporation to issue bonds, secured upon the land granted and to be granted to the Company, containing provisions for the use of such bonds in the acquisition of lands, and such other conditions as the Company shall see fit, such issue to be for $25,000,000. And should the Company make such issue of land grant bonds, then they shall deposit them in the hands of the Government, and the Government shall retain and hold one-fifth of such bonds as security for the due performance of the present contract in respect of the maintenance and continuous working of the Railway by the Company, as herein agreed, for 10 years after the completion thereof, and the remaining $20,000,000 of such bonds shall be dealt with as hereinafter provided. And as to the said one-fifth of the said bonds, so long as no default shall occur in the maintenance and working of the said Canadian Pacific Railway, the Government shall not present or demand payment of the coupons of such bonds, nor require payment of any interest thereon. And if any of such bonds so to be retained by the Government shall be paid off in the manner to be provided for the extinction of the whole issue thereof, the Government shall hold the amount received in payment thereof as a security for the same purposes as the bonds so paid off, paying interest thereon at 4 per cent. per annum so long as default is not made by the Company in the performance of the conditions hereof. And at the end of the said period of ten years from the completion of the said railway, if no default shall then have occurred in such maintenance and working thereof, the said bonds, or if any of them shall then have been paid off, with accrued interest, shall be delivered back by the Government to the Company with all the coupons attached to such bonds. But if such default should occur, the Government may thereafter require payment of interest on the bonds so held, and shall not be obliged to continue to pay interest on the money representing bonds paid off; and while the Government shall retain the right to hold the said portion of the said land grant bonds, other securities satisfactory to the Government may be substituted for them by the Company by agreement with the Government.

(18) If the Company shall find it necessary or expedient to sell the remaining $20,000,000 of the land grant bonds, or a larger portion thereof, than in the proportion of one dollar for each acre of land then earned by the Company, they shall be allowed to do so, but the proceeds thereof

over and above the amount to which the Company shall be entitled as herein provided, shall be deposited with the Government. And the Government shall pay interest upon such deposit half-yearly, at the rate of 4 per cent. per annum and shall pay over the amount of such deposit to the Company from time to time as the work proceeds, in the same proportions, and at the same times and upon the same conditions as the land grant—that is to say that the Company will be entitled to receive from the Government out of the proceeds of the said land grant bonds, the same number of dollars as the number of acres of the land subsidy which shall then have been earned by them, less one-fifth thereof that is to say, if the bonds are sold at par, but if they are sold at less than par, then a deduction shall be made therefrom corresponding to the discount at which such bonds are sold. And such land grant shall be conveyed to them by the Government, subject to the charge created as security for the said land grant bonds, and shall remain subject to such charge till relieved thereof in such manner as shall be provided for at the time of the issue of such bonds.

(19) The Company shall pay any expenses which shall be incurred by the Government in carrying out the provisions of the two last preceding clauses of this contract.

(20) If the Company should not issue such land grant bonds, then the Government shall retain from out of each grant to be made from time to time every fifth section of the lands hereby agreed to be granted, such lands to be so retained as security for the purposes, and for the length of time, mentioned in section 18 hereof. And such lands may be sold in such manner and at such prices as shall be agreed upon between the Government and the Company, and in that case the price thereof shall be paid to, and held by the Government for the same period, and for the same purposes as the land itself, the Government paying 4 per cent. per annum interest thereon. And other securities satisfactory to the Government may be substituted for such lands or money by agreement with the Government.

(21) The Company to be incorporated, with sufficient powers to enable them to carry out the foregoing contract, and this contract shall only be binding in the event of an Act of incorporation being granted to the Company in the form hereby appended as Schedule A.

(22) The Railway Act of 1879, in so far as the provisions of the same are applicable to the undertaking referred to in this contract, and in so far as they are not inconsistent with or contrary to the provisions of the Act of incorporation to be granted to the Company, shall apply to the Canadian Pacific Railway.

In witness thereof the parties hereto have executed these presents at the city of Ottawa, this twenty-first day of October 1880.

Signed: Charles Tupper, Minister of Railways and Canals.

George Stephen.   R. B. Angus.

Duncan McIntyre.   J. J. Hill.

J. S. Kennedy.   per pro George Stephen.

Morton, Rose & Co. Kohn, Reinach & Co.

by P. du P. Grenfell.

APPENDIX II

Letter to the Editor of The Globe *from George Stephen, 12 September, 1883.*

Canadian Pacific Offices,
Montreal.
10th Sept., 1883.

Sir,

I observe that two articles published in *The Globe* on Saturday, the 8th inst., contain certain statements, substantially as follows:

1. That the main line of this Company's Railway has been made to run for hundreds of miles through a country which the Company themselves declare to be unfit for settlement.

2. That the Company have refused to accept any portion of their land subsidy in the Railway belt lying along the main line west of Qu'Appelle.

The articles in question assume these assertions to be correct, and base upon them a number of observations conveying the impression that the whole of the railway belt from Qu'Appelle to Calgary is admitted by the Company to be part of the great American desert, and to fall within the exception in the contract with the Government which excludes from the land grant lands not fairly fit for settlement.

As these statements could not have been made in language better calculated to mislead the public, to injure this Company, and to retard the settlement of the North-West, even if they had been prompted by the most bitter and malignant desire to attain those objects, and as they do not merely purport to convey the opinions of *The Globe*, but profess to state the views and to describe the acts of the Company, I feel it necessary to correct any erroneous impression the articles might create by stating the facts.

I have therefore to say that the assertions in the articles in question as to the character of the land along the main line of the railway west of Qu'Appelle, and as to the views of this Company in respect of that land, are utterly and absolutely unfounded.

That this Company have not, either 'virtually' or directly, admitted or declared the lands in the railway belt west of Qu'Appelle to be in any degree unfit for settlement.

That this Company have not refused or declined to accept any land west of Qu'Appelle as a portion of their land subsidy.

I might content myself with the foregoing categorical denial of the statements made. But to prevent misconception, I desire to add that this

Company have not contemplated, and do not contemplate, refusing or declining to accept any of the uneven-numbered lots in the railway belt west of Qu'Appelle as part of their land grant, except in so far as any particular section, for some special reason, may not be fairly fit for settlement; that this Company have examined a large portion of the territory referred to, and are satisfied not only that it is in a material degree fairly fit for settlement, but that to a large extent it consists of as fine farming land as is to be found in the North-West Territories, or in any part of Canada; and as respects the portion of the territory not yet specially examined, they have no reason to doubt that it is of equally good quality.

I have further to request you to be good enough to give this letter insertion in your paper, in order that the statement of this Company may receive as wide a circulation as the articles to which it refers.

I remain, Sir,

Your obedient servant,

Geo. Stephen,

President.

APPENDIX III

Letter to the Shareholders of the Grand Trunk Railroad

London, 5 April, 1883.

Gentlemen,

At the general meeting of the shareholders of the Grand Trunk Company, held last week, the President of the Company, supported by his friends and allies, devoted a large part of their speeches to a violent attack upon the Canadian Pacific Railway Company.

Hitherto that Company has judged it better to take no notice of the incessant hostility by which it has been pursued for the last two years by journals and individuals whose relations with the Grand Trunk Company are well known; but this last attack upon its character and credit is in the nature of an official declaration of war against all Canadian Pacific interests, and cannot with propriety be ignored. I therefore propose to throw the few words of defence I have to offer into the form of a letter to the Shareholders of the Grand Trunk Company, and to send a copy to each shareholder, leaving to their sense of fair play to judge how far the Canadian Pacific Company has deserved the treatment it has met with at the hands of the Grand Trunk Company.

Let me first notice Sir Henry Tyler's complaint against the Canadian Pacific Company, that it entered upon a gigantic undertaking without coming to him, and through him invoking the aid of the Grand Trunk Company, as according to Sir Henry ought to have been done.

To this complaint of your President I reply (1) that we did not feel under any necessity to apply to him to help us. This attitude of Sir Henry Tyler shows that the Grand Trunk are still under the same illusion, that they must monopolise railway enterprise in Canada, which induced them to endeavour, in the first instance, to stifle the construction of a new direct line between Montreal and Ottawa and the North Shore Railway between Montreal and Quebec, in both of which cases the Grand Trunk failed, and have since acknowledged their mistaken policy by buying the North Shore line at a large profit to the sellers. Moreover, we did not require financial or other assistance from the Grand Trunk Company; we wanted nothing from them but peace, and to be let alone and allowed to attend to the work we had undertaken to perform.

(2) Had we been otherwise circumstanced and required help, we should not have thought of applying to the Grand Trunk Company, which appeared to us to have its hands full enough with its own affairs. The

numerous and onerous financial obligations which that Company were already under, in respect of leases and traffic guarantees (the full weight of which the shareholders have not yet begun to appreciate), to say nothing of the inevitable results of the vain and ambitious policy of universal absorption of new lines which the management in Canada were pursuing, seemed to us a task of sufficient magnitude of itself to fully employ the whole energies of that Company.

(3) Sir Henry Tyler next complains that traffic is sent by the circuitous route of Ottawa and Brockville to Buffalo, and thence to Winnipeg instead of by the more direct G.T.R. line. It is true that Montreal merchants are using this route; but this is due to the simple fact that goods sent by it reach Winnipeg in 10 days, whereas goods sent over the G.T.R. take from 4 to 8 weeks in transit, owing to the congested state of the single line between Montreal and Toronto. This, the only present through line in Canada, has to serve the traffic coming from the Western American States, in addition to the through Canadian traffic proper, and its carrying capacity is notoriously entirely inadequate to these purposes.

(4) Sir Henry, after accusing the Canadian Pacific Company of attacking his Company in its own territory, though upon what grounds he fails to point out, proceeds to say that the board of the Grand Trunk Company, as a board, have never attacked the Pacific Railway Company. The qualification is well put in, but his repudiation of hostile feelings on the part of the Grand Trunk board is too transparent to deceive anyone who has paid the least attention to what has been going on in Canada and here during the last two years. Even Sir Henry himself will scarcely pretend to say that individual members of his board, and gentlemen high in the confidence of himself and his colleagues, have not done all in their power to discredit and damage the C.P.R. Company in the eyes of the British public. If he should attempt to do so, I would refer him to the violent speech which followed his own remarks at the meeting on the 29th ult., and in which Mr. Abbott stated that he wished it to be understood that he would handle the C.P.R. without gloves, and declared that he would not hesitate to raise his voice and wield his pen with all the power he possessed to prevent it getting any money from this or any other country. Is language of this sort likely to promote feelings of good neighbourhood between the two companies?

I do not propose to notice the mis-statement of facts concerning the C.P.R. Company, made at the meeting, further than to say that we are not shirking the construction of the line north of Lake Superior. On the contrary, there are some thousands of men at work at this moment on that section, and that, difficult as that part of our task may be, the line will be finished and ready for traffic by the end of the year 1886. I will add further, that we shall this year complete 325 miles additional at the western end of the line, bringing it well into the Rocky Mountains, and that the connection with the Pacific Ocean will be made by the end of 1885.

I will now, with your permission, state as briefly as possible the object which the Government and people of Canada had in view when they decided on building a through line of railway in Canadian territory to the Pacific Ocean, setting forth as clearly as I can the position of the Company and the line of policy by which it hopes to accomplish the purpose for which it was brought into existence.

The C.P.R. is a purely commercial organization, having no ambitious designs of any kind, and harbouring no hostile feelings towards the Grand Trunk or any other Canadian company. It was created for the purpose of opening up the hitherto undeveloped North-Western territories of the Dominion of Canada, and for carrying the traffic between those territories and the Atlantic seaboard on the one hand, and the Pacific Ocean on the other, through British territory.

The Dominion Government, acting in harmony with the unanimous voice of public feeling, and aided by the cooperation of the Imperial Government, granted the following subsidies to the C.P.R. Company: $25,000,000 cash; 25,000,000 acres of good agricultural land in the fertile belt of the North West; about 713 miles of finished railway in the most difficult sections of the line, estimated to cost $35,000,000, and several other minor but important privileges. In return the present company entered into a contract with the Government of the Dominion to complete the line, and to own and operate it for ever.

Such is the nature of the enterprise which the Grand Trunk Railway Company's officials so fiercely assail, regardless of the feeling they must excite against themselves by attacking a national enterprise, which is regarded by the Canadian people as the means whereby they are to be rendered independent of United States railway lines, and to promote which the Imperial Government have already assisted the Dominion Government by a guarantee of some £3,000,000 sterling.

Let me now explain the progress already made. In the two years that have passed since they entered into this contract the Company have built and finished 760 miles of road, and have well advanced with the construction of over 250 more. They have also provided the bulk of the equipment required for the 1730 miles now ready to be operated. All this has been done out of their own resources, plus the earned share of the subsidies granted by the Government.

Excepting the issue to the public some 18 months ago of $20,000,000 of 5 per cent. bonds, secured by mortgage on the Company's land grant—not the railway—(of which bond issue over $17,000,000 have since been practically provided for by last year's land sales, amounting to about 6,450,000 acres) there was no application for public support until February last, when the Company issued in New York and Amsterdam $10,000,000 of its common stock at the price of $60 per $100 share. Something was said at the Grand Trunk meeting about London having only taken $800,000 of this issue; but it ought in fairness to have been stated that no issue was made here, and that the London subscribers had to send to Amsterdam for their shares.

In conclusion let me say that the Canadian Pacific Company is officially committed to the statement, that the whole of the main line, from Montreal to the Pacific Ocean, 2,904 miles plus some 450 miles of branches —complete and fully equipped—with the addition of about 17,000,000 acres of perhaps the finest wheat lands on the continent, will be represented by $90,000,000 of share capital, without preferences of any kind. The proprietors of this share capital will own the whole of this property, free from all encumbrances, except about $5,500,000 of mortgage bonds previously charged on the purchased lines. In other words, taking the $90,000,000 of share capital at the issue price of 60, the actual cash cost of the 3,354 miles of railway, and some 17,000,000 acres of land, will be $54,000,000—say, $16,300, or £3,260 per mile of railway, with the valuable land asset in addition. Yet, with the knowledge of these facts within their reach, our assailants at the G.T.R. meeting spoke of the shares of the C.P.R. Company as 'watered,' forgetting apparently that the nominal capital of their own and leased lines of about the same length as the C.P.R., stands at something like $280,000,000 as against our $90,000,000, while the debenture capital alone of the Grand Trunk and Great Western Railway Companies exceeds £6,000 per mile; and these debenture stocks are selling in the market about 115. Also forgetting that the £7,168,055 third preference stock of the G.T.R., with nearly £28,000,000 sterling of other preferences of the Grand Trunk and Great Western Companies ahead of it, not including the numerous traffic guarantees recently incurred, is quoted in the depressed market today at 50. What, let me ask, on this basis of value, should the shares of the C.P.R. be worth?

With these few facts I leave you to judge how far Sir Henry Tyler and his supporters, supplemented by the petty annoyances of your general manager in Canada, to which we have been exposed ever since we came into existence, are likely to succeed in crushing or even permanently injuring the C.P.R. Company.

Gentlemen, there is a much better policy to be pursued, one that would benefit Canada as well as its two great railway enterprises, if your officials had only the wisdom to see it and were in a frame of mind to follow it.

I am, gentlemen, yours truly, George Stephen.
President, Canadian Pacific Railway Coy.

APPENDIX IV

Confidential Memorandum by Mr. George Stephen, President of the C.P.R.

Explaining a Scheme for the Settlement of Irish Families in the Canadian North West.

Colonial Office, March 1883.
CO812/26. Misc. No. 49.

For the sum of £1,000,000 sterling, ten thousand small farmers with their families averaging five persons to each family, say fifty thousand people in all, can be comfortably brought from their homes in Ireland to the New Canadian North-West, and each family provided with 160 acres of the finest wheat growing lands, a comfortable wooden house, a cow, and the implements necessary to enable them to begin the cultivation of their land, including the cost of ploughing and seeding a few acres for their first year's crop.

The money required, to be provided by the Government and advanced by way of loan, to the North-West Land Company of Canada, and to such other Corporations interested in the Settlement of the Canadian North-West, as might wish to join in the enterprise, and be able to furnish the Government with such security for the repayment of the loan as might be required.

The loan to be for ten years without interest.

In consideration of this loan, the Land Company undertake the work of transplanting and settling in the North-West, under the supervision of the Government, these 10,000 families, assuming all the risks incident to the business, and the responsibility of the repayment of the money advanced by the Government.

The Land Company would take a lien on the 160 acres of land given to each family to the amount of £100, on which the emigrant would be charged interest at the rate of six per cent. per annum after the first two years of his settlement; the emigrant to have the right to pay off the principal at any time.

The chief inducement to the Land Company to undertake this work lies in the increased value that would be given to its own lands adjoining those upon which the emigrants settled.

This scheme is based on the assumption that the emigrants sent out are fit for agricultural work, and have energy and ability to take care of themselves, after getting the fair start thus provided for them.

It will thus be seen that the redundant population of Ireland may be materially reduced without further cost to the Government than the Interest on £100 for ten years for each family—say £2 10s. per annum or £25 for the whole ten years.

APPENDIX V

Sir George Stephen to the Shareholders of the C.P.R. Company, 12
September, 1887. (From *Montreal Gazette* 17 September, 1887.)

To the Shareholders—

In view of the exaggerated accounts and persistent mis-statements which have been sent out regarding the railway agitation at Winnipeg, the directors of the Company have thought it due to the Shareholders to publish a brief statement of facts for their information.

On the 21st of October, 1880, the contract for the construction of the C.P.R. was signed, and for the purpose of carrying it out the Canadian Pacific Railway Company was incorporated on the 17th of February, 1881.

Article 15 of the contract provided that for twenty years the Dominion Government should not authorize the construction of any line of railway running south from the main line of the Canadian Pacific Railway to any point within fifteen miles of the international boundary.

A Legal Contention

It is asserted and widely believed that this clause has no effect in the original province of Manitoba; but the British North America Act, which settled and defined the constitution of Canada, distinctly assigns to the jurisdiction of the Dominion Parliament all matters not specifically delegated to the Provincial Legislatures, and the power to legislate concerning railways extending beyond the international boundary, or intended to connect with other lines at such boundary, is nowhere in the constitution given to the provinces.

Whether or not the fifteen mile limit applies to the original province of Manitoba, the matter of a railway connection at the international boundary is clearly within the control of the Dominion and as clearly beyond the power of the province.

The Object of Monopoly

The object and spirit of the fifteenth clause of the contract with the company was the temporary protection of the interests of the Dominion, in the North West, as well as the protection of the Canadian Pacific Railway from the encroachment of lines from the south, during the infancy of the enterprise. Could connections be made with the American railway system at the southern boundary of the original province of Manitoba, the clause would be meaningless, for once across the boundary line there would be practically no limit to the extensions that might be made.

The Company's Return

The company required protection because it was bound under its contract to make an enormously expensive railway through what was thought to be an unproductive wilderness north and east of Lake Superior. It was, also, bound to take over and work the line then being built by the Government from Lake Superior to Red River, through a similarly unpromising district, and it was required to give security for the working of the entire line, when completed. It was not expected at the time that sufficient local traffic could be developed for many years to make the section from Lake Nipissing to Red River, nearly eleven hundred miles, self-sustaining, and that it must depend for its support upon the through traffic to and from the great prairies beyond, and this traffic had yet to be created as the settlement of the prairies had then scarcely begun. Railway lines were pushing northward from Chicago and St. Paul towards the Manitoba boundary, threatening to tap the prairie section of the Canadian Northwest and to deprive the Eastern Section of the railway of the traffic so necessary to its support and efficiency as part of the through line.

It was, therefore, on the part of the company, deemed to be absolutely necessary to the procuring of the requisite capital proposed to be invested, and, generally, to the success of the enterprise, that the traffic of the territory to be developed by the railway should be secured to it for a reasonable period, and the term of ten years from the time fixed for the completion of the railway was agreed upon. *Without this provision for protection the necessary capital could not have been secured and the railway could not have been made.*

The Political Aspect

The Government had strong reasons, of a more exclusively public nature, for this protection. It was a political necessity that the detached provinces should be connected and bound together by a railway, and the older provinces were to be heavily taxed for the building of it. Political reasons alone would not justify the heavy burden it would put upon the country, but a vast territory was to be opened up, and the older provinces looked to the extension of their trade and manufactures over the entire northern half of the continent, to justify the expenditure.

Their interests required protection, and the protection afforded to the Company protected them as well. It was most important to the whole country that the railway, when made, should be in a position to efficiently serve the purposes for which it was intended, and the need of protection was generally recognized. Indeed, the same protection was insisted upon by the Government in respect of the Canadian Pacific Railway when it was commenced as a public work long before the Company was thought of.

The Northwest

Winnipeg at the time was a mere village, and the settlements in Manitoba were mainly confined to a narrow fringe along Red River. The province hailed the signing of the contract with satisfaction, and hardly a voice was raised in objection to the so-called 'Monopoly Clause.'

The Company set about its work, and completed it in less than half the time required by the contract. Feeling that the protective clause in its contract placed upon it a moral obligation to provide railway facilities as rapidly as possible in southern Manitoba, where the making of railways was to some extent restricted, the company, almost simultaneously with the commencement of work on its main line, laid out and commenced work on a system of branch lines extending south and south-west from Winnipeg; and up to this time it has expended on branch lines in Manitoba in addition to those previously made by the Government, more than $5,700,000.

Building Branch Lines

Partly in view of the same moral obligation, but chiefly for the purpose of promoting the development of the country, the company made its rates both for freight and passengers on a scale far below the rates of any of the railways in the United States similarly situated. The immediate effect of the opening of the railway between Lake Superior and Winnipeg was an enormous reduction in the rates theretofore paid by the province to and from the east over the American lines. For the chief products, and for fuel and the commodities most essential to the growth of the country, the rates were made especially low, and year by year, as the traffic has increased these rates, in whole or in part, have been reduced, until they are now, in many cases, less than one-half the rates originally authorized. The charges that the rates are excessive or unreasonable is simply untrue.

The Traffic Charges

The average earnings of the company for the past three years have been as follows:

	1884	1885	1886
Freight per ton per mile	$1.45	$1.20	$1.10
Passengers per mile	2.60	2.45	2.10

And omitting the through traffic to and from the Pacific from the figures of 1886, they stand: $1.14 per ton per mile for freight and $2.13 per mile for passengers, a lower average than is shown by any important American line, aside from the old Trunk lines in the east.

It has been the aim of the company to so adjust its tariffs that the settlers in the Canadian Northwest should receive more for the products of their farms and pay less for fuel and no more for the other necessaries of life than settlers similarly situated in the United States; and that it has succeeded in this is clearly shown by a comparison of prices with the neighbouring sections of Minnesota and Dakota. The company has also dealt in the most liberal manner with all the independent railway enterprises in the Northwest, and the building and operation of at least two of these would have been impossible but for its co-operation and liberality.

The Country's Benefit

The development of the prairie section west of Winnipeg has been rapid, and on the section from Winnipeg eastward to Lake Nipissing, where little was at first expected, a valuable local traffic from the forests and mines is growing up, giving promise that even this part of the line will, before long, be self-supporting. It may, therefore, be argued that the protection afforded by the contract is no longer necessary; but it should be remembered that the company, encouraged and aided by the growth of its traffic, and on the faith of this protection, has expended a vast amount of money on local lines in Manitoba, and, unless prevented by the acts of the province itself, will yet expend a large amount in the completion of the system of branch lines it has planned, and has been carrying out as rapidly as its means would permit; and it should also be remembered that all of the 433 miles of branch lines operated by the company in the Northwest are in Manitoba; that all but sixty-five miles were paid for with the company's money, and that many miles were made prematurely at the urgent solicitation of the provincial Government and without expectation of immediate profits.

But, notwithstanding the liberal policy of the company as regards branch lines, and independent lines, and rates of transportation, notwithstanding that the tariff rates of the company have as yet been approved by the Government only from year to year, and are subject to annual revision, and notwithstanding that no complaint of these rates has ever been made to the Railway Committee of the Privy Council, the natural and inevitable consequences of over-speculation have been mistaken by many people in Winnipeg, and some other towns in Manitoba, for the need of railway competition. This idea has been fostered by individuals with selfish ends to serve; by towns seeking advantages over others in trade; by local politicians striving for popularity, and by politicians at large for party ends. The usual means have been employed for creating and keeping up a ferment—the cry of monopoly and extortionate rates; sensational articles in the local press; unfair and false comparison of rates; inflammatory speeches, and appeals to prejudice. The local political parties have vied with each other in securing to themselves the support of the malcontents, and this has resulted in the undertaking by the provincial Government to construct a line of railway to the international boundary, where it has agreed to make a connection with a line advancing northwest from the Northern Pacific railway, and which is supposed to be building under the auspices of that company. The acts of the local Government providing for the railway in question, are in direct violation of the British North America Act and beyond the powers of a province, and are consequently without warrant of law.

The Injunction

In attempting to proceed without legal right, the province has been checked by a temporary injunction, and it is not to be believed that in the event of a permanent injunction being granted by the courts, the local Government will set the law at defiance. Nor can it be expected that the wishes of even a majority of the 100,000 people of Manitoba will prevail against the interests of the 5,000,000 people of the Dominion.

Independent of any constitutional question, and particularly in view of the heavy expenditures by the company in making branch lines largely at the instance of the local Government, and of the other great expenditures that have been made by the company for the development of the province, the action of that Government in attempting to divert its traffic by building a railway to the boundary, however insignificant that railway may be, is unfair, unjust, and a breach of faith with the company. The service of the company has given universal satisfaction, and if the rates were oppressive no complaint has ever been laid before the constituted authorities that the facts might be authoritatively brought out and redress obtained.

It would be absurd to urge that the completion of the 66 miles of railway undertaken by the Government of Manitoba would ruin the vast Canadian Pacific system, but its construction would be a violation of the contract with this company, and the directors feel it to be their duty to maintain the rights of the company in the matter, in every legitimate way.

The Government's Action

That the country will carry out the contract with the company in good faith, the shareholders may rest assured. The Parliament of Canada, at its last session, sustained the Government by an extraordinary majority in the determination to prevent, if only as a matter of public policy, the building of railways in the Northwest to the international boundary and the prompt action of the Governor General in disallowing the acts of the Manitoba Legislature relating to the Red River Valley railway, followed by active steps of the Minister of Justice to stop the work by injunction, is sufficient evidence of the intention of the Government in this regard.

The present agitation in Winnipeg is chiefly damaging in its effect on the province itself. The intemperate, sensational and ridiculous utterances of a section of the local press are reprinted and read abroad with alarm, and the effect upon emigration and upon the credit of every enterprise in the province, has already been most serious. Your directors believe, however, that this agitation, like those which have preceded it, will disappear as soon as the people of the country come to understand the facts, and discover the motives of those by whom it was created.

APPENDIX VI

Sir George Stephen to the Shareholders of the C.P.R. Company, on his resignation from the Presidency, 7 August 1888. (From C.P.R. Reports, 1889.)

From the time when I became a party to the contract with the Dominion Government for the construction of the Canadian Pacific Railway, and consented to accept the position of President of the Company, it has always been my intention to relinquish the active chief control of the affairs of the Company as soon as the task which I then undertook should be completed. This task was partially finished when the line was opened for traffic through to the Pacific Ocean over two years ago; but at that time so much remained to be done towards the firm establishment of the enterprise, and its future development and success, that, in deference to the wishes of my colleagues I consented to continue for a time in office. Warned now by the state of my health, finding that the severe and constant strain which I have had to bear for the past eight years has unfitted me for the continuous and arduous duties of an office in which vigour and activity are essential; feeling the increasing necessity for practical railway experience, and believing that the present satisfactory and assured position of the Company offers a favourable opportunity for taking the step I have so long had in contemplation, I have this day resigned the Presidency of the Company, which I have had the honour to hold since its organization.

In taking this step it may not be out of place to say that my pecuniary interest in the enterprise remains undiminished, and that the welfare of the Company is, and always must be, to me, a matter of the deepest possible interest; and that as a member of the Board of Directors I will always be ready to aid and cooperate with my colleagues in everything calculated to protect and promote the interests of the Shareholders.

In resigning the position of President of the Company, it is, to me, a matter of the greatest possible satisfaction to be able to say that, in my successor, Mr. Van Horne, the Company has a man of proved fitness for the office, in the prime of life, possessed of great energy and rare ability, having a long and thoroughly practical railway experience and above all an entire devotion to the interests of the Company.

In conclusion, I cannot refrain from congratulating the Shareholders upon the arrangements recently completed by Sir Donald A. Smith and myself, which will have the effect of securing to the C.P.R. the permanent friendship of the two new and important American lines extending from

Sault Ste. Marie to Minneapolis and St. Paul, on the one hand, and to Duluth on the other, and reaching a traffic the importance of which it would be difficult to overestimate.

It is also a matter of congratulation that arrangements have been practically settled with the Wabash Railway for a permanent connection between the Detroit River and Chicago, and the southwest; and further, that the long-pending negotiations with the Imperial Government for the establishment of a first-class steamship line between Vancouver and Japan and China have at last been concluded.

Index